Teresa of Avila
and the Politics
of Sanctity

Teresa of Avila and the Politics of Sanctity

Gillian T. W. Ahlgren

Cornell University Press   Ithaca and London

This book is published with the aid of a grant from the
Program for Cultural Cooperation between Spain's Ministry
of Culture and United States universities.

First published 1996 by Cornell University Press
First printing, Cornell Paperbacks, 1998

Library of Congress Cataloging-in-Publication Data

Ahlgren, Gillian T. W., 1964–
    Teresa of Avila and the politics of sanctity / Gillian T. W.
Ahlgren
        p.   cm.
    Includes bibliographical references and index.
    ISBN 0-8014-3232-4 (cloth : alk. paper)
    ISBN 0-8014-8572-x (pbk. : alk. paper)
        1. Teresa, of Avila, Saint, 1515–1582. 2. Christian women saints—
Spain—Biography. 3. Counter-Reformation—Spain. 4. Women—
Religious life—Spain—History. I. Title.
    BX4700.T4A45   1996
    282'.092—dc20
    [B]   95-42066

Printed in the United States of America

Cornell University Press strives to use environmentally responsible suppli-
ers and materials to the fullest extent possible in the publishing of its
books. Such materials include vegetable-based, low-VOC inks and acid-
free papers that are recycled, totally chlorine-free, or partly composed of
nonwood fibers.

Cloth printing   10 9 8 7 6 5 4 3 2 1

Paperback printing   10 9 8 7 6 5 4 3 2 1

Contents

Acknowledgments

It is certainly a great pleasure for me to be able to thank some of the people who have given me support and nurturance over the years I have been working on Teresa. Grover Zinn first introduced me to Teresa and the mystical tradition more broadly during my undergraduate years at Oberlin College. Harriet Turner guided my first intense readings of Teresa in Spanish. Marcia Colish helped turn my musings into more discerning questions. Bernard McGinn instilled in me a keen sense of the discipline of mystical theology and has encouraged me to appreciate Teresa's contributions as a theologian. Ulrike Wiethaus has consistently challenged me to reconceive notions of gender and society in my research. I owe a great debt of gratitude to all of them.

Others have been supportive as well. A Xavier University Faculty Development summer grant enabled me to complete chapter 6. My thanks to colleagues at Xavier University who have given advice, support, promptings, and suggestions. In particular, Bill Madges and Carol Winkelmann have read and commented on various parts of my research over the past several years, and Rosie Miller has been a lively conversation partner. Special thanks go to Sidnie Reed, our interlibrary loan specialist.

In Spain my thanks go to the personnel at the Biblioteca Nacional and the Archivo Histórico Nacional in Madrid and to friends there who have made my stays rich and enjoyable. Special thanks to Miguel Angel Tabladillo López for help and support.

Unless I indicate otherwise, all references to Teresa's works are to the definitive critical edition: Teresa de Jesús, *Obras completas*, edited by Enrique Llamas, Teófanes Egido, Daniel de Pablo Maroto, José Vicente Rodríguez, Fortunato Antolín, and Luis Rodríguez Martínez, under the direction of Alberto Barrientos (Madrid, 1984). The modern chapter and paragraph numbers provided in the notes will guide readers to the appropriate passages in most other editions and English translations. The translations here are my own.

This book has also been a family affair. My mother, Barbara Donne, made editorial suggestions. My husband, Scott Campbell, and our son, Matthew—born in the midst of it all and toddling through the revision process—have been there to show me that there is indeed life after Teresa!

G. T. W. A.

Cincinnati, Ohio

Abbreviations

AHN   Archivo Histórico Nacional, Madrid
exp.   expediente
exp. s.n.   expediente sin número
Inq.   Inquisición
leg.   legajo
lib.   libro

BAC   Biblioteca de Autores Cristianos

BAE   Biblioteca de Autores Españoles

BMC   *Biblioteca mística carmelitana*, ed. Silverio de Santa Teresa, 35 vols. (Burgos: El Monte Carmelo, 1934–49)

BN   Biblioteca Nacional, Madrid

CE   Teresa de Jesús, *El camino de perfección*, El Escorial version

CV   Teresa de Jesús, *El camino de perfección*, Valladolid version

Llamas   Enrique Llamas Martínez, *Santa Teresa de Jesús y la Inquisición española* (Madrid: Editorial de Espiritualidad, 1972)

Obras completas   Teresa de Jesús, *Obras completas*, ed. Enrique Llamas Martínez, Teófanes Egido, Daniel de Pablo Maroto, José Vicente Rodríguez, Fortunato Antolín, and Luis Rodríguez Martínez, under the direction of Alberto Barrientos (Madrid: Editorial de Espiritualidad, 1984)

Teresa of Avila
and the Politics
of Sanctity

Introduction

Teresa de Jesús (1515–82) is widely considered to be one of the most important saints of the Counter-Reformation. She actively promoted mystical prayer, reformed the Carmelite order, and wrote mystical treatises. To many Catholics her canonization, just forty years after her death, seemed inevitable, yet Teresa was subjected to close scrutiny throughout her life and could not be confident that her books would survive her.

Teresa wrote literally thousands of folios about her mystical experiences, despite her superiors' suspicion and distrust. As scholars explore more fully the climate of Counter-Reformation Spain, the irony of Teresa's achievements becomes clearer. Indeed, Teresa wrote two of her most important works, the *Vida* and *El camino de perfección,* while her contemporaries Luis de Granada, O.P. (1504–88), and Juan de Avila (c. 1499–1569) were scrambling to revise books prohibited by the Valdés Index in 1559.

The strategies that enabled Teresa's works to survive have been examined in detail by other scholars.[1] Here I want clearly to situate those works in their theological and ecclesiastical milieu. Teresa lived and died during the Inquisition, when all writings were closely scrutinized, when women lacked theological authority, and when canonization was a highly political process.

The challenges Teresa encountered and the very climate of sixteenth-century Spain shaped both her message and the way she expressed it. Over the course of her life Teresa was called upon to defend the legitimacy of her mystical experience, her reform agenda, and, indeed, her very self. As she realized how rooted such criticisms were in misogynist assumptions, Teresa began to take on the defense of women in general, arguing for a greater and more explicit role for women within the Christian tradition. Remaining a "daughter of the church" was perhaps the single most difficult thing Teresa accomplished.

As I have struggled to understand this truly enigmatic woman, I have repeatedly been struck by the wide range of reactions she elicited from her contemporaries. Revered and hailed by some church figures as an extraor-

1. See Rosa Rossi, *Teresa de Avila: Biografía de una escritora,* trans. Marieta Gargatagli (Barcelona, 1984); and Alison Weber, *Teresa of Avila and the Rhetoric of Femininity* (Princeton, 1990).

dinary and gifted mystic, she was sharply criticized as either a fraud or an unbearably arrogant woman by others. On many occasions Teresa's life, her reform efforts, and the legacy of her mystical works were nearly cut short. One of her most useful skills was the ability to court people whose theological and political perspectives differed from her own.

The support that enabled Teresa to function as a reformer and writer— an extensive network of confessors, religious communities, patrons, and church officials—suggests that community structures provided forms of protection as well as challenge. Indeed, insofar as religious communities and friendships encouraged mutual tolerance and nurturance, they served to counter the relationships of domination and submission that structured the Spanish and ecclesiastical cultures.[2] Yet patriarchy had pervasive effects on the lives of religious women, perhaps the most important of which has been identified by Gerda Lerner: even Teresa, whose vulnerability as a public figure must have made the emotional and psychological support of her religious community all the more valuable to her, deliberately put herself in conversation with men and chose an active, public apostolate even after she had founded a movement of cloistered contemplatives.[3] Thus Teresa's own remedy for her situation was to assimilate herself to patriarchal culture even as she challenged it. Although her convents represented a spiritual haven of sorts for women, they were still built on many patriarchal assumptions.

Teresa's life spans a critical period in Spanish history. At her birth in 1515, many important advances in humanism were under way: the founding of the University of Alcalá, the preparation of the Complutensian Polyglot Bible, and the translation of medieval mystical works into the vernacular. Through the 1540s and 1550s, however, in response to political problems encouraged by new theological currents, the Iberian Peninsula began to close its doors to intellectual contributions from Germany and the Low Countries. Reforms adopted at the Council of Trent (1545–63) were enforced very unevenly in Catholic Europe; indeed, Spain's idiosyncratic enactment of Tridentine Catholicism was the subject of much scholarly debate.

Teresa observed the growth of systematic censorship with increasing discomfort. When the Valdés Index of Prohibited Books appeared in 1559, Teresa recognized the problems it would cause "unlettered" people in the realm of spiritual development, and sought to fill this vacuum with her

2. See Ulrike Wiethaus, *Maps of Flesh and Light: The Religious Experience of Medieval Women Mystics* (Syracuse, 1993), p. 3.

3. See Gerda Lerner, *The Creation of Feminist Consciousness: From the Middle Ages to 1870* (New York, 1993).

own literary efforts.[4] She wrote the first version of her *Vida* in 1562. As she continued to write, however, she was challenged by the increasing vigilance of the Inquisition's censors, who excised passages they considered dangerous. In 1574 the Inquisition undertook a thorough review of the *Vida*, and never returned the manuscript to her. Teresa's response to the appropriation of her "little book" was the theological tour de force known as the *Moradas*, which she wrote in 1577. Although the *Moradas* escaped the censors, it did not circulate in published form until Teresa's complete works were printed in 1588, six years after her death. The public appearance of her mystical corpus, however, provoked another investigation by the Inquisition. And so the "difficult times" that plagued Teresa's life continued after her death.[5]

I seek to contextualize the life of Teresa the woman and the meaning of Teresa the saint within the Counter-Reformation agenda by exploring the complex and conflicting notions of female sanctity at work in sixteenth-century Spain. I approach this task by sketching the evolution of Teresa's spirituality and theology within a patriarchal climate of opposition, analyzing her struggles as exemplary of those of other women in Counter-Reformation Spain. The portrait of Teresa I draw is, then, an attempt to understand sanctity both as an internal process of spiritual maturation in response to a specific sociohistorical context and as a negotiated set of social relationships. Finally, I view sanctity from the perspective of two institutions, both of which assumed the responsibility, in different ways, of determining sanctity: the Spanish Inquisition and the papacy, through the canonization process. Throughout this process I emphasize the reconstructing of Teresa, following the insights of Aviad Kleinberg, who observed that "the status of saint was conferred upon a person in a gradual process that involved disagreement and negotiation, as well as collaboration and even collusion."[6]

Simply stated, my argument consists of four major points. First, institutional desire to control religious experience and theological writing was the most significant factor in Teresa's career as writer and reformer. She began to write in response to the dearth of mystical texts in Spain after the appearance of the Valdés Index. Her books, written in the vernacular and designed to stimulate readers to pursue holiness and mystical union, were

---

4. To Teresa and her contemporaries, "unlettered" people were those who could not read Latin. Teresa, like most women and indeed most men outside the church, was unlettered in this sense. Though she was extremely well read, she knew Latin only phonetically and could not read theological treatises in Latin.

5. Teresa described the spiritual climate of her day as *"tiempos recios."* See *Vida* 33:5.

6. Aviad M. Kleinberg, *Prophets in Their Own Country: Living Saints and the Making of Sainthood in the Later Middle Ages* (Chicago, 1992), p. 4.

essential resources for the contemplative life of the newly reformed Carmelite order. Second, her quest for survival as an articulate, spiritually experienced woman in the context of patriarchal control and suspicion of mysticism forced her to develop complex strategies of humility and obedience, through which she appeared to conform to the models of religiosity prescribed for women. Third, though officials of the Inquisition found several aspects of Teresa's mystical experience and some of her mystical doctrine disturbing, her model of sanctity had great popular appeal. So that, fourth, her canonization in 1622 represents the Pyrrhic victory of those who campaigned for official recognition of her sanctity: Teresa's popularity overcame the posthumous criticisms of her work, but the canonized Teresa bore little resemblance to the Teresa who wrote books, debated theologians, and counseled men and women alike.

Teresa's vocation was deeply rooted in the historical circumstances of her day, particularly in the various manifestations of the Catholic/Counter-Reformation in Spain: the reform of religious orders, the Council of Trent, censorship of many religious texts, and the Spanish Inquisition. The different ways in which women and men experienced these historical circumstances are the focus of chapter 1. Next I consider the many ways the Inquisition and its Valdés Index of Prohibited Books influenced Teresa's motivations and decisions as an author. Writing to evade censorship was a constant challenge for her. In chapter 2 I retell the story of Teresa's life and vocation from this perspective.

Teresa's struggle for theological authority and the rhetorical strategies she developed to guarantee her right to write are the focus of chapter 3. In chapter 4 I examine elements of her mystical doctrine to elucidate further the concrete theological and rhetorical strategies that Teresa adopted to ensure the survival of her thought: she produced new treatises precisely at times when she was concerned about the suppression of her books; she developed an increasingly complex system for encoding her doctrine; and she attempted to establish norms for the discernment of spirits, thereby sharing strategies for the survival of women's vision.

In chapter 5 I review the various arguments made for and against her mystical doctrine during the Inquisition's posthumous procedure against her *Obras completas*. It was during this debate that officials acknowledged the institutional advantages in recognizing Teresa's mystical way.

Finally, in chapter 6 I demonstrate how Teresa's survival strategies were exaggerated in the persona canonized by the Roman Catholic Church. The woman who emerges from contemporary descriptions of Teresa in the testimonials gathered for her canonization process differs significantly from the saint described in the official canonization vita. I also discuss the variety of responses to Teresa's personality and contrasting views on what specifically made her an appropriate candidate for sainthood.

In all, Teresa emerges as an indomitable woman, navigating her way through perilous waters, somehow managing to best or charm the men who wished to control her overtly through criticism and censorship and more covertly through their assumptions of women's inferiority. It is this rugged tenacity, her *determinada determinación,* that enabled her to survive her era and keeps her alive in our own.

1

Women and the
Pursuit of Holiness
in Sixteenth-Century Spain

Striving for spiritual perfection—always a difficult enterprise—proved particularly challenging in sixteenth-century Spain. As the century advanced,
European nations developed their own approaches to questions of political
and ecclesial structures; and from this plurality of contemporary models,
Spain emerged by mid-century as the country most clearly aligned with the
Tridentine agenda. Spain acquired this reputation through its attachment to
an idiosyncratic orthodoxy that evolved slowly, from a brand of humanism
that allowed for individual theological speculation and spiritual experimen-
tation to a more rigid model of clerical catechetical control that in many
ways discouraged the "new spirituality," with its emphasis on mental
prayer.[1]

It is clear that the series of inquisitions that the Spanish church directed
against certain groups of people had a cumulative effect on the nature and
practice of Roman Catholicism in Spain. The first attack, which continued
throughout the sixteenth century but was particularly sharp through the
1520s, was against *judaizantes,* people accused of continuing to practice Judaism after their conversion to Catholicism. Because accusations of "Ju-
daizing" tended to be based on such practices as cleaning and preparing the
home for the Sabbath, abstaining from pork, avoiding eating in neighbors'
homes, and directing prayers to the omnipotent God (without cultivating a
relationship with Christ or seeking the intercession of saints), this campaign
tended to encourage a formulaic social expression of Catholic ritual. The
second campaign, against *luteranos*—a generic term that encompassed not

---

1. The historians Donald Weinstein and Rudolph Bell characterize the Catholic Reformation as "above all else a reformation of the episcopacy, a rededication of the bishop to the care
of souls, the nurturing of his flock, the reforming of his clergy, and the monitoring of correct
doctrine. . . . Reformation Catholicism rejected all . . . experiments with religious democracy
and reaffirmed the most extreme version of clerical authority and practice": *Saints and Society:
The Two Worlds of Western Christendom, 1000–1700* (Chicago, 1982), pp. 225–26. For more
specifics on post-Tridentine reform, see Sara T. Nalle, *God in La Mancha: Religious Reform and
the People of Cuenca, 1500–1650* (Baltimore, 1992).

only followers of Luther but anyone who expressed disrespect for the papacy, the sacraments, purgatory, or the clerical state in general—began in the 1520s, reached its peak from 1559 through 1565, and lingered on through the 1570s. The harsh treatment of *luteranos* encouraged a deferential attitude toward ecclesiastical authority and limited public criticism of the church. Finally, the movement against *alumbrados,* people accused of having been falsely "enlightened" by prayer, was certainly the most important with respect to women. *Alumbrados* had made two major errors: they had been deceived in prayer and they had had too much spiritual pride to admit that they had been so deceived. The campaign against the *alumbrados* had the double effect of redefining prayer as essentially vocal and as not an authoritative source of spiritual knowledge and of encouraging clerical mediation and sometimes control over the spiritual lives of confessees.

The evolution of Spanish orthodoxy had very different effects on women than it did on men. By placing all spiritual authority in the clergy, from which women were barred, the Catholic Reformation denied women the power of spirituality. In fact, a clear enunciation of male and female roles figured prominently in sixteenth-century religious debate. Though they would not describe their activities this way, most sixteenth-century authors and ecclesiastical figures were engaged in the construction of a gender ideology. In Spain, many men wrote treatises on the "estates," describing the ideal Christian virgin, wife, and widow. Luis de León's *Perfect Wife* is an excellent example of this genre. Other men contributed their views on women with varying degrees of candor in treatises on spirituality, the discernment of spirits, and witchcraft.

Thus increasingly throughout the sixteenth century Spanish women were confronted with theological writings about "womanhood," an ideal created by men which many women found difficult or even undesirable to achieve. They were characterized as *mujercitas,* "little women," a term that signaled women's political, social, and spiritual powerlessness. The Dominican theorist Martín de Córdoba, who wrote his *Jardín de las nobles donzellas* in the late fifteenth century, was one of many writers to declare that women were unable to control their passions because they were less rational than men: "Reason is not so strong in them as in men, and with their greater reason men keep carnal passions in check; but women are more flesh than spirit, and therefore are more inclined to the passions than to the spirit."[2] Assumptions of women's intellectual inferiority led to the belief that

---

2. Martín de Córdoba, *Tratado que se intitula Jardín de las nobles doncellas,* ed. Fernando Rubio (Madrid, 1946), p. 91: "En ellas no es tan fuerte la razón como en los varones, que con la razón que en ellos es mayor, refrenan las pasiones de la carne; pero las mujeres más son carne que espíritu; e, por ende, son más inclinadas a ellas que al espíritu."

women were easily confused and deceived by visionary and revelatory experiences. Authors of treatises on the discernment of spirits advised male confessors to judge women's visions carefully before they accepted their validity. Finally, as authors of books on witchcraft argued, women were unable to make sound moral judgments, so they were acutely vulnerable to temptation by the devil. Martín de Castañega, for example, devoted an entire chapter of his *Tratado de las supersticiones y hechicerías* (1529) to six reasons "why among these diabolical ministers there are more women than men."[3]

On another level, sixteenth-century Spain has long fascinated scholars of mysticism because of the proliferation of mystical literature in an age that was not hospitable to it. In many ways the early sixteenth-century reappropriation of the mystical tradition provided a common denominator for spiritual men and women, but men and women relied on different forms of mystical experience, had differing theological preparation and perspectives, and had unequal access to public roles. Caroline Bynum has noted the ambivalence with which church authorities confronted women mystics and the misogyny that led them to accuse such women of witchcraft. She sees here the roots of "the witch-hunting theology" of the fifteenth century.[4]

By the sixteenth century, then, the climate of Spain seemed to encourage women visionaries yet to accord them an increasingly ambivalent reception. Women were conceded an increasingly specific intercessory role in the redemptive process—their private prayers and penances could speed the purification of souls in purgatory—yet the more charismatic the woman, the more dangerous she seemed to the institutional church.[5]

3. See Martín de Castañega, *Tratado de las supersticiones y hechicerías* (Madrid, 1946), pp. 37–38. Castañega appears to have been highly influenced by the infamous *Malleus maleficarum* (1486), which was available in many sixteenth-century Castilian editions. Castañega attributes women's proclivity for witchcraft to these factors: (1) Because Christ denied women the power to administer the sacraments, the devil granted them more of his authority. (2) Like Eve, women are more easily deceived by the devil. (3) Again like Eve, women are curious to understand things that are beyond their nature to comprehend. (4) More inclined to chatting than men, they share secrets among themselves and recruit other women to the trade. (5) More vengeful than men and with fewer opportunities to get even with their enemies, women are more inclined to seek out the devil for help in avenging themselves. (6) Less educated than men, women who cast spells are classified as "witches," whereas men who do the same thing are low-level "scientists." Castañega's thought makes an interesting comparison with ideas in the *Malleus,* pt. 1, bk. 6.

4. Caroline Walker Bynum, *Holy Feast and Holy Fast: The Religious Significance of Food to Medieval Women* (Berkeley, 1987), p. 22.

5. For a review of several aspects of the medieval mystical tradition, see ibid.; Lerner, *Creation of Feminist Consciousness;* Bernard McGinn, *The Growth of Mysticism: From Gregory the Great through the Twelfth Century* (New York, 1994); Elizabeth Alvilda Petroff, ed., *Medieval Women's Visionary Literature* (New York, 1986); Wiethaus, *Maps of Flesh and Light.*

The Counter-Reformation reformulated such contradictions in ways that increasingly placed women at an institutional disadvantage. The sixteenth-century gender ideology was critical to the attempts to maintain religious, social, and political order. Women were at once virtuous and evil in ways that men were not. Men defined and honored themselves by a negative: they were not women. It was their lack of femaleness that justified their authority.[6] In the face of such assumptions, women found their religious influence declining over the course of the century. From a position of credibility and relative authority in the first several decades, when Spain was open to such spiritual innovations as the thought of Erasmus and the prayer techniques of Franciscan reformers,[7] women's religious experience became subjected to increased scrutiny, and religious women lost a great deal of control over their lives. Not until we recover the stories of women during those years can we get a clear picture of sixteenth-century Catholic reform and its implications for the Christian tradition.[8]

The Campaign against the Alumbrados

The flowering of mysticism in sixteenth-century Spain depended heavily on the spiritual revival of the Franciscan reform movement, initiated at the turn of the fifteenth century under Cardinal Francisco Ximénez de Cisneros (1416–1517). Cisneros held positions of significant power: confessor to Queen Isabella, he was the archbishop of Toledo, the vice-regent of Spain, and inquisitor general. As provincial of the Franciscan order and founder of the University of Alcalá, Cisneros was an extremely influential force in Spanish religious reform.[9] He was able to effect change on many levels from his various positions of religious authority. He regularly took stands on controversial religious issues and often supported *beatas,* laywomen who

6. See Mary Elizabeth Perry, *Gender and Disorder in Early Modern Seville* (Princeton, 1990). The idea that patriarchal control of women is particularly rigid during times of political and social transition is not limited to the sixteenth century. See, for instance, Mary Douglas, *Purity and Danger: An Analysis of Concepts of Pollution and Taboo* (London, 1966), and Gerda Lerner, *The Creation of Patriarchy* (New York, 1986).

7. See Marcel Bataillon, *Erasmo y España,* trans. Antonio Alatorre (Mexico City, 1986); first published in French in 1937. The "openness" was relative. Spanish humanism should not be confused with religious tolerance. During this "open" period, when vernacular treatises made it possible for the laity to engage in theological discussion, anti-Semitism was increasing.

8. Among works that examine the effects of this shift on Spanish women are Electa Arenal and Stacey Schlau, *Untold Sisters: Hispanic Nuns in Their Own Works* (Albuquerque, 1989), and Richard L. Kagan, *Lucrecia's Dreams: Politics and Prophecy in Sixteenth-Century Spain* (Berkeley, 1990).

9. On Cisneros, see Melquíades Andrés Martín, *Los recogidos: Nueva visión de la mística española (1500–1600)* (Madrid, 1975); Bataillon, *Erasmo y España,* pp. 1–71; and Pedro Sáinz Rodríguez, *La siembra mística del Cardenal Cisneros y las reformas en la Iglesia* (Madrid, 1979).

had achieved local reputations for sanctity, when their authority was questioned.[10] Cisneros was especially supportive of people who sought to follow the mystical way, and apparently he was little troubled by the ecstatic visions and revelations that came to them.[11]

Although Cisneros's reforms were principally concerned with the spiritual life of the reformed Franciscan order, they had far-reaching effects on the Spanish population. Among his reforms was the requirement that Franciscans engage in one and a half hours of mental prayer daily. To make this experience meaningful, Cisneros commissioned Castilian translations of medieval mystical texts, including those of Augustine, Gregory the Great, Cassian, Bernard of Clairvaux, John Climacus, Angela of Foligno, and a popularized version of Pseudo-Dionysius' *Mystical Theology* known as the *Sol de contemplativos.*[12] These vernacular translations had the additional effect of facilitating major developments in lay spirituality and allowed women increased access to the mystical tradition.

The school of mystical prayer initiated by the Franciscans involved a technique known as *recogimiento,* withdrawal from worldly concerns, in which individuals turned away from external distractions and gradually centered their souls in prayer, particularly in meditation on the Passion. *Recogimiento* has been described as "a method by which the soul seeks God in its own heart, in such total detachment from the world that it puts aside the thought of everything created and even all reasoned thought."[13]

The modern definition of the Franciscan method of prayer as *recogimiento* distinguishes it from the *dexamiento* of the *alumbrados,* or illuminati; yet the boundary between the two types of prayer was not clear, and indeed may not even have existed. Marcel Bataillon writes: "One cannot distinguish between *recogidos* and *dejados* until 1523, when coexistence and fellowship were no longer possible and each movement went its own way." The *alumbrados* were so closely associated with the Franciscans, Bataillon claims, that they lacked only the order's official patronage.[14] The early sixteenth-century

10. Among the *beatas* he supported were María de Toledo, founder of the convent of Santa Isabel de los Reyes, and María de Santo Domingo, of Piedrahita. See Mary E. Giles, *The Book of Prayer of Sor María de Santo Domingo* (New York, 1988).

11. A good example of Cisneros's tolerance of ecstatic experience is shown in his publication of Vincent Ferrer's treatise on the spiritual life in 1510. This version omitted chapters in which Ferrer warned against trusting visions and ecstasy. See Bataillon, *Erasmo y España,* p. 170.

12. See Melquiades Andrés Martín, *La teología española en el siglo XVI,* 2 vols. (Madrid, 1976), 1:111.

13. Bataillon, *Erasmo y España,* p. 167. Francisco de Osuna is considered the most prominent expositor of this method.

14. Ibid., pp. 116, 179.

tendency to use the terms interchangeably and loosely is reflected in the trial of María de Cazalla, who testified in 1529 that people used the term *alumbrado* to designate anyone who was more withdrawn (*recogido*) than most, or who avoided bad company.[15]

The origins and practices of both the *recogido* and the *alumbrado* movements are heavily indebted to new vernacular translations of classic mystical texts from the medieval tradition.[16] Their adherents should be viewed as early reformers who practiced and preached a more disciplined approach to lay spirituality. They shared their society's optimism about the possibility of advancing in spirituality and receiving divine inspiration. Before the first trial of *alumbrados* in 1524–25, as we shall see, many laypeople had preached and achieved religious authority. As the *alumbrados* became the

15. AHN, Inq., leg. 110, no. 6, fol. 72v: "Este nombre de alumbrados se suele imponer agora y en el tiempo que esta testigo dispuso a cualquier persona que anda mas recogida que los otros o se abstiene de la conversacion de viciosos, como es publico y notorio." Later she testified that contemplative religious persons in Guadalajara were often called *alumbrados* ("este nombre se suele poner muchas veces a las personas recogidas y devotas en guadalajara" [fol. 74r]) because they were withdrawn or did good works ("porque andaban recogidas o hazian buenas obras" [fol. 75r]). A transcription of this document is available in Antonio Márquez, *Los alumbrados: Orígenes y filosofía (1525–1559)* (Madrid, 1980), with commentary on pp. 77–78; commentary is also found in Bataillon, *Erasmo y España*, pp. 470–74; and José González Novalín, "La Inquisición española," in *La Iglesia en la España de los siglos XV y XVI*, vol. 3, pt. 2, of *Historia de la Iglesia en España*, ed. Ricardo García-Villoslada (Madrid, 1980), pp. 148–51.

16. The question of the origin of the *alumbrados* is complicated, but every historian who touches on this theme seems obliged to examine it. Early scholarship suggested that the *alumbrados* developed spontaneously (see Fidèle de Ros, *Un maître de Sainte Thérèse: Le père François d'Osuna, sa vie, son oeuvre, sa doctrine spirituelle* (Paris, 1936), p. 78; Miguel Mir and Justo Cuervo, eds., "Los alumbrados de Extremadura en el siglo XVI," *Revista de Archivos, Bibliotecas y Museos* 9 (1903): 204), but it is difficult to believe that a movement that had so much in common with other early reform movements arose independently. This theory takes no account of the doctrine of the *alumbrados* prosecuted by the Inquisition. Other authors have noted parallels between the *alumbrados* and some continental mystics. Pierre Groult argued that the *alumbrado* movement owes its origins to fourteenth- and fifteenth-century Flemish mystics. See his "Courants spirituels dans la Peninsule Iberique aux XVᵉ, XVIᵉ et XVIIᵉ siècles," *Lettres Romances* 9 (1955): 218–21. Citing the familiarity of Pedro Ruiz de Alcaraz with the Italian mystics, Pedro Sáinz Rodríguez argued for the movement's origins in Italian mysticism. See his "Influencia de los místicos italianos en España," in *Corrientes espirituales en la España del siglo XVI: Trabajos del Segundo Congreso de Espiritualidad de Salamanca*, (Barcelona, 1963), 2:546–47. Both schools seem to have had their influence. It is easy to see parallels between the teachings of the *alumbrados* and the school of the *Devotio moderna*, which could act as a bridge between Spain and the Lowlands. Alcaraz referred to Pseudo-Dionysius to explain the practice of *dexamiento*, the suspension of one's own will in an effort to know God's, and claimed that it was essentially the same as the teachings of such medieval mystics as Bernard of Clairvaux, Bonaventure, Angela of Foligno, and Jean Gerson. See Márquez, *Los alumbrados*, p. 121. If the *alumbrados* themselves saw their movement as consistent with medieval mystical teachings, this is perhaps the best avenue for modern historical interpretation of the movement.

targets of the Inquisition, however, the *recogimiento* movement also lost ground, and by 1559, when the Valdés Index was issued, it had all but disappeared.

Accusations against a group of Christians in Guadalajara in 1519 signaled the beginning of serious trouble for Spanish lay spirituality. This group met in the palace of the Mendozas to discuss the Bible and the contemplative books that poured out of the University of Alcalá in the early sixteenth century.[17] They eventually became known as the first *alumbrados,* since they claimed to have received spiritual enlightenment from their religious experiences.[18] Heavily influenced by the Franciscan reform movement, the thought of Erasmus,[19] and the Christian mystical tradition at large, these early *alumbrados* attacked clerical privilege and other trappings of the institutional church while encouraging individual, unmediated experiences of God in prayer.

This emphasis on revelation and charismatic gifts rather than on title, office, or academic education put women on an equal footing with men, and many of the first *alumbrados* prosecuted by the Inquisition were women. Isabel de la Cruz, María de Cazalla, and Francisca Hernández all achieved significant influence as preachers and teachers, though they had no university training in theology. These women elaborated theological perspectives out of their own mystical experience, and gained numerous fol-

---

17. Several members of this group were "New Christians," or converts from Judaism, who probably joined these groups in their attempts to understand the complexities of the Christian mystical tradition. As these people traveled about the region to organize meetings for spiritual advancement, the presence of *conversos* among them must have made their activities seem even more suspect to the authorities.

18. For a brief but solid English-language introduction to the *alumbrado* movement, see Alastair Hamilton, *Heresy and Mysticism in Sixteenth-Century Spain* (Toronto, 1992).

19. *Alumbrados* recognized their dependence on Erasmus when they emphasized inner intentionality over religious ceremony and personal piety over scholastic reasoning. When Alcaraz was accused of having little respect for the practice of counting prayers against a rosary, for example, he argued that prayer should be mental, unceremonial, and devoid of selfish interest, and he referred to the *Enchiridion* to support his opinions regarding the importance of intentionality in external acts. Curiously, however, the early *alumbrados* exhibited none of Erasmus's humanism. Alcaraz taught that one need not be literate to know the love of God, and in fact that the spiritual and the intellectual were not compatible. Time devoted to the pursuit of human knowledge, he said, was time stolen from God, for all Christians must hold to the words of the Gospel: "You have hidden these things from the learned and revealed them to the humble" ("el tiempo que uno da a las ciencias humanas, es tiempo robado a Dios, puesto que todos los cristianos deben aspirar a aquello del Evangelio: 'escondiste estas cosas a los sabios, y las revelaste a los humildes'"). See Márquez, *Los alumbrados,* p. 244. And indeed, according to Isabel de la Cruz, acquired knowledge (*ciencia*) was enough to prohibit learned clerics from attaining a state of perfection in prayer (ibid., p. 266). Márquez discusses the anti-intellectual tendencies of the early *alumbrados* on pp. 169–72.

lowers.[20] Francisca Hernández, for example, was credited with several miracles, including the cure of a Franciscan after a four-year illness.[21]

In the wake of the *comuneros* uprising and the controversy over the spread of Lutheranism in northern Europe, the Spanish elite understood the early *alumbrados* to be indicative of the kind of political and religious chaos that the teachings of Erasmus and Martin Luther encouraged. They turned to the Inquisition to stop its spread efficiently.

In 1525, after more than six years of inquiry, the Inquisition published the first edict against the beliefs and teachings of the *alumbrados*. This edict, written as a general reprimand of *alumbradismo*, was extremely significant in the history of Spanish spirituality.[22] Besides elaborating a list of theological errors committed by the *alumbrados*, the edict cast public doubt on internal revelation and was used as a resource for inquisitors for decades to follow. Among other things, according to the edict, *alumbrados* denied the existence of hell; argued that the sacrament of penance was not of divine origin; claimed that becoming lost in prayer to God superseded any other Christian activity, including fasting and good works; argued against religious processions and the veneration of religious statues; denied the need for indulgences; and would not take oaths.[23]

20. See John Longhurst, "La beata Isabel de la Cruz ante la Inquisición (1524–1529)," *Cuadernos de Historia de España* 25–26 (1957): 279–303; Milagros Ortega Costa, *Proceso de la Inquisición contra María de Cazalla* (Madrid, 1978); and Angela Selke, *El Santo Oficio de la Inquisición: Proceso de fray Francisco Ortiz (1529–1532)* (Madrid, 1968).

21. Selke, *El Santo Oficio*, p. 41.

22. The best critical edition of this edict is found in Márquez, *Los alumbrados*, pp. 229–38. Márquez's study is an extensive analysis of the Edict of 1525, the Inquisition's first important document characterizing the *alumbrados* as heretics. Unfortunately, Márquez does not allow for exaggeration or distortion. He assumes, for instance, that the inquisitors "constructed a model on the basis of facts that were real but disconnected, supplied by the people" (p. 66), but of course an accusation is not necessarily a "real fact."

23. Other beliefs also seem to stem directly from Luther's thought, especially rejection of the idea that good works were necessary for salvation. This teaching is reflected most obviously in the edict's proposition 33: "That those who love their soul or do something for their own salvation lose it, and that losing it in God and in God's love wins them more; and they ceased to do good works, as they were engaged in higher endeavors" (ibid., p. 236). For the *alumbrados* any act arising from the soul was not good in itself because the soul always acts out of self-interest (ibid.). To what extent the early *alumbrado* movement was a Spanish expression of Lutheranism is a matter of some debate. Some of Luther's early works were available briefly in Spain, but they were quickly banned. The "Lutheran thesis" was first argued by Angela Selke de Sánchez in "Algunos aspectos de la vida religiosa en la España del siglo XVI: Los alumbrados de Toledo" (Ph.D. diss., University of Wisconsin, 1953). Márquez finds no evidence that Luther's works were available in Spain at such an early date, and considers the *alumbrados* to have had more in common with radical reformers of the spiritualist orientation, particularly Kaspar Schwenkfeld, though he knows of no interchange between the two groups (*Los alumbrados*, pp. 152–55). Márquez points to the absence of Luther's Christology from the *alumbra-*

The *alumbrados* were also accused of teaching that *dejamiento*, or the giving over of one's own will to God, was the only way to obtain pardon for sins. *Dexados* had no need for confession of sins, fasts, penance, or any other pious acts. Their practice of prayer was quietistic: no amount of thought, not even the contemplation of the Passion of Christ, could help the soul initiate or sustain the union of wills in *dejamiento*. In this state of abandonment, any act that impeded communication between the soul and God was an act of disobedience to God. The soul thus instructed by the love of God acted purely through God and had no need of the institutional church. These doctrines were attributed primarily to Pedro Ruiz de Alcarez and Isabel de la Cruz of Toledo.[24] The Edict of 1525 and the inquisitional procedures against the two appear to have been highly successful, for the Toledo group disintegrated. The encounter between the Inquisition and this group of dedicated Christians was extremely important in the evolution of sixteenth-century spirituality, for it fed the authorities' growing suspicion of nearly *any* form of religious experience, particularly one that involved direct access to God. Long after *alumbradismo* had all but disappeared, the inquisitors continued to see signs of it in people and teachings that had no connection to it: Even Ignatius of Loyola was suspect.

Suspicion of mystical experience in general was a hallmark of the theologians popularly known as *letrados*, or "lettered ones," who understood religious faith as a matter of doctrine rather than of personal experience. In general, they discouraged speculation on theological issues among the laity and suggested that the pursuit of virtue ought to be the main focus of their devotion. The *letrados* were opposed by the *espirituales,* who focused less on doctrine than on mystical prayer, and taught that all Christians had a responsibility to grow in knowledge of self and of God—in short, to pursue Christian perfection, not just Christian morality. These two currents of thought might coexist uneasily in the same religious order. Many Dominicans were *letrados,* for example, but others were *espirituales.* The distinction between the two groups lies in two things: their conception of the Christian vocation vis-à-vis contemplative prayer and their understanding of the nature of faith as experiential or doctrinal. The learned *letrados* were always ready to advise the inquisitors in their judgment of cases, and by mid-cen-

---

dos' beliefs, but one would not expect to find any carefully developed Christology in a religious group that deprecated theological discussion. In any case, Lutheran pamphlets that might have been available to the *alumbrados* were not aimed specifically at developing a particular Christology. The Lutheran thesis merits further attention.

24. The charges against these two *alumbrados* are found in Márquez, *Los alumbrados,* pp. 244–57, 265–71. On the deprecation of sacraments, see pp. 247–51. Accusations that Isabel stressed obedience to the will of God rather than the will of prelates are on pp. 275–76.

tury they were well on their way to achieving control over theological discourse in Spain, though some *espirituales* continued to hold that theological learning that was not rooted in a lived experience of God was of little value.

Since the *letrados* were oriented toward orthodoxy and dogmatic theology, their greater influence on the inquisitors resulted in a concerted effort to root out unorthodox expressions of prayer in Christian circles. Thus when the word *alumbrado* emerged again after the appearance of the Valdés Index, it was a convenient way to accuse people, especially women, of false revelations and even of having been deluded by the devil.

Accusations of *alumbradismo* appeared sporadically through the next decades, then swelled into another wave in the 1570s.[25] These later groups, made up primarily of women associated with a male spiritual director, were active in southern Spain: Seville, Córdoba, Llerena, and Baeza. They attracted attention because their experience of ecstasy in prayer seemed too physical, and they were accused of various sorts of sexual misconduct. Contemporary critics stressed the moral deficiency of the women and men involved and faulted their spiritual practices rather than their orthodoxy per se.[26] Prosecution of *alumbrados* in the late sixteenth century is probably best understood as an attack on women's ecstatic experience and charismatic power.

Inquisitional activity against Lutheranism peaked in the 1550s and 1560s, then declined, but *alumbradismo* and witchcraft—crimes of which women were accused significantly more often than Lutheranism—continued to cause institutional concern. The second wave of *alumbradismo*, which continued through the 1620s, reflects the Inquisition's growing tendency to exert control over gender roles and to challenge women's claims to religious authority.

Institutional Control over the Diffusion of Ideas

Another means of social and intellectual control was the Inquisition's policy of censorship. Censorship was a critical strategy in an era in which the press had become the most formidable instrument for the diffusion of ideas. Yet

25. According to Márquez, this second wave had nothing to do with the earlier one; it is neither historically nor doctrinally legitimate to use the same word to describe the Toledo movement of the 1520s and the Llerena movement of the 1570s. For him the *alumbrado* phenomenon ended in 1559. See Márquez, *Los alumbrados*, pp. 28–30.

26. For more information on these later groups, see V. Beltrán de Heredia, "Un grupo de visionarios y pseudoprofetas que actúa durante los últimos años de Felipe II: Repercusión de ello sobre la memoria de Santa Teresa," *Revista Española de Teología* 7 (1947): 373–97 and 9 (1949): 483–534; Alvaro Huerga, *Historia de los alumbrados (1570–1620)*, 5 vols. (Madrid, 1974–94); Mir and Cuervo, "Los Alumbrados de Extremadura"; Luis Sala Balust, "En torno al grupo de alumbrados de Llerena," in *Corrientes espirituales en la España del siglo XVI: Trabajos del II Congreso de Espiritualidad* (Madrid, 1963), pp. 509–23.

censorship certainly affected different groups of people—literate and illiterate, clerical and lay, male and female—in disparate ways.

The Fifth Lateran Council established the initial guidelines for the censorship of books containing propositions considered contrary to the Catholic faith. Leo X placed the Inquisition in charge of this project. In the early sixteenth century, censorship took the form of edicts that prohibited the circulation of specific works.[27] The theoretical framework for censorship was already in place when the works of Martin Luther began to test its practical efficacy. According to J. M. de Bujanda, over 300,000 volumes of Luther's works were sold throughout Europe between 1517 and 1520.[28] When in 1521 the papal nuncio Aleandro reported that various of Luther's works had been translated into Castilian to be sent to Spain,[29] Cardinal Adrian of Utrecht, in his capacity as inquisitor general, ordered the search and seizure of all of Luther's works that could be found in Spain. The historian José González Novalín characterizes this measure as launching one of the efforts that the Spanish church most consistently applied throughout the sixteenth century: the seizure of books it considered heretical.[30]

Over time individual edicts and lists of suspect books gave way to the Index of Prohibited Books issued in 1559 by the inquisitor general Fernando de Valdés and republished in 1560. According to Virgilio Pinto Crespo, with the publication of the Valdés Index the Inquisition entered a new phase.[31] The most obvious novelty is the Index's length: it lists some 253 titles, fourteen editions of the Bible, nine editions of the New Testament, and fifty-four books of hours. Spiritual and mystical treatises specifically banned include Luis de Granada's *Libro de la oración, Guía de pecadores,* and *Manual de diver-*

---

27. These edicts were both a practical application and an extension of the theoretical framework established by the "Catholic monarchs," Ferdinand and Isabella, whose *Pragmática* of 1502 required official permission before books could be published or imported. For a modern transcription and analysis of this document, see J. M. de Bujanda, *Index de l'inquisition espagnole: 1551, 1554, 1559* (Sherbrooke, Québec, 1984), pp. 121–22, 165–213.

28. Ibid., p. 12. Bujanda also notes that it took only one month for all of Europe to gain access to copies of the 95 theses.

29. Among the works were probably Luther's *Commentary on Galatians* and *On Christian Liberty.* See González Novalín, "La Inquisición española," p. 179.

30. González Novalín, "La Inquisición española," p. 182. In my discussion of censorship I focus mainly on the index of 1559. For a more detailed analysis of the development of censorship in the early sixteenth century, see three works by Virgilio Pinto Crespo: *Inquisición y control ideológico en la España del siglo XVI* (Madrid, 1983); "Biblias publicadas fuera de España secuestradas por la Inquisición de Sevilla en 1552," *Bulletin Hispanique* 69 (1962): 236–47; and "Nuevas perspectivas sobre el contenido de los índices inquisitoriales hispanos del siglo XVI," *Hispania Sacra* 33 (1981): 593–641; and J. Ignacio Tellechea Idígoras, "La censura inquisitorial de Biblias de 1554," *Anthologica Annua* 10 (1962): 89–142.

31. Pinto Crespo, *Inquisición y control ideológico,* p. 150. Pinto Crespo summarizes the evolution of the Valdés Index on pp. 149–77.

sas oraciones; Juan de Avila's *Audi, filia;* Erasmus's *Enchiridion;* Juan de Caza-lla's *Luz del alma;* and Bernabé de la Palma's *Via spiritus.*

More important, the Valdés Index contains many general prohibitions designed to raise religious scruples in readers' minds.[32] The Index required all readers to analyze the books they read to make sure they conformed to its standards. Indeed, the Index decreed that everyone had the responsibil-ity, under pain of excommunication, to submit to the Inquisition any book that contained "false, evil, or suspicious doctrine," and reserved the right to add books to the list as necessary. In summary, the Valdés Index of Prohib-ited Books was not merely a list of books prohibited to the public; it was an edict intended to limit the scope of religious speculation and to define reli-gious faith and practice very narrowly as the province of an educated elite whose task was not speculation but transmission of dogma.

If Pinto Crespo is right in identifying the Inquisition with ideological control, he is also right in identifying censorship not only with prohibition but also with teaching. The great importance of the Valdés Index lies in the change in the idea of censorship itself: "Censorship must be not just con-crete prohibitions but a plan to define a clear and precise dividing line be-tween orthodoxy and heterodoxy and an instrument to keep that line from shifting."[33] The Valdés Index also reflects the state's concession to the In-quisition of the leading role in the definition of ideological orthodoxy.[34]

The advances in censorship produced by the Valdés Index escalated with the appearance of the Index of 1583–84, which exceeded the old one in its rigor and norms for further censorship.[35] Known as the Quiroga Index, it was the result of over fourteen years of study and preparation and a com-prehensive synthesis of the Valdés Index and other sixteenth-century in-

---

32. In addition to specific works, the Valdés Index lists types of books that may not be printed: books printed after 1525 that do not include the name of the author, the press, and the date and location of the printing; books by known heretics; partial or whole translations of the Bible; books of hours that mention "superstitious practices"; books in Arabic or He-brew, or that tell of Muslim or Jewish practices; books regarding witchcraft or superstition; books critical of the Disputation of Regensburg; books with introductions, dedications, com-mentaries or annotations by heretical authors; and manuscripts that touch on the biblical tra-dition or the sacraments or the Christian religion, be they sermons, letters, treatises, or prayer manuals. The Index also prohibits the publication of any figure or image that is "inappropri-ate or injurious" to the Virgin Mary or the saints. See Ricardo García-Villoslada, ed., *La Igle-sia en la España de los siglos XV y XVI,* vol. 3 of *Historia de la Iglesia en España* (Madrid, 1980), pt. 2, pp. 706–17.

33. Pinto Crespo, *Inquisición y control ideológico,* p. 171.

34. See José Martínez Millán, "El catálogo de libros prohibidos de 1559: Aportaciones para una nueva interpretación," *Miscelánea Comillas* 37 (1979): 179–80.

35. The Index of 1583–84 is reproduced in F. H. Reusch, *Die Indices librorum prohibitorum des sechzehnten Jahrhunderts* (1886; Tübingen, 1961), pp. 377–477.

dexes.[36] With the Quiroga Index, censorship became the norm to which literary creativity had to conform. The Quiroga Index, Pinto Crespo observes, reflected

> a conscious grasp of the catalog's value as a tool of censorship. It served to justify such activity, enlarge its field of action, and define its objectives more precisely. It was the most scrupulously worked-out catalog of the sixteenth century and in some ways can be considered a model. It was also one of the first manifestations of the advent of the religious program designed at Trent.[37]

The most important result of these two indexes was an atmosphere that stifled the production of spiritual tracts. Melquíades Andrés Martín has identified two distinct waves of spirituality in sixteenth-century Spain, separated by the Valdés Index.[38] The first, based mainly in the writings of the reformed Franciscans, cultivated the ground for the flowering of mysticism in the second half of the sixteenth century. The reforms of religious orders in Spain enacted in the first half of the century called for spiritual literature that fostered individual religious growth: lives of Christ and of the saints, tracts on the interior life and methodical mental prayer. This literature formed a sort of mystical vocabulary, the lexicon that facilitated the expression and analysis of such experience.

The strides in spirituality made in the reforms of the first half of the sixteenth century had much to do with the flowering of mysticism in the second half. As Melquíades Andrés explains, the *recogimiento* codified by Francisco de Osuna, Bernardino de Laredo, and Bernabé de la Palma "became the common mystical way in Spain, accepted by Santa Teresa, San Juan de Avila, San Francisco de Borja, San Pedro de Alcántara, and some Jesuits and Dominicans."[39]

---

36. Important indexes that contributed to the Quiroga Index include the Index of the Council of Trent (1564); the Antwerp catalog of 1570, developed from the Trent Index and the deliberations of a committee of theologians headed by the Spanish Augustinian Benito Arias Montano; and the Portuguese Index of 1581.

37. Virgilio Pinto Crespo, "La censura: Sistemas de control e instrumentos de acción," in Angel Alcalá et al., *Inquisición española y mentalidad inquisitorial* (Barcelona, 1984), p. 281.

38. The first period, 1523–59, saw the publication of a great number of books on withdrawal from worldly concerns, which were seized upon by the great mystics in the second period. This period of relative freedom in spiritual inquiry ended with the appearance of the Valdés Index, which attempted to stop the circulation of such books. In the second period (1580–1625) the works of Teresa and John of the Cross gained a following among the laity. The works of other mystics, such as Juan de los Angeles, Bartolomé de los Mártires, and Antonio Sobrino, also circulated. According to Andrés, this was the moment of "maximum vitality . . . among the Discalced Carmelites and other religious orders that accepted the contemplative reforms." A third period toward the end of the seventeenth century produced other mystics but lies beyond the scope of this book. See Melquíades Andrés Martín, *Los recogidos: Nueva visión de la mística española (1500–1700)* (Madrid, 1975), pp. 40–45.

39. Ibid., p. 41.

The advances in mystical techniques and analysis made by Teresa and John of the Cross are directly related to the spiritual tracts that circulated during the first half of the sixteenth century.

The Valdés Index of 1559 interrupted this flourishing by making it difficult for both authors and publishers to produce books that put advanced spiritual techniques in the hands of the masses. According to Melquiades Andrés, the Valdés Index "tried to banish affective spirituality in its various manifestations, encouraging the traditional spirituality of the practice of virtues and the destruction of vices over other ways of spirituality considered mystical."[40] Teresa of Avila's experiences bore witness to the growing intensity of censorship during her lifetime. In both *El camino de perfección* and the *Vida* Teresa criticized the banning of texts she considered orthodox and fundamental to the soul's spiritual growth. At the same time, Teresa recognized that censorship would continue to control the religious sphere in which her reforms must exist, and she urged her readers to develop their own spiritual resources rather than rely solely on written texts.

As the new mystical pathways opened in the first half of the century narrowed to a dogmatic and disciplined orthodoxy, so did the range of subjects appropriate for theological debate. Internal rules governing style as well as content constrained the few authors who wrote spiritual tracts in the second half of the century. If the works were to survive intact, certain topics had to be handled with extreme care, and authors used language to hide rather than reveal their intent. The long-term effects of such carefully systematized censorship are difficult to assess because we have no way of knowing what literature never made its way from the inquisitors' hands to the printing press. Three major trends are apparent, however: fewer books explored contemplation; fewer religious books were issued in the vernacular; and books written by women disappeared.

The Valdés Index encouraged a distinction between books published in Latin and those issued in the vernacular, thus determining the potential audiences of the works available. Instructional books, such as catechisms and moral treatises, were published in the vernacular; theological discourse was limited to Latin. The priorities of the press had changed, and vernacular translations of speculative theological works were no longer available. One result of this new orientation was the monopoly of the presses by university-trained, ordained theologians: the teaching office had become strictly sacerdotal. No books by female authors

---

40. Melquiades Andrés Martín, *La teología española en el siglo XVI,* 2 vols. (Madrid, 1976), 1:362.

emerged from the presses in Alcalá, for example, between 1550 and 1600.[41]

The inquisitors considered some issues particularly sensitive. The subject of divine revelation, for instance, raised questions that could provoke dangerous answers: What was its importance? How could one know if its origins were really divine and not diabolic? How did it fit into the religious life in general and in the sacramental experience of the recipient? Authors of mystical treatises recognized the difficulties their subject matter inevitably entailed, and they crafted their works accordingly, as carefully in style as in content. At a time when all personal religious experience was suspect, *alumbrados* took care to write of their religious experience in words of impeccable orthodoxy.

For women the indexes of prohibited books posed special problems of literacy and lexicon. Because most women did not read Latin, the Valdés Index systematically denied them the texts and vocabulary they needed to describe their religious experience in orthodox terms. Thus it was difficult for them to challenge confessors who gave them poor spiritual counsel and to avoid pitfalls in any sort of religious discourse, particularly when they sought to describe mystical experience. Modern scholars with hindsight readily distinguish between prayer techniques such as *dejamiento* and *recogimiento*, but then a significant amount of debate was necessary to define *dejamiento* and its heterodox assumptions. Such discussions of prayer encompassed many gray areas that necessitated a technical vocabulary. Because many women did not conform their expression of their experience to scholastic categories (or found that their experience did not conform to them), they were vulnerable to the scrutiny of the Inquisition's censors. As the genres of theological discourse shifted from speculative and mystical treatises to dogmatic texts, the technical terms used to describe mystical states were not accessible to vernacular writers. Religious women, increasingly pressured by their confessors into experiential exegesis, scrambled to find a vocabulary that would separate them from innovators and establish them within orthodox circles.

Control of the printed word was an important first step in determining and circumscribing the very nature of religious inquiry in sixteenth-century

41. Works by Angela of Foligno, Clare of Assisi, and Catherine of Siena were issued elsewhere before 1559, but I have not seen any of these works issued between 1550 and 1600 by any other press, nor do I know of any new *published* literature by women during this time period, with the exception of Teresa's works. For a review of sixteenth-century published literature, see, for example, Mariano Alcocer y Martínez, *Catálogo razonado de obras impresas en Valladolid, 1481–1800* (Valladolid, 1926); Juan Catalina García López, *Ensayo de una tipografía complutense* (Madrid, 1889); and Cristóbal Pérez Pastor, *La imprenta en Toledo: Descripción bibliográfica de las obras impresas en la imperial ciudad desde 1483 hasta nuestros días* (Madrid, 1887).

Spain. Censorship and the environment it engendered determined both the content of religious treatises and the types of theology and methodologies their authors explored. Finally, censorship effectively barred women from the written expression of their ideas and kept them from an important means of public self-construction.

Holy Women Challenged

The encounter between the Inquisition and the *alumbrados* represents a key moment in the shifting attitudes toward humanism, subjectivity, and mystical experience, all of which continued to lose ground in Spain after the 1520s. As the institutional church struggled to control the vernacular terms of spirituality, women were challenged in ways that men were not in their efforts to maintain the integrity of their religious authority. Though all internal religious experience was suspect to some degree by the 1540s, the instrumentality of the female visionary model—certainly the most accessible for spiritual women—underscored the precariousness of women's religious authority. Since the source of women's authority was external revelation or reflection on experience, and since it rested on a charismatic gift, it had to be examined for validity. As attitudes toward revelation changed, so inevitably did the authority of women's voices.

The downfall of Magdalena de la Cruz in the 1540s was a result of suspicion about women's spiritual experiences and a confirmation for religious hierarchs that women were not reliable spiritual leaders. Magdalena de la Cruz was tried by the inquisitional tribunal of Córdoba in 1546 for entering into a pact with demons. Before her ordeal, Magdalena had been abbess of the convent of Santa Isabel Francisca in Córdoba and was well respected for her penitential practice and spiritual gifts. A contemporary reported that "she would go without eating or drinking for many days; she slept on the floor on a hard mat; she knew about things that had disappeared from the house; she always wore a *cilicio*,[42] she was observed levitating in prayer; she transported herself from time to time; she knew who was coming to see her and where they were from."[43] When she was tried in 1546, Magdalena confessed that she had entered into a pact with a demon at the age of twelve. He promised to heap great honors upon her, she said, and he brought a

42. *Cilicio* is often translated as "hair shirt," and that may be the appropriate translation in this case; but the word can also refer to a penitential device formed of metal. I have chosen not to translate *cilicio* to avoid forcing on it a meaning it may not have.

43. Testimony of Luis de Zapata in Jesús Imirizaldu, *Monjas y beatas embaucadores* (Madrid, 1977), p. 33. "Estaba sin comer ni beber muchos días; dormía en el suelo en una seca estera; decía las cosas que se habían hurtado en la casa; traía perpetuo cilicio; veíanla estar en oración en una vara del suelo en alto; transportábase de cuando en cuando; decía quién la venía a buscar y de qué parte."

naked black man and invited her to engage in carnal sin. The black man was ugly, though, so she took the demon as her lover instead.[44] She admitted that she had faked her religious experiences, and the court sentenced her to reclusion in her convent as the lowest-ranking member of her religious community. During the second half of the sixteenth century, Magdalena de la Cruz was often held up as a warning of the danger and public scandal a woman could cause.

The doctrine of women's intellectual and moral inferiority—explicit in contemporary treatises on witchcraft but also present in other theological treatises, catechisms, and pious literature—attacked women's capacity to discern between divine and diabolical inspiration.[45] Thus women had a difficult time overcoming the assumption that, no matter how accomplished they were, they could always be "instruments of the devil." Religious and social controls over women emerged to protect society from female power, which was, by definition, rarely virtuous. Men, Mary Elizabeth Perry observes, "did not deny that women actually had power. . . . Women who succumbed to their weak and sinful natures held the power of evil, it was believed; and when they lost their fear and timidity, there was no one stronger or less afraid, or more infused with power to seduce, ensnare, and infect."[46] It was in the public interest, then, to limit women's public roles and freedom of movement. The confinement of holy women emerged in discussions of religious orders at the Council of Trent and was

44. Ibid., 47: "Tenía familiar dende que fue de cinco años y cuando le via de esta edad pensaba que era angel hasta que de doce años que confesó ser demonio y hizo pacto y convenencia con él y él prometió de sustentarla por gran tiempo en grandes onrras, y este diablo trijole un negro desnudo combidandola a deleites carnales; y ella como le vio tan feo huyó del y su familiar enojóse con ella y luego volvió a ella haciendo paces y en este día que hizo estas paces, tuvo deleites carnales hasta el día que lo confesó y en esto de carnalidades manifestó muy grandes cosas las quales verán en su sentencia." Imirizaldu attributes this description to another member of the religious community at Isabel Francisca.

45. Women's moral and spiritual inferiority was commonly assumed in early modern Spain. See, e.g., Clemente Sánchez de Vercial, *Libro de los exemplos por A.B.C.*, ed. John Easton Keller (Madrid, 1986), esp. pp. 235–39; Castañega, *Tratado de las supersticiones;* Diego de Simancas, *Institutiones catholicae* (Valladolid, 1552), chap. 20; Juan de Horozco y Covarrubias, *Tratado de la verdadera y falsa prophecia* (Segovia, 1588); Pedro de Ribadeneyra, "Tratado de la tribulación," in *Obras escogidas del padre Pedro de Ribadeneira de la Compañía de Jesús*, ed. Vicente de La Fuente, BAE 60 (Madrid, 1868); Pedro Navarro, *Favores del rey del cielo* (Madrid, 1622); Sor Magdalena de San Gerónimo, *Razón y forma de la galera, y casa real, que el Rey N.S. manda hazer en estos reinos para castigo de las mugeres vagrantes y ladronas, alcahuetas, hechizeras, y otras semejantes* (Salamanca, 1608); Bartolomé Alcaraz, *Chrono-historia de la Compañía de Jesús en la provincia de Toledo*, 2 vols. (Madrid, 1710); and Jerónimo de Sepúlveda, "Historia de varios sucesos del reino de Felipe II, 1584–1603," *Ciudad de Dios* 115 (1918).

46. Perry, *Gender and Disorder*, p. 8.

enforced by papal bull in 1566, but Spanish society was already moving in that direction. Indeed, gender ideology was pursued with grim determination.

> The fact that women and men did not always behave according to gender beliefs did not prevent lay and secular officials from repeatedly invoking these beliefs. Nor did they hesitate even when their gender ideals seemed completely incongruous with actual living conditions. In fact, gender beliefs that women required special protective enclosure seemed to be even more strongly invoked as men's preoccupation with wars and colonizing required women to participate more actively in the life of the city.[47]

Controls over women spanned a wide range of institutions with varying degrees of formality, from legislation governing women's commercial activities to guild policies to social practices connected with marriage and widowhood.

The controls exerted over women who aspired to holiness were equally diverse and pervasive. The symbols chosen to promote conceptions of womanhood, primarily the Virgin Mary and other female saints, emphasized the primacy of humility and obedience. By the end of the sixteenth century, Perry observes, the predominant images of Mary showed her as either innocent maiden or sorrowing mother. These images of purity, passivity, and social withdrawal appear "to reflect a need for social control, a concern for order that rested squarely on gender prescriptions."[48] Holy women were accused of spiritual arrogance when they spoke of their mystical experiences and what had been revealed to them. Over the course of the sixteenth century, the religious virtue of humility prescribed for women was defined in practice as withdrawal from the public sphere and dissociation from their own experience, authority, and power.

The enforced claustration of nuns clearly moved this agenda forward, but an alternate form of religious life for women, that of the *beata*, was not so easily controlled by ecclesiastical policy. A peculiarly southern European expression of the eremitical tradition in female monasticism, the *beata* had become a fixture in the religious landscape of Spain. Yet her autonomy was increasingly perceived as a lack of allegiance to the institutional church, and many *beatas* found themselves under investigation by the Inquisition. The church actively worked to destroy the credibility of these religious women, Perry finds, "using community rituals that transformed them from a symbol

47. Ibid., p. 9. Perry describes the narrowing of women's social roles on pp. 14–32.
48. Ibid., p. 43.

of holiness into one of illusion and deceit."[49] Kept in isolation as befitted weak women who had no male protector, subjected to relentless interrogation, their writings confiscated, the *beatas* were taught humility. The effects of the Spanish Inquisition on women require further investigation, but it is not too early to conclude, as Perry does, that "a major concern was to curb popular religious figures who had developed so much power independent of lay or ecclesiastical discipline."[50] Such a conclusion suggests that women, who by social definition were already disfranchised by both secular and religious sources of institutional power, could not achieve any real form of charismatic power without being challenged by the Inquisition.

Sixteenth-Century Definitions of Sanctity

Controlling ideas and written expressions of spirituality was an important task of the Inquisition, but its control of orthodoxy would have been incomplete without regulation of religious praxis. Thus inquisitors designed investigative techniques to scrutinize religious behavior for possible prosecution. The fact that the Spanish Inquisition could verify the "objective" authenticity of religious experience during the lifetime of a saint introduced a new dynamic into the relationship between saints and their contemporaries.[51] Popular acceptance of a saint could not guarantee the survival of his or her reputation for sanctity. Many religious—women in particular—found their credibility attacked by an inquisitional procedure.

In this climate, people who wanted to realize their spiritual aspirations found it helpful to display virtues well established within the Christian tradition—ascetic discipline, humility, charity, obedience. For both men and women, accepted practice shifted over the course of the century, so that ho-

49. Mary Elizabeth Perry, "Beatas and the Inquisition in Early Modern Seville," in *Inquisition and Society in Early Modern Europe,* ed. Stephen Haliczer (London, 1986), p. 148. See also Perry, *Gender and Disorder,* pp. 109–17. The loss of autonomy that spiritual women experienced was replicated in the secular realm. Perry has also noted the increasing tendency of Spanish institutions to control women's sexual expression by containing unmarried, sexually active women in brothels, prisons, or Magdalen houses. See Mary Elizabeth Perry, "Magdalens and Jezebels in Counter-Reformation Spain," in *Culture and Control in Counter-Reformation Spain,* ed. Anne J. Cruz and Perry (Minneapolis, 1992), pp. 124–44.

50. Perry, *Gender and Disorder,* p. 104.

51. The Inquisition's scrutiny of religious behavior calls into question Kleinberg's theory that religious authenticity is irrelevant in the communal recognition of sanctity. See Kleinberg, *Prophets in Their Own Country,* p. 7: "From a social point of view, saints exist in a Berkeleyan world—if they are not seen they do not exist. . . . For others, saints are what they are seen and believed to be, not what they actually are. The saints' inner lives and sincerity, important though they may be in theory, are of little concern to society, because they are beyond its reach. In other words, the charismatic need not believe in the authenticity of his powers to succeed in his role. The sincere ecstatic and the successful imposter play exactly the same social role and belong in the same social category."

liness became a more difficult endeavor than ever. Moreover, in many ways these changing perceptions of holiness tended to separate men's and women's avenues for religious expression.

First, the renewed emphasis on evangelization, partly a product of continuing expansion into the Americas and partly a result of Protestant advances, allowed men much greater access to areas outside Spain and steered them toward new approaches to monastic discipline. Geographical mobility, though not entirely denied to religious women, was limited because of the push toward the cloister.[52] The post-Tridentine trend toward the claustration of women was not always successful in decreasing women's sphere of influence. Women found creative ways to establish public support for their religious endeavors. Further, the life of the cloister enabled some women to form communities of mutual support in their efforts for spiritual advancement. Such, of course, was Teresa's vision of the Discalced Carmelite order.

After Trent the Spanish church became more clericalized. Tridentine ecclesiology encouraged emphasis on the sacraments, and the demand for confessors increased. The new emphasis on catechesis called for priests who could explain Christian doctrine.[53] Most parish priests understood their doctrinal duties in a very rudimentary sense: help parishioners to memorize the Our Father, the Hail Mary, and the Ten Commandments; explain the essentials of the mass; and go over the sacraments and mortal sins.[54] In Cuenca, Sara T. Nalle finds, "a generation of persuasion and enforcement" had to pass after Trent before people were taught their prayers.[55] Mystical doctrine and even the basics of mental prayer, however, were completely beyond Catholic education.

Though women were denied the kind of teaching authority a theologian, *letrado,* or even cleric would have, they were able to establish some forms of charismatic authority through direct experiences of divine revelation, such as visions. As with other spiritual currents, however, sympathy toward ecstatic

52. Convents for women were established in the Americas fairly early in the years of Spanish domination.

53. See Jean Pierre Dedieu, " 'Christianization' in New Castile: Catechism, Communion, Mass, and Confirmation in the Toledo Archbishopric, 1540–1560," in Cruz and Perry, *Culture and Control,* p. 4: "The Spanish bishops showed more concern for catechesis than did the fathers of Trent. . . . Many catechisms were being edited throughout Spain, earlier than in other Catholic countries."

54. A council in Toledo in 1565–66 ordered priests to teach the catechism on Sundays. In 1568 the archbishop of Toledo forbade communion to anyone who did not know the formula for the sign of the cross, the Paternoster, the Ave Maria, or the Salve Regina. For other examples, see ibid., pp. 4–6.

55. Nalle, *God in La Mancha,* p. 132. Nalle explores catechesis at the parish level on pp. 104–33.

experiences shifted through the century. Early in the century people had revered women whose experiences of God were clear (and therefore author-itative), but embodied prayer came increasingly to be viewed with suspicion. Juana de la Cruz (d. 1534), a nun at the Franciscan convent of Santa María de la Cruz near the village of Cubas, was accorded special license to preach in the diocese of Toledo during the 1520s because she went into a state of ec-stasy at the pulpit.[56] She was revered as God's messenger, a true preacher of God's word because God spoke through her inert body, and both Cisneros and Charles V consulted with her. By the 1570s, however, as prosecution of *alumbradas* became more frequent, women's reliance on ecstasy as a confir-mation of their access to God became an increasingly fragile link to religious authority. It certainly no longer allowed women access to the pulpit.

The narrowing of women's religious roles was clearly part of the Counter-Reformation agenda. The claustration of women in convents permitted their pursuit of holiness to be monitored and controlled. Claustration produced a definite gender differentiation in the patterns of holiness. Weinstein and Bell identify a "masculine type" of saint as the "holder of temporal or ecclesiasti-cal power, missionary to the heathen and fiery preacher of the word . . . a par-adigm reflecting both societal values and church regulations." Women took a far less public role: "Apart from the hospice, the theater of their activity had to be the cloister or the contemplative's cell."[57]

This public circumscription of women's religiosity led to a strong associ-ation of women with penitential practice. The model of the eremitical lifestyle reemerged with a plethora of artistic representations of Jerome and Mary Magdalene. Both men and women were encouraged to imitate these "desert dwellers," but women could embrace this lifestyle only in a convent. In her *Book of the Foundations* Teresa describes Catalina de Cardona (d. 1577) as a woman of "terrible" penances.

> She said she spent eight years in that cave, many days eating nothing but herbs and roots from the field. . . . She disciplined herself with a large chain, and these flagellations often lasted an hour and a half or two hours. Her *silicios* were so harsh that a woman told me that when she was returning from a pilgrimage she spent the night with her, and when she lay down to sleep, she saw [Catalina] take off the *silicios* covered with blood and clean them off.[58]

---

56. A manuscript collection of her sermons is available at the library in El Escorial. For more information on Juana de la Cruz, see Ronald E. Surtz, *The Guitar of God: Gender, Power, and Authority in the Visionary World of Mother Juana de la Cruz (1481–1534)* (Philadelphia, 1990). Surtz has transcribed some of Juana's sermons.

57. Weinstein and Bell, *Saints and Society,* pp. 237, 229.

58. *Fundaciones* 28:27: "Dijo que había estado ocho años en aquella cueva, y muchos días pasando con las yerbas del campo y raíces. . . . Las disciplinas eran con una gran cadena, y dura-

Catalina's severe penitential practice certainly made an impression on Teresa, but her religious practices—and certainly her charisma—were considered problematic because Catalina was not cloistered.

Pressured to associate herself with a religious order, Catalina finally assumed a Carmelite lay habit, but she would not submit to claustration. Catalina was not opposed to living in a community—her cave became the meeting place for a small school of spiritual disciples—but she objected to cutting off regular contact with outsiders. The growing need to control female religiosity led the Spanish Inquisition to try Catalina on at least one occasion. Catalina was probably considered prideful because she would not take a nun's vows and was overly committed to her disciplines. Catalina's penitential practice was not enough to overcome the institutional church's rejection of the independence a woman required to live the eremitical life.

Another of Teresa's contemporaries, the *beata* Francisca de Avila, faced great hostility after she founded a *beaterio* in Toledo for young women of poor families. Many people followed Francisca's advice and listened as she described her visions; twenty-six of them testified against her during her four-year trial, and the Inquisition condemned her in 1578. Francisca's reform efforts thus failed to achieve new opportunities for other women.[59]

Clearly the challenges women faced in their pursuit of holiness were formidable. Unable to define "holiness" for themselves, they were often also unable to conform to male definitions of female religious behavior. Thus religious accomplishment in or out of the convent involved a tremendous amount of politicking. In a very real sense, attitude was everything. The proper attitude toward religious authority—expressed primarily through obedience to institutional policy, opinion, and superiors—was essential to survival.

The trends toward narrowing orthodoxy, the hierarchical ordering of institutions, and the patriarchal repression of women are interrelated, at once responses to the dramatic changes of the sixteenth century and a new orientation of the Counter-Reformation church. Fear of sociopolitical change, a clear reality with the advances of Protestantism, was addressed (however inadequately) through the promulgation of institutions, regulations, and socioreligious practices that controlled women.

The Inquisition's concerns about Teresa cannot be separated from the climate of suspicion that surrounded religious experience. Various tribunals

---

ban muchas veces dos horas y hora y media. Los silicios tan asperísimos, que me dijo una persona, mujer, que viniendo de romería se había quedado a dormir con ella una noche, y héchose dormida, y que la vió quitar los silicios llenos de sangre y limpiarlos."

59. The transcript of Francisca's trial is found in AHN, Inq., leg. 113, no. 5.

sensed that the line between Teresa and the *alumbrados* was not at all clear. Isabel de la Cruz, one of the *alumbrados* of the Guadalajara circle, like Teresa, came from a family of *conversos*. The beginning of her religious life, too, was plagued by poor health and trancelike states that remind us of the experiences Teresa describes in the early chapters of her *Vida*. Both women read voraciously, and looked to the contemporary religious literature for spiritual advice. Indeed, some time ago Pierre Groult observed that Teresa had read more or less the same books as the *alumbrado* Pedro Ruiz de Alcaraz.[60] Both Teresa and the *alumbrados* were concerned about hypocrisy in regard to prayer. Both saw mental prayer as superior to vocal, and Teresa's comments in the *Moradas* regarding the contemporary practice of reciting prayers as penance—"Prayer must be done with reflection; because prayer that takes no notice of who is being addressed and who is asking what of whom—I don't call that prayer, no matter how much the lips move"[61]—recall the scorn of the *alumbrados* for Christians who pray as if to dispatch a duty.

The major difference between Teresa and the *alumbrados* lay in institutional allegiance. Although several *alumbrados* were affiliated with the Franciscans, they did not focus their reform efforts within any religious order or structure. Indeed, whereas Teresa's prayer life led her to more serious dedication to the reform of the Carmelite order, the *alumbrados* seem to have located the key to reform outside the monastic life—indeed, outside the institutional church—and inside the individual. From the perspective of institutional officials, reform movements, as innocent as they may seem, could not be separated from the control of orthodox structures because they might quickly draw support from the nobility and lead to uprisings. But even affiliation with the institutional church did not guarantee orthodoxy, as demonstrated by the proceedings against Francisco de Ortiz, one of the most promising Franciscan preachers of his day, and the notorious case of Archbishop Bartolomé de Carranza of Toledo.

Teresa is distinguished from the *alumbrados* not only by her obedience to her superiors and devotion to the sacraments but by her education. The many *conversos* among the *alumbrados* lacked the theological and devotional background assumed by the religious works they read. Teresa's background at the convent of Santa María de la Gracia, a sort of finishing school for young women of sufficient means, gave her a foundation in religious life that enabled her to interpret her spiritual experiences along orthodox lines.

---

60. Pierre Groult, *Les mystiques des Pays-Bas et la littérature espagnole du seizième siècle* (Louvain, 1927), p. 163.

61. *Moradas*, 1:1.7: "Oración ha de ser con consideración; porque la que no advierte con quien habla y lo que pide y quién es quién pide y a quién, no la llamo yo oración aunque mucho menee los labios."

Further, her extensive reading in classic spiritual texts gave her a theological background as strong as that of many of her male peers.

Teresa realized that the boundary between what the Inquisition considered orthodox and unorthodox was extremely hazy. During Teresa's beatification process the Carmelite nun Ana de la Trinidad testified that a representative of the Inquisition, Alvaro de Quiñones, visited Teresa anonymously to warn her to remember Magdalena de la Cruz, "whom the people had taken for a saint, whereas the devil had her completely under his control." With no slightest change of expression Teresa replied very humbly, "I never remember her without trembling."[62] Indeed, Teresa's anxiety over her standing as a good Catholic is reflected in her last words of thanksgiving: "I give you many thanks for having made me a daughter of your Church and that I have ended my days in her. At last, Lord, I am a daughter of the Church."[63]

Teresa's literary vocation thus can be viewed as an attempt to counter the suspicions cast on women's religious experience by the Inquisition's procedures against the *alumbrados* in several ways: (1) by offering explanations of the technique of mystical prayer; (2) by presenting an alternative to the potentially confusing mystical doctrine of the leading representative of the *recogimiento* school, Francisco de Osuna; (3) by emphasizing the importance of the sacramental life of the church; and (4) by recovering the role of revelations and visionary experience in the mystical life.

Though Teresa never used the term *alumbrados,* the effects of the movement were probably the most important influence on her literary objectives. The suspicions of prophecy and of women's religious experience which the movement had inflamed affected Teresa's credibility. Thus her apologia was at once personal—she had to legitimize her religious authority and defend her orthodoxy—and theoretical in its justification of her epistemology and the mystical experience in general. In her works Teresa devoted a significant amount of time to the theological problems generated by the *alumbrados*: the role of visions in religious experience; the discernment of spirits; the spiritual and moral debility of women in this area; and the importance of

---

62. Ana de la Trinidad, *Proceso de Salamanca* (1591), in *BMC* 18:43–44: "Vínola una vez a hablar don Alvaro de Quiñones, sin quererse dar a conocer, y díjola, porque le respondía, que se acordase de Magdalena de la Cruz, a quien la gente había tenido por santa y el demonio tenía muy rendida y sujeta. La Madre no se alteró poco ni mucho de aquella comparación, antes con mucha humildad respondió: 'Nunca vez me acuerdo de ella que no tiemble.'"

63. "Muchas gracias os doy que me habéis hecho hija de vuestra Iglesia y que acabe yo en ella. Al fin, Señor, soy hija de la Iglesia." Many witnesses cite these words that Teresa spoke on her deathbed. See the Alba *Proceso* of 1592 in *BMC* 18, particularly the testimony of Constancia de los Angeles, Isabel de la Cruz, Juana del Espíritu Santo, Catalina Bautista, María de San Francisco, and Mariana de la Encarnación.

the sacraments and allegiance to the institutional church.[64] As well, Teresa's detailed and precise explanations of mystical experience were meant to distinguish the experiences she described from those of the *alumbrados*.

Recognition of the censors' suspicions is readily apparent in Teresa's works. First, her language was as exact as possible; lacking formal theological training, she made no attempt to employ technical terms, but she did explain mystical phenomena as thoroughly and accurately as possible in an effort to separate herself from the *alumbrado* movement and the contemporary suspicions of mystical experiences, especially those with a sensory element. Second, Teresa was very careful about the literary and theological sources she mentioned. Many of her favorite authors appeared on the Valdés Index, and there was always the possibility that other authors might seem suspect in the future. Third, she employed a series of rhetorical devices to justify her right to write as an "unlettered woman." Finally, and most important, Teresa practiced a sort of self-censorship; her allusions to controversial subjects, such as her *converso* origins, permitted contemporary readers (especially those who knew her) to understand the subtext, but she never spoke openly enough to attract attention.

Sixteenth-century Spain would not seem to be fertile ground for a flowering of mystical literature. Ironically, however, the same period that saw the rise of a rigid system of religious repression also witnessed what was one of the most fecund eras in the history of Christian mysticism. Religious reform movements of the first half of the century had encouraged the circulation of spiritual treatises in the vernacular. When religious practices were scrutinized by the Inquisition, many men and women responded to the challenge by developing their internal piety even as they attempted to conform to ever-changing lines of orthodoxy.

Both the suspicion of mystical experience in general and the appearance of the Valdés Index played important roles in the evolution of Teresa's literary vocation. Her inner experience of God stood in direct contrast to the Inquisition's warnings against the *alumbrados*, signaling to her that not all spiritual gifts were delusions. As she reflected on this experience, in consultation with numerous books (some of which were later placed on the Index and taken away from her) and spiritual directors, Teresa grew increasingly confident in the validity of her religious experience. She wanted to provide a coherent, orthodox mystical treatise to dispel institutional fears about spirituality. Besides, as she grew in her conviction that contemplation was

---

64. Since Teresa viewed the *luteranos* as people whose lack of respect for institutional authority threatened the unity of the church, her comments in this regard were equally a message to them.

the key to religious reform, Teresa needed an authoritative text for the spiritual development of the Discalced Carmelites.

Teresa's primary importance in this era of Christian spirituality was her ability not only to rewrite her own life but in effect to rewrite charismatic experience so that it would fit within the parameters of Tridentine Catholicism. She responded to the challenge posed by distrust and repression of mystical experience by developing new resources for Catholic spiritual reform. Her mystical works argued quite forcefully that charismatic experience did not have to be viewed as a potential danger to the institutional church, but could instead be an important source of Roman Catholic identity.

2
Filling the Void:
The Vocation
of Teresa de Jesús

Few of the many biographies of Teresa de Jesús incorporate the historical realities of her day in their analysis of her personality.[1] At root this problem is one of sources: most biographers rely heavily on Teresa's own descriptions of herself without verifying and modifying them by reference to other historical sources, and often fail to understand the significance of details poignantly absent from Teresa's works, such as her *converso* background. Because Teresa never mentions it, some historians still claim that she did not know about it.[2]

By the same token, many biographies do not give details of Teresa's problems with the Inquisition, and literary critics rarely take into account the effect of contemporary censorship on the style and content of her works. During her lifetime Teresa was denounced to the Inquisition on at least six occasions. These accusations attacked both her person and her writings, raising suspicions about the orthodoxy of her mystical experiences and her use of prophecy. These encounters played an important role in shaping Teresa's public persona.

1. Teófanes Egido calls for a new biography, one that refuses to "perpetuate the image of the saint isolated in a greatness that never manages to situate itself within [contemporary] social, economic, political, and psychological conditions": "El tratamiento historiográfico de Santa Teresa: Inercias y revisiones," in *Perfil histórico de Santa Teresa,* ed. Egido (Madrid, 1981), p. 22.
2. I believe one of the most important aspects of recent Teresian scholarship is the examination of Teresa's *converso* background and its possible influences on her religious vocation. See ibid., pp. 13–31; Narciso Alonso Cortes, "Pleitos de los Cepedas," *Boletín de la Real Academia Española* 25 (1946): 85–110; Teófanes Egido, "Ambiente histórico," in *Introducción a la lectura de Santa Teresa,* ed. Alberto Barrientos (Madrid, 1978), pp. 53–88; Egido, "La familia judía de Santa Teresa," *Studia Zamorensia* 3 (1982): 449–79; José Gómez Menor, *El linaje familiar de Santa Teresa y de San Juan de la Cruz: Sus parientes toledanos* (Toledo, 1970); Dierdre Green, *Gold in the Crucible: Teresa of Avila and the Western Mystical Tradition* (Longmead, 1989), pp. 77–119; Francisco Márquez Villanueva, "Santa Teresa y el linaje," in *Espiritualidad y literatura en el siglo XVI* (Madrid, 1968); and Homero Seris, "Nueva genealogía de Santa Teresa," *Nueva Revista de Filología Hispánica* 10 (1965): 363–84.

In the most serious case against Teresa, which developed in Seville in 1576, the actual accusations do not survive. Several retractions of accusations made against her by Carmelite nuns in 1578–79 are available, and it is through these retractions that we must reconstruct the events in Seville.[3] The original documentation of other procedures against Teresa is similarly inaccessible. Documentation of posthumous inquiries into Teresa's orthodoxy after the publication of her complete works in 1588 is more accessible. Several *memoriales*, or briefs, written by theologians regarding Teresa's mystical theology are available in the Archivo Histórico Nacional and have been transcribed in Enrique Llamas's *Santa Teresa y la Inquisición española*. We also have contemporary accounts of the "difficult times" that Teresa and her Discalced Carmelites encountered. María de San José, Jerónimo Gracián, and others wrote about the difficulties "nuestra santa Madre" experienced in Seville and other places. Finally, we can extrapolate somewhat from the trials of other women in approximately the same situation as Teresa.

Because many documents have not survived, the story of Teresa's problems with the Inquisition can perhaps never be written in its entirety.[4] I suggest, however, that Teresa's interaction with the Inquisition—both direct and indirect—was the most significant influence on her career as a writer. Concern over the lack of treatises on contemplation caused by the Valdés Index led Teresa to write her *Vida* and other works so that the Carmelites would have the books necessary for their spiritual development. Continued accusations to the Inquisition caused Teresa to change the style, content and rhetorical strategies of her works. Engaged in a struggle for survival, Teresa alternately criticized contemporary religious strictures and made great protestations of allegiance both to institutions at large and to persons who might protect her from such strictures. Teresa's quest for the authority that would justify her religious experiences, her reform movement, and her orthodoxy makes sense only when it is viewed against the backdrop of the Inquisition.

3. Transcriptions of these retractions are available in Llamas.
4. Though many authors accept Llamas's *Santa Teresa y la Inquisición española* as the authority on the subject, there are several problems with it. First, it focuses on Carmelite documents without reading them in dialogue with inquisitional records and the trials of other women. In fact, Llamas states clearly (p. 389) that Teresa's problems with the Inquisition have "no historical connection" with those of her contemporaries. Second, Llamas's apologetic tone interferes with his efforts to put events in perspective. It may be tempting to think that Teresa's canonization demonstrates her ultimate "victory" over the Inquisition, but it is worth remembering that during her lifetime and for years after her death, neither Teresa's orthodoxy nor the legitimacy of her reforms was a given. Later works that discuss Teresa's difficulties with the Inquisition rely solely on Llamas's analysis. See, e.g., Green, *Gold in the Crucible*, pp. 120–52, and Alison Weber, *Teresa of Avila and the Rhetoric of Femininity* (Princeton, 1990), esp. pp. 120–21, 153–54.

Further, Teresa's encounters with the Inquisition make it clear that her drive to found new convents was spurred by the wish to create havens of sorts for women who were striving for spiritual perfection, a goal that many theologians and inquisitors alike doubted that women could achieve. Her writings were her efforts to overcome the effects of the Valdés Index and provide the guidance these women needed. Her activities on both fronts, then, should be seen as acts of resistance to an increasingly clerical, patriarchal, and authoritarian Counter-Reformation church.

The responses to Teresa's agenda were quite mixed. Although she had the approbation or support of many influential religious figures, all of her books were subjected to close scrutiny by the Inquisition's censors, and she was asked to rewrite several parts of them. The most problematical areas were her presumed arrogance for teaching mystical theology, her criticism of the Inquisition, her defense of women's pursuit of mystical perfection, and her discussion of mystical experience as a source of religious knowledge.

It was not only her writings that drew attention to Teresa; in fact, she became suspect because of her visibility as a reformer in what seemed to some people blatant disrespect of the norms established at the Council of Trent for the strict claustration of religious women. Since Teresa's efforts at reform were resisted on several fronts, the Inquisition was frequently informed of her activities. Although she may have been somewhat naive at first, Teresa soon came to realize that her relationships with inquisitional officials, members of the ecclesiastical hierarchy, civil authorities, and her own reformed Carmelite nuns would determine the survival of her life's work. The growing intensity of Teresa's encounters with the Inquisition reflects the problems that her spirituality and message embodied in sixteenth-century Spain.

Vocation: Reformer and Writer

Just as Teresa was discovering and living her double vocation as reformer and writer, the Valdés Index threatened her entire reform agenda. The spiritual formation of her Discalced Carmelites depended on access to mystical treatises that could orient and guide their immersion in contemplative prayer. Teresa stepped into this vacuum by telling her life story in a book she referred to as *The Story of God's Mercies,* or her *Vida.*[5] The *Vida* describes quite poignantly Teresa's journey toward discerning her calling and the obstacles she overcame to achieve her goals.[6]

5. Ironically, it was the *Vida* that caused the most trouble with the Inquisition because many of Teresa's contemporaries did not believe it should circulate.

6. We are concerned here only with specific moments in Teresa's life. Readers interested in a more general biography of Teresa may consult Marcelle Auclair's now quite dated but once

Most readers of the *Vida* recall Teresa's story of her conversion before a statue of Christ in chapter 9. Scholars date this event about 1554. At that time Teresa had been a nun at the convent of the Encarnación about twenty years, and she saw clearly the limitations to her spiritual growth posed by her affiliation with the Carmelite order and that particular convent. Thus the conversion experience identified the beginning of her commitment to founding new options for women in religious life.

The life of contemplation to which Teresa committed herself before the statue of Christ was impossible in her present situation. The convent of the Encarnación had fallen on difficult times. Because the house was overcrowded and revenues were limited, the wealthier nuns were encouraged to leave the convent to live with family or friends. Divisions along lines of economic status were so exacerbated that some of the poorer nuns showed signs of malnutrition. "Parlor conversations" with wealthy benefactors interrupted the sisters' liturgical duties and prayer time. Looking back on this time, Teresa noted how important silence and solitude were if one were to make progress in prayer:

> When one begins to give oneself to God, there are so many backbiters that in self-defense one must seek company until they become strong enough not to be overwhelmed by suffering; if not, they will find themselves in great conflict. It seems to me that this is why some saints used to go to the desert.[7]

Teresa's reading of the hermit tradition and early founders of the Carmelite order gave her ideas about how to reformulate religious life so that it would support the nuns' contemplative vocation.

Her experience of prayer was calling Teresa to a new religious rigor that required a change in atmosphere and attitude. It is not possible to say exactly when Teresa decided to return to the Carmelites' primitive rule, although the idea had attracted her for many years. According to several contemporaries, the decision to reform the order was born of her near-death experience in 1538–39. "While she was unconscious," said Beatriz de Mendoza, "Our Lord had told her what to do about the Order she founded, because later she began to speak about it with great fervor. . . ."[8]

---

classic *Teresa of Avila* (New York, 1959); E. Allison Peers's still useful *Mother of Carmel* (London, 1946); Rowan Williams's compact but solid *Teresa of Avila* (Harrisburg, Pa., 1991); or the more detailed, three-volume study by Efrén de la Madre de Dios and Otger Steggink, *Santa Teresa y su tiempo* (Salamanca, 1982–84).

7. *Vida* 7:22: "Si uno comienza a darse a Dios hay tantos que murmuren, que es menester buscar compañía para defenderse, hasta que ya estén fuertes en no les pesar de padecer; y si no, veranse en mucho aprieto. Paréceme que por esto debían usar algunos santos irse a los desiertos."

8. *BMC* 18:397: "En aquel tiempo y desmayo le había Nuestro Señor mandado lo que toca acerca de la Orden que fundó, porque luego ella empezó a tratar de ello con gran fervor. . . ." See also the testimony of Ana María de Jesús in *BMC* 19:442.

Other witnesses describe conversations at the Encarnación in which Teresa spoke of the lives of the earliest Carmelites and suggested a return to the primitive rule of Carmel. The concrete planning for the founding of San José, the first Discalced Carmelite convent, probably began in 1560–61.[9]

Teresa's reform ideals fit into the larger context of the Catholic Reformation and concern over the spread of Protestantism. According to her contemporaries, Teresa felt this tension acutely and wished she had the freedom to travel to other countries to speak stirring words and convert Protestants back to Catholicism. In her testimony for Teresa's canonization María de San José Salazar explained Teresa's dilemma: "In particular she wanted to oppose the heresies in France, but as a woman she could not oppose them with sermons."[10] Instead, Teresa established as one of the Discalced Carmelites' special missions the support of the efforts of friars and priests through their prayers.[11]

As Teresa's reform agenda emerged, she advocated the vocation of Christian perfection, achieved through virtue and contemplation, as the only model that would save the church from the Reformation crisis. Teresa was convinced, J. Mary Luti writes, that

> the mortal danger in which [she] saw the Church engulfed on all sides could be remedied . . . ultimately only by holiness. . . . The reverence she felt for the expertise of the theologian and preacher at the service of the Church, her enormous desire to assist them in their work, and her recasting or augmenting of the purpose of the reformed monastery of San José to accord with this desire were predicated only partially upon a simple acceptance of their institutional authoritative role and admiration for the extent of their learning. What made Teresa most enthusiastic about *letrados* was the explosive potential for good in the Church and the world contained in the combination of learning *and holiness*.[12]

9. In *Vida* 32:10 Teresa describes a conversation in her cell regarding the reform of the order. According to Otger Steggink, this conversation, which probably took place in 1560, gave Teresa the resolve she needed to go ahead with the reform of the order. See Otger Steggink, *La reforma del Carmelo español: La visita canónica del general Rubeo y su encuentro con Santa Teresa (1566–1567)* (Rome, 1965), p. 357. By 1561 Teresa was working out the arrangements for the purchase of the convent with her brother-in-law, Juan de Ovalle.

10. *BMC* 18:489: "El motivo con que Nuestro Señor movió a la dicha madre Teresa a fundar estos monasterios en el rigor de la primera Regla del Carmen fué para se oponer en particular a los herejes de Francia, pues como mujer no podía oponerse a ellos con sermones."

11. When Juan de Ovalle was asked to explain the purpose of Teresa's reforms, he said she wanted "to unite souls to pray to Our Lord for the conversion of the heretics [in France, Germany, and England] and for the prelates of the Church." ("El principal intento que había tenido a hacer estas fundaciones, era ver la perdición de Francia y Alemania e Inglaterra, para en estas casas juntar algunas almas que suplicasen a Nuestro Señor por la reducción de estos herejes y por los prelados de la Iglesia"): *BMC* 18:126–27.

12. J. Mary Luti, "Teresa of Avila, 'Maestra Espiritual' " (Ph.D. diss., Boston College, 1987), pp. 117–18; emphasis hers.

Thus in Teresa's conception of the Discalced Carmelite order there was a recognition of the clear differences between male and female religious vocations and yet an attempt to have the two sexes work together in the pursuit of Christian perfection. If the Jesuits were emerging as the post-Tridentine male ideal, she offered the Discalced Carmelites as the model for women. Teresa's reforms resonated with the Tridentine decree on the claustration of religious women. Strict enclosure reinforced the contemplative vocation of her nuns, yet Teresa grounded this prayer in active missionary work. If they could not preach, Carmelite women could support the missionaries' efforts by prayer and penitential acts.

Yet prayer, penance, and monastic reform were not Teresa's only ways of realizing her desire to do missionary work. Her literary vocation was perhaps the strongest response to the growing need for Catholic identity. At the same time, it was an attempt to overcome the circumstances that marginalized spiritual women. In the end, Teresa expressed her desire to convert souls by her literary works, whose purpose was less to describe her own experiences than to teach and compel. Yet she encountered as much resistance to her literary endeavors as to her reform efforts.

Reflection on her reform ideals led Teresa to acknowledge the important role that religious books had played in her own spiritual development. Her vocation as an avid reader of pious books crystallized during several months of illness in 1532. While staying with her uncle Pedro de Cepeda, a widower who lived in Hortigosa, she read the letters of St. Jerome, and they strengthened her decision to become a nun.[13] Indeed, during this time reading was one of the few things that Teresa's fragile health permitted: "I suffered from fevers and fainting spells; ever since my health has been poor. Becoming fond of good books gave me life."[14]

13. Teresa's reference to Jerome's letters appears in *Vida* 3:7. Letter 14, to Heliodorus the monk, and letter 22, to Eustochium, probably had the most influence on Teresa. See Víctor García de la Concha, *El arte literario de Santa Teresa* (Barcelona, 1978), pp. 54–55. Several editions of Jerome's letters would have been available to Teresa. García de la Concha argues for the translation by Alonso Alvarez de Toledo, printed in Seville in 1527. Both A. Morel-Fatio and Guido Mancini cite the translation by Juan de Molina printed in Valencia in 1520. See A. Morel-Fatio, "Les lectures de Sainte Thérèse," *Bulletin Hispanique* 10 (1908): 45; and Teresa de Jesús, *Libro de la Vida,* ed. Guido Mancini (Madrid, 1982), p. 313. Efrén and Steggink cite a 1532 reissue of the Molina translation: *Santa Teresa y su tiempo,* 2:165.

14. *Vida* 3:7: "Habíanme dado, con unas calenturas, unos grandes desmayos; que siempre tenía bien poca salud. Dióme la vida haber quedado ya amiga de buenos libros." See also *Vida* 6:4. Teresa's continued medical problems reached a crisis in 1538 or 1539, when she was in a coma for four days. The nuns thought she was dead, but her father refused to let them bury her. When she regained consciousness, Teresa found wax in her eyes, one of the preparations for burial. See *Vida* 5:9.

Although the influence of contemporary spiritual classics on Teresa's thought is beyond the scope of this work, we should note that Teresa grounded her texts in the authority of accepted theological treatises. Thus, in addition to patterning her *Vida* on Augustine's *Confessions,* Teresa used concepts from the then-popular *Tercera parte del libro llamado Abecedario espiritual,* written in 1527 by Francisco de Osuna.[15] She incorporated Osuna's terminology when she described movement in prayer, such as the soul's "rise above itself" and its "entrance into itself," although she refined his definitions somewhat. As one of the masters of the *recogimiento* school, Osuna provided Teresa with several theological terms for her mystical experience, helping her to differentiate her experience from that of the *alumbrados.*[16] Another Franciscan of the *recogimiento* school, Bernardino de Laredo, provided Teresa with further justification for the orthodoxy of her mystical experience. When her confessors could not understand the intricacies of her experience, Teresa marked passages of Laredo's *Subida del Monte Sion.* This book was particularly helpful in the difficult question of the role of the soul during contemplation and what exactly it meant "not to think about anything."[17]

Books were also an important part of Teresa's reform, helping the nuns in their spiritual formation. In the *Constitutions* for the Discalced Carmelites Teresa recommends that the following books be made available to the nuns for their pious reading: the *Vita Christi* by the Carthusian Ludolph of Saxony, translated by Ambrosio Montesinos and edited in four volumes in Alcalá in 1502–3; the *Flos sanctorum;* the *Contemptus mundi,* or *The Imitation of Christ,* by Thomas a Kempis; the *Oratorio de religiosos* by the Franciscan Antonio de Guevara, published in Valladolid in 1542; and books by Luis de Granada and Pedro de Alcántara.[18] Teresa also expressed affection for Cassian's *Collations.*[19]

15. Teresa mentions the *Third Spiritual Alphabet* in *Vida* 4:7.

16. For more on Francisco de Osuna and his influence on Teresa, see Efrén and Steggink, *Santa Teresa y su tiempo,* 1:239–50; García de la Concha, *El arte literario,* pp. 65–74; Fidèle de Ros, *Un maître de Sainte Thérèse: Le père François d'Osuna, sa vie, son oeuvre, sa doctrine spirituelle* (Paris, 1936); Rossi, *Teresa de Avila,* pp. 37–42.

17. Teresa mentions the *Subida* in *Vida* 23:12. For the influence of Laredo on Teresa see García de la Concha, *El arte literario,* pp. 74–78. The third Franciscan author Teresa mentions is Alonso de Madrid, whose *Arte de servir a Dios,* published in Seville in 1521, she recommends to those who have reached the first level of prayer. See *Vida* 12:2.

18. See *Constitutions* 8. These books would have included Granada's *Libro de la oración y consideración* (Salamanca, 1554); *La guía de pecadores* (Lisbon, 1556); and *El memorial de la vida cristiana* (Lisbon, 1565); and probably Alcántara's *Tratado de la oración y meditación* (Lisbon, 1556). These two authors found themselves on the Valdés Index of 1559, to Teresa's distress. On the censorship of Luis de Granada, see Justo Cuervo, *Luis de Granada y la Inquisición española* (Madrid, 1915).

19. See the testimony of Petronila Bautista in *BMC* 19:584.

As this list reveals, Teresa was an avid reader of most of the spiritual treatises then available in the vernacular. Despite her inability to read Latin and
her lack of training in the scholastic method of the universities, Teresa had
certainly read as much as many of her better versed confessors, perhaps
more. The absence of technical terms in her works and her own protestations of ignorance must not mislead us into thinking that Teresa's spiritual
experiences were intellectually foreign to her. Although some of her mystical experiences preceded her reading of any of the books she recommended
in the *Constitutions*, for Teresa mystical experience and the reading of spiritual books were complementary activities.[20] Lacking a teacher of contemplative technique, Teresa actively searched for guidance in contemporary
spiritual literature. As she reflected on this time period, most likely between
1535 and 1554,[21] Teresa wrote:

> It seems to me now that the Lord meant me not to find anyone to teach me
> [mental prayer], because it would have been impossible, I think, to persevere the
> eighteen years I bore this trouble, and in such great [spiritual] drought, for not
> being able to discuss [anything]. Throughout all of this, if I had not just received
> communion, I never dared to begin to pray without a book; for my soul feared
> to be in prayer without one as much as if I had to fight against many enemies.[22]

Teresa's vocation as a writer is tightly bound to her vocation as a reformer, for her objectives could be realized only by monks and nuns with an

---

20. See, e.g., *Vida* 4:7: "Comenzó el Señor a regalarme tanto por este camino, que me hacía
merced de darme oración de quietud, y alguna vez llegaba a unión, aunque yo no entendía qué
era lo uno ni lo otro, y lo mucho que era de preciar." Before Teresa experienced these spiritual
gifts, she had already read Jerome's letters, Gregory's *Moralia*, and Osuna's *Third Spiritual Alphabet*.

21. Many scholars take 1554 to be the date of Teresa's conversion before the statue of Christ
at the pillar, but the chronology of the conversion experience is still controversial. Critical in the
dating of the conversion is the appearance of a Castilian translation of Augustine's *Confessions* in
1554; this date is most likely the earliest acceptable one. Silverio de Santa Teresa, however, locates
the conversion in 1553; see his *Historia del Carmen descalzo en España, Portugal y América*, 15
vols. (Burgos, 1935–52), 1:331. Miguel Mir and Jerónimo de San José claim that the statue conversion occurred in 1555: Miguel Mir, *Santa Teresa de Jesús*, vol. 1 (Madrid, 1912), p. 180. The
historians who argue for 1554 follow Efrén and Steggink, *Santa Teresa y su tiempo*, 1:328–29. On
the basis of six chronological calculations of events mentioned in the *Vida*, Juan Ignacio Ugarte
Grijalba argues that the statue conversion did not occur until 1556: *La segunda conversión: Estudio de la renovación de la vida espiritual, en Santa Teresa de Jesús* (Lima, 1979), pp. 19–25.

22. *Vida* 4:9: "Ahora me parece que proveyó el Señor que yo no hallase quien me enseñase;
porque fuera imposible—me parece—perseverar dieciocho años que pasé este trabajo, y en
estos grandes sequedades; por no poder—como digo—discurrir. En todos estos, si no era acabando de comulgar, jamás osaba comenzar a tener oración sin un libro; que, tanto temía mi
alma estar sin él en oración, como si con mucha gente fuera a pelear." Although I have translated "tener oración" as "to pray," it means literally "to have prayer," and carries the implication
of receiving a spiritual gift or being engaged in mystical prayer.

advanced spiritual foundation in the techniques of mental prayer, an important part of the Discalced Carmelite vocation.[23] This education, like Teresa's own, must be based on the reading of spiritual books and personal experience within the religious community. With the publication of the Valdés Index in 1559, however, many of the spiritual treatises that had given Teresa guidance in her early years were suddenly prohibited. Teresa lamented the appearance of that index: "When they took away many books written in the vernacular, so they would not be read, I was very sorry, because some of them gave me pleasure, and I could not read them in Latin. But the Lord said to me, 'Don't be distressed, I will give you a living book.' "[24] The "living book" was probably the mystical doctrine that Teresa and other *espirituales* had experienced and in fact themselves embodied. J. Mary Luti explains:

> The notion of the "living" or "true" book ran like a vein through the various wings of the sixteenth century affective prayer movement, emphasizing in dramatic fashion the thoroughgoing interiority of the movement and its consequent ability to transcend the difficulties imposed by the *letrados'* insistence that religious experience conform to their interpretation of Scripture and scriptural imperatives. Moreover, by depending upon the knowledge the living book communicated, they could, for example, as in Teresa's case, survive the intended mortal sounding when the Inquisition took the books away."[25]

Teresa's grief was not solely for her own access to such texts. As we have seen, by the time the Valdés Index appeared, Teresa had basically accomplished her own literary and spiritual formation. Part of what saddened her was that the texts that had helped her interpret her mystical experiences

23. Teresa's concern for promoting an atmosphere conducive to reflection and contemplative prayer are apparent in her *Constitutions,* first written in 1563. The *Constitutions* ordered strict enclosure in the convent and prohibited private property. These principles freed the nuns from temporal concerns and allowed them to follow the communal life with more complete dedication. To maintain the self-sufficiency of the convent and to encourage charity among the sisters, Teresa ordered that the communities remain small. Finally, to encourage the nuns in their dedication to prayer, Teresa ordered the reading of spiritual literature, examination of conscience, a regular liturgical life with mass and communion, and continued silence, broken only during the time for recreation. As an integral part of the life of prayer, Teresa implemented increased mortification: strict adherence to fasts and abstinences, increased application of discipline, austerity in the habit, and manual labor during free time. Teresa's first *Constitutions* were approved by a papal brief dated July 17, 1565. Teresa revised them in 1567, and adapted them from time to time to the circumstances of some of her later foundations. See the interesting portrait of the first Discalced communities in Steggink, *La reforma del Carmelo español,* pp. 388–409.

24. *Vida* 26:5: "Cuando se quitaron muchos libros de romance, que no se leyesen, yo sentí mucho, porque algunos me daba recreación leerlos, y yo no podía ya, por dejarlos en latin, me dijo el Señor: 'No tengas pena, que Yo te daré libro vivo.' "

25. Luti, "Teresa of Avila," p. 114.

would now be denied to her contemporaries. As the passage suggests, however, Teresa was beginning to realize her own vocation as a writer: instead of having to rely on the external authority of other texts, her own experience of the contemplative life, in the form of a living book, would provide her with teaching authority. The prohibitions in the Valdés Index were a major motivation for Teresa to move from reading books to writing them.

Not long after the statue conversion, Teresa began to record her experiences and her prayer techniques so that her confessors might evaluate the state of her soul.[26] These descriptions gave Teresa an opportunity to analyze and systematize her experience of God; over time she learned to describe it more carefully, while avoiding technical terms that might be considered inappropriate and perhaps dangerous for a woman to use. Thus by 1561, when Teresa began her *Vida,* she had already written several "relations," or "accounts of conscience." The earliest extant relation was most likely written in 1560, though she says she wrote several earlier relations, the first of them shortly after the statue conversion.[27]

Capitalizing on her relations, Teresa undertook to write the complete story of her life, and finished the first version early in 1562, just before she founded the first Discalced Carmelite convent, San José.[28] Teresa gave the book to her confessor, García de Toledo, to read and comment on. García did not hesitate to show it to his friends, among them Pedro Ibáñez, another Dominican confessor; Alvaro de Mendoza, bishop of Avila; and Pedro Domenech, rector of the Jesuit house in Toledo. In 1564 García returned the manuscript with the readers' request for revisions. In the second version of the *Vida* she tried to make her experience of prayer more objective, probably adding what we now know as chapters 11–22, which cause some loss of literary flow. With these alterations the work became less an account of Teresa's conscience or general confession than a treatise on prayer.[29] This second version was finished in 1565, and Teresa submitted it to her new confessor, Domingo Báñez, for his consideration.

26. Teresa also sought the advice of spiritual "experts," including Juan de Avila and Pedro de Alcántara. She remained particularly devoted to her Jesuit confessors, explaining that they were the first to give her proper spiritual direction. See *Vida* 23:9, 15–18.

27. See Enrique Llamas Martínez, "Cuentas de conciencia," in *Introducción a la lectura de Santa Teresa,* ed. Alberto Barrientos (Madrid, 1978), pp. 375–76. Basing his calculations on conversion in 1554, Llamas claims that Teresa wrote her first relation in 1554–55, for the edification of her counselors. Teresa describes it in *Vida* 23:10–14. When she began to confess to her new Jesuit confessor, she wrote another relation (see *Vida* 23:15). Neither of these relations is extant. According to Llamas, both were either lost or incorporated in the *Vida.*

28. See Maximiliano Herráiz García, *Introducción al 'Libro de la Vida' de Teresa de Jesús* (Desierto de las Palmas, Castellón, 1981), p. 51.

29. If I am correct in believing that Teresa consciously patterned her *Vida* on Augustine's *Confessions,* the first version probably shared more of the *Confessions'* structure.

The second version—the *Vida* as we know it—is divided into three sections.[30] The first twelve chapters give an account of Teresa's struggles in prayer as a model of what spiritual progress the soul can accomplish through penitence, meditation, and other pious activities. Chapters 11 and 12 summarize these acts, moving them from the specific (Teresa's own experiences) to the general and forming a bridge between the section on Teresa's experience and the treatise on prayer in chapters 11–22.[31] In chapter 11 Teresa presents the metaphor that leads us through this second section, the metaphor of the soul as a garden and the four ways it can be watered. In chapter 23 she takes up the story of her life, which she continues to the end of the book (chap. 40). Here the struggles Teresa describes in the first section are resolved, as her life is now not her own but what God lives through her: "It's a new book from here on—I mean a new life. The one up to now was mine. The one I have been living since I began to explain these things about prayer is what God lived in me, as far as I can understand."[32]

Given the general suspicion of women's spiritual experience, we can expect that a nun's account of her life would have to be carefully constructed to survive the attacks it would generate. Teresa's *Vida* was a defense of her way of prayer, her vocation, and her entire persona. Luti suggests that Teresa "used *The Book of Her Life* as a key piece in a long process of establishing, in a world of male preeminence, her identity, reputation and credibility as an authority on the spiritual life, a teacher of mystical prayer." In the *Vida* Teresa made public, in a new way, the reform agenda she embodied, an agenda that included not only the reform of the Carmelite order but also the establishment of a place for women's mystical experience in the church. "Teresa fully understood the power of the word, and especially of the published word, to spark the transformation of women, men and institutions."[33]

During the time between the two versions of the *Vida* Teresa was involved in the arduous task of founding and administering the Discalced convent of

---

30. Herráiz García presents a structural interpretation of the *Vida* similar to the one that follows in respect to contrast and harmony, but his divisions are different. Herráiz García discerns four parts in the *Vida:* chaps 1–10 which present an open contrast between Teresa and God; chaps. 11–22, the treatise on prayer; chaps. 23–31, the beginning of harmony between God and Teresa; chaps. 32–40, a deepening of that harmony. The division between pts. 3 and 4 seems artificial to me. See Herráiz García, *Introducción al 'Libro de la Vida,'* pp. 80–85.

31. See *Vida* 12:1: "What I have tried to explain in this last chapter . . . is how much we ourselves can accomplish" ("Lo que he pretendido dar a entender en este capítulo pasado . . . es decir hasta lo que podemos nosotros adquirir").

32. *Vida* 23:1: "Es otro libro nuevo de aquí adelante, digo otra vida nueva. La de hasta aquí era mía. La que he vivido desde que comencé a declarar estas cosas de oración, es que vivía Dios en mí, a lo que me parecía."

33. Luti, "Teresa of Avila," p. 277.

San José in Avila. The date of the papal brief approving a new branch of the Carmelite order was February 7, 1562, while Teresa was in Toledo; she did not receive it until she returned to the Encarnación at the beginning of July. The year before, Teresa's sister and brother-in-law, Juana de Ahumada and Juan de Ovalle, had moved from Alba de Tormes to Avila in order to purchase a home for the new convent.[34] According to Teresa,

> Everything was done under great secrecy, because otherwise nothing could have been done, since the town was very much against the idea, as became apparent later. The Lord ordained that a brother-in-law of mine became sick, and his wife was away, and he was in such need of care that they gave me permission to be with him. At this time no one knew anything, though a few people suspected something but could not believe it. It was astonishing that he was sick only as long as was necessary for this business, and as soon as he had to be well, so I could leave him and he could leave the house freely, the Lord granted him a prompt recovery.[35]

The convent was founded on August 24, 1562, but that same day Teresa was called back to the Encarnación by the prioress, who did not recognize the new establishment.

The resistance that Teresa encountered at the founding of San José came from two quarters: the nuns at the Encarnación and the citizens of Avila. The nuns objected to San José because it competed with them for the favor of Avila's almsgivers. The townspeople rejected Teresa's idea of founding the convent without an endowment, since there was no guarantee that the nuns could support themselves and municipal resources were dwindling. As Jodi Bilinkoff observes:

> Avila's principles, in short, possessed a vested interest in perpetuating the sociological system that Teresa of Jesus had come to reject. Elites undoubtedly realized that if upper-class women accepted the discalced reform, they might see their daughters starve or, perhaps even worse in their eyes, sever the bonds of family and honor essential to the ordering of life as they knew it.[36]

34. See the testimony of Juan de Ovalle in *BMC* 18:125: "Vino para este efecto a la ciudad de Avila con su mujer e hijos y su casa, el año de mil y quinientos y sesenta y uno. . . ."

35. *Vida* 36:3: "Todo se hizo debajo de gran secreto; porque, a no ser así, no se pudiera hacer nada según el pueblo estaba mal con ello, como se pareció después. Ordenó el Señor que estuviese malo un cuñado mío, y su mujer no aquí, y en tanta necesidad, que me dieron licencia para estar con él; y con esta ocasión no se entendió nada, aunque en algunas personas no dejaba de sospecharse algo, más aún no lo creían. Fue cosa para espantar, que no estuvo más malo de lo que fue menester para el negocio, y en siendo menester tuviese salud para que yo me desocupase y el dejase desembarazada la casa, se la dió luego el Señor, que él estaba maravillado."

36. Jodi Bilinkoff, *The Avila of Saint Teresa: Religious Reform in a Sixteenth-Century City* (Ithaca, 1989), p. 140. For more details on the resistance of some *abulenses* to the convent of San José, see ibid., pp. 137–40. The townspeople's concerns were not entirely unfounded: traditionally, economic hardships often led to problems in the community and served to counter reform efforts. See Bataillon, *Erasmo y España*, pp. 4–5.

Teresa's insistence that the convent be founded in poverty was based on her desire to follow the tradition of apostolic poverty associated with the friar movements.[37] She received moral support from Pedro de Alcántara and financial support from the Poor Clares in Avila, whose convent was known as las Gordillas. Not surprising, when she defended her decision in the *Vida*, she told of several visions she had received on this subject, one of them from Saint Clare herself.[38]

When her detractors heard that Teresa was justifying her reform decisions on the basis of visions, they threatened her with the Inquisition.[39] "In addition," Teresa says, "the devil began to make people here think I had seen some revelation in this business, and they came to me in great fear to tell me that these were difficult times and they might stir up something against me and go to the inquisitors." This prospect, however, did not at all frighten Teresa.

> This seemed so funny to me, it made me laugh, because in this matter I was never afraid, it was well known that in matters of the faith, I would die a thousand deaths before I'd go against even the least ceremony of the church, or against any truth in the Sacred Scriptures. And I said that . . . if I thought there was any reason [to fear the Inquisition], I would go to them myself, and that if such an accusation were raised, the Lord would free me and I would profit from it.[40]

Teresa could claim to be amused at this stage of her career, but, she never again mentioned the Inquisition overtly, much less flippantly.[41]

---

37. See Bilinkoff, *Avila of Saint Teresa*, pp. 123–25.

38. See *Vida* 33:13.

39. Although Bilinkoff understands Teresa's emphasis on mental prayer and divine revelations to be another reason for opposition to Carmelite reform at large, I am inclined to see this as a smoke screen for the economic issues involved. In other words, recognizing Teresa's visionary experience as a potential vulnerability, some townspeople were willing to exploit the contemporary suspicion of women's religious experience to hold back Teresa's reforms.

40. *Vida* 33:5: "También comenzó aquí el demonio de una persona en otra procurar se entendiese que había yo visto alguna revelación en este negocio, e iban a mí con mucho miedo a decirme que andaban los tiempos recios y que podría ser me levantasen algo y fuesen a los inquisidores. A mí me cayó esto en gracia y me hizo reír, porque en este caso jamás yo temí, que sabía bien de mí que en cosa de la fe contra la menor ceremonia de la Iglesia que alguien viese yo iba, por ella o por cualquier verdad de la Sagrada Escritura, me pondría yo a morir mil muertes; y dije que de eso no temiesen, que harto mal sería para mi alma si en ella hubiese cosa que fuese de suerte que yo temiese la Inquisición; que si pensase había para qué, yo me la iría a buscar; y que si era levantado, que el Señor me libraría y quedaría con ganancia." Here Teresa refused to admit to having used revelation to justify her decisions as founder, but she did not hesitate to do so on another occasion. Indeed, the revelation she describes in *Vida* 32:11 may well be the same one she denies here.

41. The only exception is in Teresa's *Vejamen*, a satirical debate over interpretations of a scriptural passage. This work was never meant to circulate. In it Teresa wrote: "I ask God to give me the grace not to say anything that might merit my denunciation to the Inquisition." Written in Toledo, right after her difficulties with the Inquisition in Seville, this is eloquent testimony to Teresa's wry sense of humor.

The municipal junta discussed the new convent of San José at great length a few days later. The testimony of Domingo Báñez—who at the time did not know Teresa personally but later became one of her confessors—helped her reform gain credibility in the eyes of the council members.[42] Teresa received permission from the provincial of the order, Angel de Salazar, to move back to San José in December 1562, and she was named prioress there the following month.

The resolution of the problems surrounding the convent of San José was a significant victory for Teresa. Her activities as a writer and a founder were bound up in the same reform agenda; success on one front and success on the other added up to the same thing. "Her reputation," Luti explains, "was now tied to a project; that project was linked to the practice of contemplative prayer; and, in its origins at least, it would be women who would be practicing that controverted form of devotion. The reform would not go down easily."[43] Through the convent of San José and the writing of her *Vida* Teresa had entered the public forum, and she would now experience continual problems with the Inquisition. A nun with remarkable experiences of prayer was cause enough to attract the Inquisition's attention; one who ventured into the public arena of financial deals and establishment of convents could become a threat.

When Teresa submitted the second version of her *Vida* to Domingo Báñez in 1565, she was already involved in the production of another book, a treatise on prayer which she called *El camino de perfección,* directed specifically to the reformed Carmelite nuns. Taking advantage of her situation as prioress, in the *Camino de perfección* Teresa continued her ongoing dialogue with her reformed sisters and made available to them information included in the *Vida* which Teresa doubted they would be able to read: "A few days ago I wrote a certain account of my life. Since my confessor may not want you to read it, I will put down here a few things about prayer similar to what I say there and others that also seem to me to be necessary."[44] Teresa's uncertainty about whether Báñez would approve the *Vida* dates the first version of the *Camino* in late 1565 or early 1566.[45] At that point, she sub-

---

42. For a summary of Báñez's remarks, see Francisco de Santa María, *Reforma de los descalzos de Nuestra Señora del Carmen de la primitiva observancia,* 2 vols. (Madrid, 1644–55), 1:160–62. See also Efrén and Steggink, *Santa Teresa y su tiempo,* 1:432–34, esp. n. 82.

43. Luti, "Teresa of Avila," p. 192.

44. *Camino de perfección,* Prologue:4: "Pocos días ha escribí cierta relación de mi vida. Porque podrá ser no quiera mi confesor la leáis vosotras, pondré algunas cosas de oración que conformarán con aquellas que allí digo y otras que también me parecerán necesarias."

45. According to Efrén and Steggink, Teresa finished the book in 1564; according to Tomás Alvarez she finished it in 1566. See discussions in Teresa de Jesús, *Obras completas,* ed. Efrén de la Madre de Dios and Otger Steggink (Madrid, 1974), p. 193; and Teresa de Jesús, *El camino de perfección,* ed. Tomás de la Cruz, 2 vols., facs. ed. (Rome, 1965), 2:15–29.

mitted the manuscript to García de Toledo, who read it and marked certain passages for elimination or change. Teresa took the censor's advice seriously and reduced the book's seventy-three chapters to forty-two.[46] The comments of García de Toledo account for only part of the editing process, for Teresa's alterations go far beyond the censor's requirements.[47]

The Valdés Index encouraged this sort of self-censorship. Writers learned to ponder the implications of what they wrote. Did their work accord with common theological assumptions about the church, the human condition, the activity of grace, and so forth? After subjecting the *Camino* to such scrutiny, Teresa refined many of her comments on the most sensitive issues. She also sought to distance herself from the intense theological debates then stirring the universities by declaring her audience to be limited to cloistered women.

Teresa's reform began to gain credibility when in 1566 the general of the Carmelite order, Juan Bautista Rubeo, came to Spain from Rome for an apostolic visit. This was the first official visit ever conceded to Spain, as Teresa noted in the *Foundations:* "Our generals always reside in Rome, and none of them ever came to Spain."[48] Rubeo's purpose was to make sure the Spanish Carmelites were conforming to the order's rule.[49] He arrived in Avila on February 18, 1567, and visited first the convent of the Encarnación and then the reformed convent of San José. He spent a week with Teresa, and he was so impressed by her reforms that on April 27 he authorized her to found more reformed convents throughout Castile.[50]

46. According to Efrén and Steggink, Teresa produced the second version in 1569, but Tomás Alvarez, citing the lack of information regarding further foundations, dates it before the second foundation in Medina del Campo, or sometime in 1566. See his edition of *Camino de perfección,* pp. 30–35.

47. In its second version, according to Maximiliano Herráiz García, the *Camino* "lost freshness and spontaneity, bold and ironic expressions," but it "gained in doctrinal clarity, in broadening of some subjects and deepening of others": *Introducción al "Camino de perfección," de Santa Teresa* (Desierto de las Palmas, Castellón, 1981); p. 21.

48. *Fundaciones* 2:1: "Siempre nuestros generales residen en Roma, y jamás ninguno vino a España." Rubeo was general of the Carmelites from 1562 to 1578.

49. The apostolic visit followed a set formula. The general was met by the relevant dignitaries of the city or town he visited and led to the monastery or convent of his order. There he gave an exhortatory speech to the monks or nuns gathered in the choir. General Rubeo seems to have stressed the importance of dress standards as a reminder of the religious state. After the general congregation, Rubeo called in the monks or nuns one by one to ask them about the religious observation in the convent and about their possessions; he was particularly insistent that the Carmelites relinquish all private property, as he believed it exacerbated differences among the religious. A notary wote down the responses of the religious during these interviews. For more information, see Steggink, *La reforma del Carmelo español.*

50. The exclusion of Andalusia from this license was to cause problems for Teresa in Beas and Seville (1575). In another patent, dated August 16, 1567, Rubeo authorized Teresa to found two monasteries for men. See Joaquin Smet, *Los Carmelitas: Historia de la Orden del Carmen,* trans. Antonio Ruiz Molina, 2 vols. (Madrid, 1987–90): 2:50–55.

On August 13, 1567, Teresa set out for Medina del Campo, at that time a commercial center of some importance, with an influential *converso* community. The town had welcomed the Jesuits in 1553, and as Teresa's confessor Baltasar Alvarez was now installed there as rector of the Jesuit house, Teresa could depend on his assistance in founding a new convent. According to Francisco Márquez Villanueva, the town's acceptance of the Jesuits, the only other religious order with a flexible policy on the admission of *conversos*, ensured the Carmelites' success, for it implied that the Carmelites, too, would receive *converso* recruits, along with the donations made by their families.[51] Teresa met with the same sort of opposition she had encountered in Avila. This time, however, accusations were mixed with comparisons with Magdalena de la Cruz.[52] The Dominican Pedro Fernández testified on Teresa's behalf, and the town council commissioned Luis de Santander to examine Teresa and her project before they would approve it.[53]

The convent was successfully established on August 15, 1567. From then on, Teresa was continuously involved in travel and other preparations for founding new reformed houses. From February 1569 to January 1571 she founded six houses in some of the most important centers of Castile: Valladolid, Toledo, Pastrana (two houses), Salamanca, and Alba de Tormes.

The convents in Pastrana were to bring Teresa many problems. Both houses were financed by the prince and princess of Eboli, Ruy Gómez de Silva and Ana de Mendoza y de La Cerda. From the beginning Teresa's relationship with Ana de Mendoza was difficult. Wary of permitting the princess to have too much control over the nuns' house, Teresa founded it with an endowment, thus guaranteeing the nuns' financial independence.[54] The power struggle between Teresa and Ana reached a new level when people began to compare the experiences Teresa described in the *Vida* with those of the *alumbrada* Magdalena de la Cruz.[55]

We do not know if the townspeople of Avila made good on their threats to accuse Teresa before the inquisitors. At any rate, the first known occasion of Teresa's problems with the Inquisition came at Pastrana. Unfortunately, the details of the affair are sketchy and the Inquisition left no documents on it. Teresa herself mentions nothing about the 1570 encounter with the In-

---

51. See Márquez Villanueva, "Santa Teresa y el linaje," pp. 154–55.

52. See the testimony of Domingo Báñez in *BMC* 18:11: "Un religioso de cierta orden hombre de autoridad y predicador dice mucho mal de la Madre Teresa de Jesús, comparándola a Magdalena de la Cruz, una burladora que hubo en tiempos pasados en Córdoba, quizá con algún celo de que a Dios dará cuenta."

53. See Luis de Santander's testimony in *BMC* 19:165.

54. See Efrén and Steggink, *Santa Teresa y su tiempo,* 2.2:252. Teresa had made the same arrangements in Malagón.

55. See Francisco de Santa María, *Reforma de los descalzos,* 2:305.

quisition, but in his *Memorias historiales* the early Carmelite historian Andrés de la Encarnación describes a document written by Isabel de Santo
Domingo, prioress of the Pastrana convent:

> The venerable Mother Isabel de Santo Domingo, in an account written in her
> own hand, after referring to what the Princess of Eboli said about the Saint's
> book, says: "It reached the point where the book had to be shown to the head in-
> quisitor. . . . It was submitted to Father Hernando del Castillo so he could ex-
> amine it, and God was served, as it proved her virtue more noteworthy, plus it
> was a good test of the Mother's patience."[56]

Andrés concludes that this first wave of accusations to the tribunal in Pastrana—the *Vida* was denounced as a "book of visions"—was separate from
the second wave in 1574–75, and that the book emerged intact from these
initial accusations.

> This happened in the year 1569, and the accusation the next, so it seems different
> from the one when she [Teresa] was in Beas; and it's clear that in the Pastrana
> case the original [manuscript] was returned to her, because later Father Báñez
> had it and did with it what he says in his deposition.[57]

Andrés de la Encarnación's account makes clear that the 1570 encounter
with the Inquisition was serious. Both Teresa's character and her writing
were on the line. The *Vida* manuscript was confiscated, as Teresa had feared
when she began her *Camino de perfección*. The *Vida* was the most suspect of
all Teresa's works because of its descriptions of visions, and Teresa's concern
over its survival spurred her to write several other mystical works.

Even those theologians who approved the doctrine Teresa expounded
in the *Vida* voiced some reservations about making the book available. At
the suggestion of the inquisitor Soto y Salazar, Teresa sent her manuscript
to Juan de Avila, commonly held to be one of Spain's most important
spiritual directors, for his review. He approved of her descriptions of mystical prayer and rapture,[58] but he warned her in a letter of September 12,

---

56. BN, MS. 13.483, Andrés de la Encarnación, "Memorias historiales," fol. 179r: "La Venerable Madre Isabel de Santo Domingo en una relación de su mano, después de referir lo que
la Princesa de Evoli decía del libro de la Santa[,] dice: 'Vino a términos que fue menester se
mostrase el libro al Inquisidor Mayor. . . . [S]e remitió al Padre Fray Hernando del Castillo
para que la examinase, y todo fue Dios servido, fuese para mas acreditar la virtud, mas a la
Madre eranle buenas pruebas de su paciencia.' "

57. Ibid.: "Esto vino a suceder [en el] año 1569, y la delación el siguiente, con que parece
distincta de la de cuando estaba [Teresa] en Beas; y que en la de Pastrana se le volviese el original es claro, pues depués le tuvo el P. Báñez y hizo con él lo que en sus deposiciones dixo."

58. See "Carta del venerable maestro Avila a la santa madre Teresa de Jesús, aprobando el
Libro de la Vida," *BMC* 2:208: "La doctrina de la oración está buena por la mayor parte, y muy
bien puede vuesa [sic] merced fiarse della y seguirla, y en los raptos hallo las señales que tienen
los que son verdaderos."

1568: "The book is not [suitable] to be put into the hands of many, because some words must be polished and others must be explained, and there are other things that may be beneficial to your spirit, but they would not be to those who followed them: because the ways God leads some people are not for others."[59]

Juan de Avila's own disciples ran into difficulties with the Inquisition after his death, and the fact that he had thought highly of Teresa's visionary theology became problematic. The inquisitional tribunal of Córdoba requested a report about Teresa in 1574, after noting the influence of her *Vida* on some of Juan de Avila's followers suspected of *alumbradismo*. One of the major suspects in this case was Bernardino de Carleval, rector of the University of Baeza and Avila's protégé. During his trial, Carleval referred to Teresa's *Vida* as a "book of revelations."[60] In a relation dated December 13, 1574, the tribunal was informed that Teresa had written a book of revelations better than that of Catherine of Siena, and that one of her revelations was that there were to be many martyrs in her order.[61] It is logical to suppose that the tribunal thought of her as a visionary and possibly an *alumbrada*.[62] At that time the Córdoba tribunal was embroiled in an investigation of *alumbrados* and ordered the information sent to the Madrid tribunal for further investigation.

The inquisitional tribunal of Valladolid had also received accusations against Teresa in 1575. At that time the Valladolid tribunal was involved in the trial of María de Olivares, an Augustinian nun at the convent of Nuestra Señora de Gracia in Avila, where Teresa had been interned as an adolescent.[63] The Valladolid tribunal wrote to the bishop of Avila, Alvaro de Mendoza, asking for the manuscript of Teresa's *Vida* in order to review its contents. After receiving the manuscript in late February or early March of 1575, the Valladolid tribunal assigned the censor Domingo Báñez to read it and report his findings.

59. "El libro no está para salir a manos de muchos; porque ha menester limar las palabras dél en algunas partes, en otras declararlas; y otras cosas hay que al espíritu de vuestra merced, pueden ser provechosas, y no lo serían a quien las siguiese: porque las cosas particulares por donde Dios lleva a unos, no son para otros." Juan de Avila's letter to Teresa is incorporated in Gracián's defense of her doctrine; see Teresa de Jesús, *Escritos de Santa Teresa*, ed. Vicente de La Fuente, 2 vols. (Madrid, 1952), 2:503.

60. Teresa had named Carleval as the confessor of the Discalced convent in Malagón in 1568, and he would have had access to her manuscript through Juan de Avila, who read and approved it that same year.

61. AHN, Inq., leg. 1856, no. 1, fol. 3r: "Tenía un *Libro* de revelaciones más alto que el de Santa Catalina de Sena; y, entre ellas, que había de haber muchos mártires de su Orden."

62. Perhaps a factor in their suspicions was the fact that in 1546 the Córdoba tribunal had convicted Magdalena de la Cruz of *alumbradismo*, and Teresa was often compared with her.

63. See Llamas, pp. 47–48.

Báñez had been Teresa's confessor for several years and so could judge the book's content on the basis of his conception of its author and her intent. Although Báñez generally supported Teresa's reforms, he did not approve of the circulation of her works through the new Carmelite convents. In fact, he argued with Teresa that no writings by women should circulate, and he threatened to burn the manuscript. Teresa's response was that he should think such an action over carefully and then burn the work if he thought it best. In the end, Báñez preserved the *Vida* and turned it over to the Inquisition.[64]

Báñez prepared an official censure of the *Vida* in 1575, and this document reveals the doubts Teresa's works provoked in the *calificadores*. Although Báñez admitted that he found "nothing that in my judgment is unsound doctrine," he was troubled by the book's

> many revelations and visions, which should always be feared, especially in women, who are more likely to believe they come from God and to see holiness in them. . . . Rather they should be viewed as dangerous to those who seek perfection; because Satan often transforms himself into an angel of light to fool curious souls that lack humility, as we have seen in our times.[65]

Báñez found himself in an awkward situation: he had no· wish to cast doubts on Teresa's sincerity—he admired Teresa for her obedience, penitence, charity, and other virtues—yet he felt obliged to express his reservations about her practice of teaching other women about visionary phenomena. Although he personally believed that Teresa's experiences were of divine origin, he acknowledged that "it is always more certain to maintain some reserve and awe" in judging revelations. Convinced that Teresa's sincerity would not allow her to deceive others, Báñez resolved his predicament by advising that "the book is not suitable for just anyone to read, but for learned men, experienced and of Christian discretion. It serves the pur-

---

64. Báñez himself offered this testimony during the canonization process. See *BMC* 18:10: "Todo esto contra voluntad de éste que declara, en tanta manera que se enojó con la dicha Teresa de Jesús, aunque entendía que no tenía ella la culpa, sino de quien ella se había confiado. Y diciéndole este testigo que quería quemar el original, porque no convenía que escritos de mujeres anduviesen en público, respondió ella que lo mirase bien y lo quemase si le pareciese; en lo cual conoció este testigo su gran rendimiento y humildad. Y lo miró con gran atención y no se atrevió a quemarle, sino, remitióle, como dicho tiene, al Santo Oficio."

65. "Censura del P. Báñez," in Teresa's *Obras completas*, p. 306: "Solo una cosa hay en este libro en que poder reparar, y con razón; basta examinarla muy bien: y es que tiene muchas revelaciones y visiones, las cuales siempre son mucho de temer, especialmente en mujeres, que son más fáciles en creer que son de Dios y en poner en ellas la santidad. . . . Antes se han de tener por trabajos peligrosos para los que pretenden perfección; porque acostumbra Satanás transformarse en ángel de luz y engañar las almas curiosas y poco humildes, como en nuestros tiempos se ha visto."

pose for which it was written very well, which was to permit this religious to give an account of her soul to those who have to guide her, so she would not be deceived."[66] Clearly, as Teresa suspected, if Báñez had had his way, her *Vida* would not have reached her nuns.

The support of *letrados* like Báñez, who had all but usurped the teaching office and were consulted by inquisitional tribunals throughout the peninsula,[67] was critical for Teresa's survival. Báñez's reservations about the doctrine of the *espirituales* reflects those of other *letrados*. Though Báñez believed in Teresa's sincerity, he was unsure that readers without a theological education would interpret her *Vida* in an orthodox way. Through no fault of her own, Teresa would then be associated with the *alumbrados*, who might use the text to justify their unorthodox spiritual practices. Báñez's hesitation to approve the *Vida* made Teresa and other Carmelites worry that he might burn it, and copies were made in case he gave the order.[68] These copies circulated surreptitiously after Báñez submitted the book to the Inquisition in 1575.

Two years after the Inquisition had sequestered the *Vida*, several of Teresa's supporters made a concerted effort to have it returned to her.[69] In a letter to her brother Lorenzo in February 1577 Teresa reported that Inquisitor General Gaspar de Quiroga (1507–93) had himself read the book and approved it.[70] Indeed, if we can judge by Jerónimo Gracián's account, he was favorably impressed by the book. He tells of meeting with Quiroga and Teresa in 1580 to discuss her request for permission to found a Discalced convent in Madrid, and quotes Quiroga as saying:

> "I take great pleasure in meeting her, as I have wanted to do, and she will have in me a chaplain who will help her in every way I can. And I want her to know that a few years ago they presented a book of hers to the Inquisition, and its doctrine was examined with great rigor. I myself read the entire thing; it is very sound

---

66. Ibid., p. 308: "Y resuélvome en que este libro no está para que se comunique a quienquiera, sino a hombres doctos y de experiencia y discreción cristiana. El está muy a propósito del fin para que se escribió: que fue dar noticia esta religiosa de su alma a los que la han de guiar, para no ser engañada."

67. See Luti, "Teresa of Avila," p. 99: "The power of the *letrado* to define the boundaries of acceptable religious practice according to the dictates of academic theology was joined to the power of the Inquisition to ferret out and punish heretics in an all-out assault upon innovation."

68. See the testimony of Francisco de Mena in *BMC* 18:351.

69. Llamas discusses this campaign on pp. 267–71.

70. *Letter* 183:14, in *Obras completas*, p. 1578. "De mis papeles hay buenas nuevas. El inquisidor mayor mismo los lee, que es cosa nueva (debénselos haber loado) y dijo a doña Luisa que no había allí cosa que ellos tuviesen que hacer en ella, que antes había bien que mal, y díjola que por qué no había yo hecho monasterio en Madrid."

doctrine, true and beneficial. She may send for it when she wishes, and I give her the permission she asks for, and I ask her to remember me in her prayers."[71]

Apparently, however, Teresa did not capitalize on Quiroga's support to the extent that she could have. Persuaded by Gracián to use a copy of the *Vida* owned by the Duke of Alba, Fernando de Toledo, Teresa never again saw the original manuscript, which was held by the Inquisition until shortly before its publication in 1588.

Although she could not control the fate of her *Vida*, Teresa could carry on her reforming activities in other ways. After returning to the Encarnación in Avila, now as the prioress, Teresa founded more convents, first in Beas (February 24, 1575) and then in Seville (May 29, 1575). The convent in Seville emerged against Teresa's better judgment. She wanted to open a Discalced convent in Madrid, and in prayer she found that God confirmed her decision. Gracián, however, ordered her to found a convent in Seville, and Teresa obeyed, reasoning, "I can be deceived by revelations, but never by obedience."[72] At the time Teresa arrived in Seville, the city was one of the most important commercial centers in Europe, the hub for traffic with Spanish America.[73] With this convent the Discalced reform had reached a new level of visibility throughout Spain; by straying outside the jurisdiction of the Castilian provincial, however, Teresa had paved the way for opposition by the Calced Carmelites and by Seville's tribunal of the Inquisition. The convent in Seville marks the beginning of the "years of troubles" (1575–79) to

---

71. Gracián, *Dilucidario*, 1:4, in *BMC* 15:15: " 'Mucho me huelgo de conocerla, que lo deseaba, y tendrá en mí un capellán, que la favoreceré en todo lo que se ofreciere. Porque le hago saber que ha algunos años que presentaron a la Inquisición un su libro, y se ha examinado aquella doctrina con mucho rigor. Yo lo he leído todo; es doctrina muy segura, verdadera y provechosa. Bien puede enviar por él cuando quisiere, y doy la licencia que pide y ruégola me encomiende mucho a Dios.' " This exchange is also described in the canonization testimony by Juana del Espíritu Santo; see *BMC* 18:254.

72. Many of the religious who testified in the canonization process described this episode. See, e.g., the testimony of María de San José in *Proceso de Toledo* (1595), in *BMC* 18:320–21: "Y oyó asímismo esta testigo al padre Gracián haciendo una plática en la red del monasterio de Valladolid, que estando en duda si se haría primero la fundación de monjas de Madrid o la de Sevilla, le mandó el dicho Padre, que era su prelado, que lo encomendase a Nuestro Señor, y después le dijo la dicha Madre que se hiciese la fundación de Madrid, que así lo había entendido que convenía. Y el dicho Padre le respondió, que a él le parecía que se hiciese la fundación de Sevilla, a lo cual la dicha Madre no respondió, sino dispuso las cosas para ir a la fundación de Sevilla. Y espantándose el dicho Padre cómo no le había replicado, la dijo el dicho Padre en el camino: ¿no me dijo, Madre, que había entendido de Nuestro Señor que convenía que fuésemos a Madrid? ¿cómo no me replicó nada cuando le dije que viniésemos a Sevilla? Y ella respondió: en lo que Vuestra Reverencia no me manda no me puedo engañar, y en esto sí."

73. In August 1575 one such ship brought Teresa's brother, Lorenzo de Cepeda, and his children to Seville from South America. His daughter Teresa was to live in the Discalced convent with her aunt and later to be professed.

which Teresa and other Carmelite authors refer. An analysis of those troubles is critical to an understanding of Teresa's life and literary career.

The accusations in Córdoba and Valladolid reveal the far reach of contemporary suspicions against Teresa, and the accusations in Seville highlight their pertinacity. The troubles in Seville lasted over four years, and the accusations against the nuns were the most extensive, covering questions of religious practice, morality, experience of prayer, and possible heretical ideas in the books they used for their spiritual development. Our major sources for the events in Seville are the works of the prioress of the Carmelite house there, María de San José, who wrote about the trials the nuns suffered.[74] Her testimony is confirmed by that of several other Carmelite nuns and other eyewitnesses.

According to María de San José, there were two waves of inquisitional inquests, the first in early 1576 and the second in 1578.[75] The first accusations against Teresa and the Discalced Carmelites were produced by a combination of circumstances, but most importantly by María del Corro, one of the early candidates received by the convent in 1575. María de San José describes María del Corro as "a great *beata* who had already been canonized by the whole city."[76] This novice was to provoke trouble for the entire convent. She excused herself from her monastic obligations and finally, in November, left the convent with another novice. Perhaps to protect her shattered reputation for sanctity, María del Corro went to the Inquisition and denounced the Carmelites for a variety of strange practices.[77] She was aided in this task by her confessor and other unknown witnesses.

74. See esp. María de San José, "Libro de las recreaciones," BN MS. 3508; "Ramillete de mirra," BN MS. 2176; and "Historia de los descalzos y descalzas carmelitas que fundo Santa Theresa de Jesus nuestra madre," BN MS. 2176, fols. 1–85. Modern versions of the first two works are available in María de San José, *Libro de recreaciones. Ramillete de mirra. Avisos, máximas y poesías,* ed. Silverio de Santa Teresa (Burgos, 1913). The *Persecuciones* were first published in 1599 in Julián de Avila's *Vida de la Santa Madre Teresa de Jesús,* pt. 3, chap. 1. A modern transcription of the *Persecuciones* is found in Teresa de Jesús, *Escritos de Santa Teresa,* ed. Vicente de La Fuente, BAE 53 (Madrid, 1952), pp. 555–61. If the records of the Inquisition's investigation of Teresa are extant, they have not yet been found.

75. Regarding the first accusations, she writes (BAE 53:557): "Tan recién fundado el monasterio, que no había mas de siete meses . . . y venir a nuestra casa la Inquisición." Seven months after the founding would be December 1575 or January 1576. Regarding the second wave of accusations María writes that "en este tiempo, nuestra Madre no estaba en Sevilla; había casi dos años que se había ido a Castilla." Teresa left Seville for Castile in June 1576.

76. Ibid., fol. 103r: "En este tiempo habia entrado en nuestra casa una gran beata tenida por muy santa. . . ."

77. Enrique Llamas posits that the first denunciations were made by an anonymous cleric, with María del Corro supplying the details as an eyewitness. He argues that this anonymous cleric was not the Jesuit Garciálvarez. See Llamas, p. 79. According to María de San José's *memorial* dated December 2, 1580, another Jesuit confessor, Gaspar de Hoyos, slandered

It appears that in 1575–76 the nuns were accused of believing and practicing new doctrines, similar to those of the *alumbrados* of Llerena.[78] In a letter dated 23 January 1576 the inquisitors in Seville wrote to the Consejo asking them to retrive Teresa's *Vida* from Domingo Báñez, who six months earlier had finished his examination and given his guarded approval of the book. The inquisitors explained that if they were to proceed against Teresa, they would need the book to assemble their case against her. At that point the inquisitors Carpio and Páramo believed she had committed "frauds and deceits very prejudicial to the Christian republic."[79]

The Consejo's response indicates some feeling of urgency:

> We received your letter of the 23d of last month and with it the information against Teresa de Jesús and Isabel de San Jerónimo, nuns of the Order of Carmel, which we have reviewed. After consulting with the Most Reverend Lord Inquisitor General, it seems that you must, sirs, examine the accusations that doña María del Corro has made, especially the said Isabel de San Jerónimo, one of you, sirs, going to examine her.[80]

The Consejo did not have Teresa's *Vida* sent to Seville, since they were still having it examined themselves.[81]

From what we can piece together, the accusations in Seville fell into three categories: suspicions about the nuns' religious and moral practices, suspicions about Teresa, and accusations against her writings. The first category included

---

Teresa and caused the nuns great distress ("Como a José la había Dios de levantar, mal que nos pesase. . . . Este Padre nos atormentó mucho"). This confessor may have orchestrated the accusations; in any case he most likely testified against the Carmelites. See "Declaración de María de San José" (December 2, 1580), ibid., p. 215.

78. See María de San José, "Fundación del convento de Carmelitas Descalzas en Sevilla," in Teresa, *Escritos de Santa Teresa*, BAE 53, p. 557: "She went to the Inquisition saying that we were like *alumbradas* . . . and during this time there were problems with *alumbrados* in Llerena" ("Iba a la Inquisición, diciendo que éramos como las alumbradas . . . y en este tiempo había problemas con los alumbrados en L[l]erena").

79. AHN, Inq., leg. 2946, exp. s.n.: "El libro de que el testigo segundo hace mencion tenemos relacion que esta en poder de Fray Domingo Ibañez [sic], de la Orden de Santo Domingo, morador en el monasterio de su Orden de Valladolid. Suplicamos a V. S. mande se haga diligencia en haberlo y que se nos remita, porque habiendose de proceder en esta causa, sera necesario tenerle por estar en el todo o lo mas de que se puede hacer cargo a Teresa de Jesus, que segun entendemos son embustes y engaños muy perjudiciales a la republica cristiana."

80. AHN, Inq., lib. 578, fol. 365: "Recibimos vuestra carta de 23 del pasado y juntamente la informacion contra Teresa de Jesus e Isabel de sant Jeronimo, monjas de la Orden del Carmen, que se ha visto. Y consultado con el Reverendisimo Señor Inquisidor General, ha parecido debeis, señores, examinar a los contestes que da doña Maria del Corro y especialmente a la dicha Isabel de sant Jeronimo, yendo a examinarla uno de vosotros, señores."

81. Ibid.: "Y el libro que pedis no se os envia porque se va viendo."

accusations that the nuns practiced penitence by tying each other up and applying the discipline; that they observed ceremonies of their own involving the removal of their veils; and that they failed to show reverence toward the Eucharist and engaged in other disrespectful practices.[82] Accusations of improper moral conduct, which figured more prominently in the second inquest, included the charge that they had allowed their confessor, Jerónimo Gracián, to sleep in the convent. There were also reports that Gracián took liberties with the nuns and admonished them afterward not to confess the incidents, and that he undressed before the nuns and danced naked before them.[83]

Teresa's detractors went so far as to accuse her of running a house of prostitution. According to María de San José, "The most one can decently say is what many people were claiming—that that wicked old woman, under the pretext of founding convents, brought young women from one place or another to corrupt them."[84] Charges of moral laxity and particularly sexual misconduct were frequently brought against spiritual women in the late sixteenth century. The *alumbrada* MariGomez was sentenced in the *auto* of 1577 in Llerena for just such conduct.[85]

The accusations against the Carmelites' practice of mental prayer were grounded in suspicion of mystical experience, particularly if it had a physical aspect. The reformed Carmelite constitutions allowed for ten hours of mental prayer daily; the intensity of this prayer was particularly suspect in light of the recent trials of some *alumbrados* in Andalusia. The case of Catalina Godínez, the patron of the Discalced convent in Beas, indicates that the Inquisition was unduly suspicious of many pious practices. Catalina was accused in 1574 of speaking "very intimately with Our Lord and she

---

82. See Teresa's letter to María Bautista dated April 29, 1576, in *Obras completas*, pp.1395–99. María de San José explains in her *Libro de recreaciones*, pp. 109–10: "As we were poor and did not have enough veils, and other times the sisters did not wear them to cover themselves when they received communion, we would pass them around, one to another. They said that this was a ceremony"; and "We received communion in the patio, which was very bright with the sun; to avoid the light and collect ourselves after receiving communion, each would hide herself where she could, head against the wall. . . ."

83. These accusations were retracted in 1580. See the retractions of Margarita de la Concepción, Beatriz de la Madre de Dios, Leonor de San Gabriel, and Isabel de San Francisco and the declaration of María de San José in Llamas, pp. 203–19.

84. BN MS. 2176, fol. 111r: "Lo que mas honestamente se puede decir es lo que muchos de ellos afirmaban de que trahia aquella vieja ruin en achaque de fundar conventos de una, a otra parte mugeres mozas para que fuesen malas." Diego de Yepes discusses the issue more discreetly in a letter to Luis de León: "De la Santa Madre dijeron lo último que de una mujer se puede decir." See "Relación de la vida y libros de la M. Teresa que el P. Diego de Yepes remitió al P. Fr. Luis de León (4 de Septiembre de 1588)," in *BMC* 2:492.

85. See Vicente Barrantes, "Llerena," in *Aparato bibliográfico para la historia de Extremadura*, 2 vols. (Badajoz, 1877), 2:354–55.

saw an [image of the] ecce homo sweat, and she kept herself locked in a room with it for twenty-four hours and was healed as if miraculously of an illness she had."[86] The fact that Catalina, a woman of dubious spiritual practices on no less authority than the Inquisition, had given financial support to one of Teresa's Discalced Carmelite convents did not help Teresa's case before the tribunal of Seville.

In February 1576 the inquisitors visited the Carmelites to search for information about Teresa and Isabel de San Jerónimo, who were accused of having extraordinary experiences in prayer. Isabel de San Jerónimo's experiences were particularly intense. She was known for practicing acts of humility and penitence beyond the Carmelites' already strenuous rule. In October or November 1574, Teresa was so concerned about Isabel's mental state that she sent John of the Cross to examine her and perform an exorcism, if necessary.[87]

The suspicion generated by the experiences of Catalina Godínez and Isabel de San Jerónimo must have been slight in comparison with the impression caused by Teresa's continual levitations, predictions, and recurring visions. Teresa's physical manifestations in prayer were disruptive to the entire religious community. Juana del Espíritu Santo described a night Teresa spent in the Discalced convent in Toledo, during which "the force of her love for God and her desire to suffer for him and be united with His Splendor was so great that she spent most of the night screaming and crying, unable to contain herself, until it was necessary for the prioress and other sisters to stay with her."[88] Teresa not only had had many such experiences

86. AHN, Inq., leg. 1856, fol. 4r: "Hablaba muy particularmente con Nuestro Señor y que ha visto sudar un Ecce Homo, con el cual quedó encerrada veintecuatro horas y sanó de una enfermedad que tenía, como por milagro."

87. See letter 73, to Inés de Jesús, prioress of the convent in Medina del Campo: October–November 1574, in *Obras completas*, p. 1338: "My daughter, I am very worried about Sister Isabel de San Jerónimo's illness. I am sending you Father John of the Cross to cure her. God has given him the grace to cast out demons from those people who are afflicted by them. He has just cast out three legions of demons from a person here in Avila, and he commanded them in the name of God to tell him their name and they obeyed him instantly" ("Mi hija: mucho me pesa de la enfermedad que tiene la hermana Isabel de San Jerónimo. Ahí las envío al padre fray Juan de la Cruz para que la cure, que le ha hecho Dios merced de darle gracia para echar los demonios de las personas que los tienen. Ahora acaba de sacar aquí en Avila de una persona tres legiones de demonios, y los mandó en virtud de Dios le dijesen su nombre y al punto obedecieron").

88. *BMC* 18:99: ". . . fué tanto el ímpetu de deseo y amor de Dios de padecer por él y verse con Su Majestad, que gran parte de la noche gastó con grandes gritos, ansias y lágrimas, sin poderse contener, y fué necesario que la madre Priora y otras hermanas la estubiesen acompañando." Teresa was well aware that her experiences were disruptive, and had told the nuns that if they should see her levitate in prayer, they should try to pull her back down, so as to avoid any publicity. See the testimony of María de San José in *BMC* 18:318.

but had written a book telling other women how they could have them, too. Her role as both author (and thus teacher) and founder made Teresa, in the eyes of the Inquisitors, a possible heretical dogmatizer—someone much more dangerous than a nun subject to odd but generally harmless spiritual practices.

In February and March 1576 Teresa wrote two accounts of her life and her visions, which the tribunal in Seville reviewed.[89] These accounts most likely convey the substance of what her defense before the tribunal would have been. Writing in the third person, Teresa portrayed herself as a woman who had always had "a great desire that [Christ] be praised and his church increased."[90] She described twenty-two years of spiritual struggles before she began to receive "some inner visions and revelations with the eyes of her soul, but she never saw anything with her corporeal eyes, nor did she hear anything."[91] Fearing that these visions might be caused by the devil, she began to consult with learned "spiritual men," whom she proceeded to name. The list includes many significant theologians, including *letrados* who were initially skeptical.[92] The list divides neatly into *espirituales* and *letrados*; all of the Jesuits on the list were *espirituales*, whereas the Dominicans were *letrados*. Teresa also, she explained, consulted with the inquisitor Francisco de Soto Salazar, who eventually encouraged her to write an account of her life and submit it to Juan de Avila.

Finally, Teresa described her prayer life in some detail, highlighting her willingness to submit to the judgment of orthodox theologians. "In all that has been said she subjects herself to the Catholic faith and the Roman church."[93] In summary, she reiterated that her visions were in no way imaginary but intellectual, and that they left her with greater humility and desire to serve God. In her own defense she was emboldened to suggest that the gifts she had received from God were true because they left her with increased virtue, even though they might not be comprehensible even to the-

89. See *Cuentas de conciencia* 53 ("Esta monja ha cuarenta años que tomó el hábito . . .") and 54 ("Son tan dificultosas de decir . . ."). For a study of the first document, see Tomás Alvarez, "Esta monja: Carisma y obediencia en una relación de la Santa," *El Monte Carmelo* 78 (1970): 143–62.

90. *Cuentas de conciencia* 53:1: ". . . siempre con gran deseo de que fuese alabado y su iglesia aumentada."

91. Ibid., 53:2: ". . . comenzó a parecerle que la hablaban interiormente algunas veces y ver algunas visiones y revelaciones interiormente con los ojos del alma, que jamás vio cosa con los ojos corporales ni la oyó."

92. Among others, Teresa named Francisco de Borja, Baltasar Alvarez, Pablo Hernández, Pedro de Alcántara, Domingo Báñez, Vicente Barrón, Bartolomé de Medina, Felipe de Meneses, Diego de Yanguas, and Juan de Avila.

93. *Cuentas de consciencia* 53:18: "En todo lo que se ha dicho se sujeta a la fe católica e iglesia romana."

ological experts: "Even though they may be more educated, there are things that cannot be comprehended."[94]

Teresa's self-defense is at once circumspect and spirited. She emphasized her growth in the virtues of humility and obedience and she portrayed herself as a willing servant of the institutional church. She dissociated herself from the *alumbradas* by aligning herself with the Augustinian framework for interpreting religious visions. She took refuge in the authority of renowned spiritual experts of her day. She made a good case for an institutionally acceptable "exceptional" woman.

If Teresa had been found guilty, she would have been punished in the *auto de fe* held on February 10, 1577. In fact, three women were punished as *alumbradas* that day.[95] María de Zúñiga, a fifty-six-year-old widow, was accused of saying

> that she had daily visions of Our Lord and that Saint Sebastian had appeared before her in the figure of a handsome young man, and Saint John the Evangelist, and that Our Lord had also appeared before her in her room with many choirs of angels, which she saw with her own eyes, and that one day when her confessor had not wanted her to receive communion, later that night in her dreams a priest appeared before her and said mass in her room and the host came flying into her mouth, and that the dead appeared before her saying that they needed masses said, and that she prayed for marriages and other things, and that she foretold the future and received money for it, and that she had done and said many other things that were judged to be lies, hypocrisy, and deceit.[96]

María confessed to some of these acts but denied intending any harm.

94. Ibid., 53:28: "Así como aunque más letra tengan, hay cosas que no se alcanzan."

95. Although much is said about the prevalence of *alumbrados* in the Inquisition's *autos*, these three are the only ones that appear in the records of *autos de fe* held in Seville on September 21, 1559; December 22, 1560; April 26, 1562; July 11, 1563; March 19, 1564; and November 14, 1574. According to Jerónimo Gracián, however, in the same year that Teresa was called before the Inquisition (1576), one Doña Catalina was punished as an *alumbrada*. See Carmelo de la Cruz, "Un manuscrito inédito del P. Gracián: 'Scholias y addiciones al libro de la Vida de la Madre Teresa de Jesús,'" *El Monte Carmelo* 68 (1960): 132: "Començaron entonzes en Seuilla illusiones y reuelaciones falsas y aquel mesmo año saco la Inquisicion al cadahalso una Doña Catalina por cosas de ilusiones y la açotaron siendo tenida antes de gran sancta. . . ."

96. *AHN*, Inq., leg. 2072, no. 3, fol. 27r: "Avia dicho que via cada dia la dinidad de nuestro señor y que se le avia aparescido sant sebastian en figura de un mancebo muy hermoso, y sanct juan evangelista y que tambien se le avia aparescido en su aposento nuestro señor con muchos coros de angeles al qual avia visto con los ojos corporales, y que un dia en que no avia querido su confessor que comulgase luego a la noche en sueños le aparecio un sacerdote, y le dixo misa en su aposento y la hostia se le avia venido volando hasta la boca, y que se la aparecian los diffuntos y le dezian si tenian necessidad de misas, y que hazia oracion por casamientos y por otras cosas, y dezia lo que avia de suceder por lo qual recibia dineros y que avia hecho y dicho otras muchas cosas que fueron qualificadas por embustes e ypocresias y burlerias."

The accusations against fifty-two-year-old Francisca Hernández hinged on visions she claimed to have had and the pride she took in them:

> She told a certain person . . . that she felt in her heart the burning of the Holy Spirit, and that they had found the name of Jesus written on the heart of a certain saint, and they would find more than that in her heart because God had enriched her soul with great beauty and delights and that Our Lord had appeared to her in the figure of the ecce homo, and that as a child an angel had taken her to hell and to purgatory and then they had risen up to heaven and the angel had knocked at the door but they would not let them in, and [she related] other visions and revelations that were judged to be rash fictions and illusions and that made her suspected of the errors of the *alumbrados* and *dexados*.[97]

Seven witnesses spoke against her, but Francisca denied all charges.

Finally, Francisca de Guzmán, a ninety-year-old *beata*, was accused of being under the control of an evil spirit:

> She spent much of her time in bed even though she was well and strong, and she said that God wanted her to be there, rejoicing with him, and that she should not go to mass on Sundays or feast days. And when she complained that that spirit did not let her go to church or rise from her bed, it replied, "God, whom you seek in church, do you not have him here? Why are you distressed?" And this spirit slept with her and shameful things happened between them, as if a husband were with his wife, and it did not let her pray or think good thoughts, and she took it for a great gift from God to be inflamed with this spirit. And when she told certain priests about her experiences, they helped her see the error of her ways and told her that the spirit was evil and was deceiving her and that she should have nothing to do with him and should follow the path the church teaches. She told them she understood, and she was very sorry, and she thanked God for letting her understand the truth.[98]

---

97. Ibid., fol. 27v: "[A] cierta persona . . . avia dicho que . . . sentia en el coraçon unas ynflamaciones del espiritu santo, y que a cierto santo avian hallado en el coraçon escripto el nombre de jesus, y a ella le hallarian mas que aquello porque dios le avia enrequezido el alma con grandes hermosuras y florestas y que se le avia aparescido nuestro señor en figura de Ecce homo y que siendo niña la avia llebado un angel al ynfierno, y al purgatorio, y despues subieron al cielo y llamo a la puerta el angel y no les quisieron abrir, y otras visiones y revelaciones que fueron qualificadas por themerarios enbustes y burlerias que la hazian sospechosa de estar en los herrores de los alumbrados y dexados."

98. Ibid., fols. 27v–28r: "Estubo mucho tiempo en la cama estando buena y sana y dezia que dios queria que estubiesse alli regocijandose con el, y que no oyesse missa los domingos ni fiestas y quexandose de que aquel espiritu no le dexaba yr a la yglesia ni lebantarse de alli el le respondia dios el que vas a buscar a la yglesia no le tienes aqui? Que te congojas? Y que aquel espiritu se acostaba con ella y entre ellos pasaban cosas que hera verguença dezillas como si un sposo estubiera con su esposa y que no le dexaba rezar ni pensar cosa buena y que tenia por gran merced de dios estarse abraçada con aquel espiritu. Y aviendo dado parte destas cosas esta rea a ciertos religiosos y ellos averla desengañado y dicho que aquel espiritu hera malo y la traya ylusa que se apartasse del, y andubiesse por el camino que la yglesia enseña ella les avia dicho

All three of these women were found guilty and sentenced to renounce their error *de levi* in the *auto* wearing the penitential robe, with a candle in hand. In addition María de Zúñiga and Francisca Hernandez had to wear the *soga*, a sort of metal gag, regularly inserted in the mouths of those who had uttered heresies or had blasphemed. After the procession María de Zúñiga was exiled from the city for three years. Francisca Hernández received one year of exile following one hundred lashes. Because of her advanced age, Francisca de Guzmán received one year of exile without corporal punishment.

The cases of these *alumbradas* provide some context for the Inquisition's suspicions of Teresa. To understand the accusations against her, we should examine the detailed descriptions of her visions in the *Vida*, already in the Inquisition's possession. In chapter 27 Teresa described her first vision of Christ in these terms: "While I was at prayer on the feast day of the glorious Saint Peter, I saw close to me, or I felt—to say it better—for I saw nothing with the eyes of either my body or my soul, but it seemed to me that Christ was close to me and I saw that it was He who was speaking to me, or so it seems to me."[99] Although Teresa insisted that her visions were neither corporeal nor imaginary, her descriptions of them included sensory elements, and she herself explained that the soul "feels [the presence] with its senses, or it hears it speak, or moves or touches it."[100] On another occasion, Teresa saw only Christ's hands followed by another vision of his face. These visions were meant to prepare her for the splendor of a vision of the entire resurrected Christ. She also described a vision of hell.[101]

The similarity of these visionary experiences to those of the condemned women is striking, yet the Inquisition accepted Teresa's visions as genuine, probably because of Teresa's superior education, precise vocabulary, and ability to make theological distinctions between various types of visions. As well, Teresa distinguished herself from the *alumbradas* by her repeated affirmations that any spiritual gifts given to the soul by God (visions, pleasures, etc.) were to be neither sought nor prized.[102] Social class and political connections

---

que assi lo entendia y le pessaba mucho dello y daba gracias a dios porque la avia dexado entender la verdad." Although the matter appeared to have been resolved outside the Inquisition's jurisdiction, when the Inquisition heard about the incident, it decided to try Francisca as an *alumbrada*: "Recibida esta ynformacion y votada a que se prendiesse se remitio al consejo y mando se hiziesse justicia."

99. *Vida* 27:2: "Estando un día del glorioso San Pedro en oración, vi cabe mí, o sentí—por mejor decir—que con los ojos del cuerpo ni del alma no vi nada, mas parecíame estaba junto cabe mí Cristo y veía ser El el que me hablaba, a mi parecer." Note the use of "a mi parecer," Teresa's customary way of qualifying a potentially dangerous subject.

100. *Vida* 27:3: "Siente con los sentidos, o la oye hablar, o menear o la toca."

101. *Vida* 28:1, 3; 32:1–3.

102. See, e.g., *Vida* 11:2, 15:3.

must also have played their roles. The women who were forced to abjure their errors in 1577 appear to have been of the lower social classes, or at least of families disfranchised from both the ecclesiastical hierarchy and the nobility, whereas Teresa was well connected through her family, the noble patrons of Carmelite convents, and a myriad priests, theologians, and religious.

Suspicions about Teresa and her reform movement continued to haunt the Discalced Carmelites several years after the incident in Seville. María de San José, concerned about the reputation of the convent in Seville, gathered together the four nuns whose testimony had been used against it and the five others who had testified before the tribunal. The first four retracted their earlier testimony, and the tribunal added the documents to the already closed case.

The troubles in Seville cost Teresa the favor of General Rubeo. Until then he had been very supportive of her reform effort, but now he charged that she had disobeyed his order that she limit her convents to Castile, and ordered her to choose a Discalced convent and remain there indefinitely; as far as he was concerned, she would found no more convents. According to a letter Teresa wrote to María Bautista in December 1575, she was at that time confined to the convent in Seville and unable to move about freely.[103] In June 1576, after relocating the nuns to a new house in Seville, Teresa left for Toledo, arriving there June 23. She remained there until July 1577, when she returned to San José in Avila under orders from the bishop of Avila. Teresa put her time in Toledo to good use, writing her most developed mystical treatise, the *Moradas*.

The genesis of this treatise, too, is related to Teresa's concern about the censorship and repression of her works, especially the *Vida*. Gracián describes her decision to write the *Moradas* (Mansions):

> . . . being her confessor and speaking with her once in Toledo about many things concerning her spirit, she said to me: "Oh, how well that point is written in the book of my life, which the Inquisition has!" And I said to her: "Well, since we can't recover it, write down what you remember, and other things, and write another book, and explain the basic doctrine without identifying the person who has experienced what you say there." . . .[104]

103. See Teresa's letter to María Bautista, December 30, 1575, in *Obras completas*, pp. 1380–83: "Si me dejaran, ya yo estuviera con vuestra reverencia, porque me notificaron el mandamiento del reverendísimo, que es que escoja una casa adonde esté siempre y no funde mas, que por el concilio no puedo salir."

104. Gracián, *Anotaciones al P. Ribera*, in Antonio de San Joaquín, *Año Teresiano, diario histórico, panegyrico moral, en que se descubren las virtudes, sucesos y maravillas de la seráphica y mystica Doctora de la Iglesia Santa Teresa de Jesús*, 12 vols. (Madrid, 1733–69), 7:149: "Lo que passa acerca del libro de las Moradas es, que siendo yo su Perlado, y tratando en Toledo una vez muchas cosas de su espiritu, ella me decia: O, que bien escrito esta esse punto en el libro de mi vida, que esta en la Inquisicion! Yo le dixe, pues que no le podemos haber, haga memoria de lo que se acordare, y de otras cosas, y escriva otro libro, y diga la doctrina en comun, sin que nombre a quien le haya acaecido que alli dixere; y assi le mande que escriviesse este libro de las Moradas."

Thus with Gracián's support Teresa began once again to set down her religious experience, this time in the third person, as a definitive synthesis of her mystical life.

The *Moradas* is an introduction to prayer as a continual interiorization until one reaches God, who resides in the center of the soul. To describe this process of interiorization toward ultimate union with God, Teresa uses the metaphor of a castle, based on the text "In my father's house are many mansions" (John 14:2). This inward movement is mediated by seven concentric spheres representing seven levels of proficiency in prayer. Beginners in prayer remain at the outer reaches of the spheres; progress inward involves a series of experiences, most of which are effected by God. Sprinkled throughout the treatise are counsels designed to help readers test the certainty of their experiences; after the doubts raised by the Inquisition regarding her experiences in the *Vida*, Teresa was being very careful.[105]

The theological review of the *Moradas* was effected by a sort of tribunal, consisting of Gracián, Diego de Yanguas, and Teresa herself, who met in the Discalced convent of Segovia in June or July 1580. Gracián wanted to censor some passages that Diego de Yanguas defended. In the end, Gracián wrote, "we took out some, not because they were bad doctrine, but because they were profound and difficult for many to understand. And because of the zeal I had for her, I tried to make sure there was nothing in her works that anyone could stumble over."[106] The censored passages were so few that they were simply crossed out in the manuscript, and it continued to circulate.

The *Moradas* was a theological tour de force, particularly in light of the papal nuncio Sega's criticism of Teresa as "a troublesome, restless, disobedient, and stubborn female, who under the guise of devotion invented bad doctrines, running around outside the cloister against the order of the Tridentine Council and prelates, instructing like a teacher in defiance of what St. Paul taught, who ordered women not to teach."[107]

---

105. *Moradas* 6:3, e.g., outlines signs that God gives the soul so it will know whether or not the "interior voice" that calls it proceeds from God or from the devil.

106. See Gracián, *Anotaciones*, p. 150: "Después leímos este libro en su presencia el padre fray Diego Yanguas y yo, arguyéndolo yo muchas cosas de él, diciendo ser malsonantes, y el padre fray Diego respondiéndome a ellas, y ella diciendo que las quitásemos; y así quitamos algunas, no porque fuese mala doctrina, sino alta y dificultosa de entender para muchos, porque con el celo que yo la quería procuraba que no hubiese cosa en sus escritos en que nadie tropezase."

107. Francisco de Santa María, *Reforma de los descalzos de Nuestra Señora del Carmen de la primitiva observancia, hecha por Santa Teresa de Jesús* (Madrid, 1644–55), 1:556: "Fémina inquieta, andariega, desobediente y contumaz, que a título de devoción inventaba malas doctrinas, andando fuera de la clausura contra el órden del concilio tridentino y prelados, enseñando como maestra contra lo que San Pablo enseñó, mandando que las mujeres no enseñasen."

Shortly after she finished the *Moradas*, Teresa had another encounter with the Inquisition. This incident is strikingly similar to the one with María del Corro in Seville. This story is found in the autobiography of Ana de San Bartolomé, who served as Teresa's nurse during the last four years of her life. As Ana records the incident, one of the nuns at the convent, who "claimed to have [great experiences] in prayer although she didn't have a single one," told her confessor that Ana was confessing her sins to Teresa. "She had the prioress and her confessor fooled, and they thought highly of her . . . and she told the confessor that I confessed with Mother Teresa, and to watch and see how she was fooling him and I was too, and that this was a case for the Inquisition."[108] Ana denied the accusation, but the inquisitors questioned Teresa about it. "With this and other accusations the Inquisitors came one day for the Saint and carried out an investigation, and seeing that it was not true, they dropped [the charges]. . . ."[109] Although Ana's description leaves the impression that the problem was short-lived, her own chronology suggests that the accusations may have taken up to two years to resolve.[110]

On October 4, 1582, Teresa called the Discalced nuns together to instruct them one last time. As she died, Teresa thanked God that she died "a

108. Ana de San Bartolomé, *Autobiografía* (Madrid, 1969), p. 58: ". . . [F]ingía que estaba contenta tenía oración, y no tenía ninguna. A la Priora y al confesor los engañaba, y queríanla mucho . . . y dijo al confesor que yo me confesaba con la Madre Teresa, que mirase que le engañaba y que yo lo estaba también, que aquello era caso de Inquisición." According to Ana, the nun involved was a cousin of a friend of Teresa's, so Teresa hesitated to banish her from the convent. See ibid., p. 57: "era sobrina de un amigo suyo." This incident happened shortly after Teresa fell and broke her arm (December 24, 1577). Ana's original account is BN MS. 19.389, "Cartas y cinco opúsculos que se conservan originales en el convento de Salamanca."

109. Ibid.: "Con estas y otros dichos los Inquisidores venían un día por la Santa y hacían las informaciones y viendo que no era verdad lo dejaron y como nuestra Santa estaba segura y libre de lo que la acusaban estaba contenta [que] se le ofreciese aquella afrenta."

110. Ana implies that the problem was not solved when Teresa left San José to found more convents in 1580. See BN MS. 19.389, fol. 46r: "She [Teresa] was sorry about the trouble this sister gave me, for she said things about me that ill became a nun, and the confessor and the prioress were on her side. And a few days later the Saint was forced to leave to found convents, and she was happy to be able to take me out of there for the grief that sister gave me" ("Ella sentia bien el travajo, q[ue] esta h[erma]na me dava q[ue] me tratava mal de palabras q[ue] no eran bien sonantes a una religiosa y el confessor y la priora estavan en su opinion y a pocos dias fuele forsoso a la S[an]ta salir a las fundaciones y estava contenta de sacarme de alli por la pena q[ue] me dava aquella h[erma]na"). In 1580 Teresa received a patent from Angel de Salazar, the Carmelite provincial, to continue founding new convents. In her final wave of foundings, Teresa traveled to Villanueva de la Jara (convent founded February 25, 1580), Palencia (December 29, 1580), Soria (June 3, 1581), and Burgos (April 19, 1582). She was unable to found a convent in the growing new center of Madrid, though she never gave up hope. See, e.g., her negotiations with Dionisio Ruíz de la Pena in her letter dated June 30, 1581; in *Obras completas*, pp. 1948–50.

daughter of your church." Teresa's last words reflect her problematic status in the church because of her encounters with the Inquisition. Indeed, during her lifetime Teresa never received a verdict from the Inquisition on the *Vida* or any of her other books.[111] Inquisitional officials held onto the manuscripts of the *Vida*, the *Moradas*, and the *Camino de Perfección* until 1586, when the Carmelites were preparing to publish all of Teresa's works.[112]

Conclusions

Although Teresa's troubles with the Inquisition did not begin until 1570, they were the logical outgrowth of difficulties she had encountered since her conversion experience: doubts about the validity of her mystical experiences, resistance to the reforms she wanted to make in the Carmelite order, and challenges to her authority as both writer and reformer. Without more documentation we cannot claim to understand the dynamics of each of the Inquisition's cases against Teresa. We can say, however, that in nearly all instances the inquisitors conducted their inquiries in response to specific complaints about Teresa or her Discalced Carmelites; they did not single Teresa out for attention.

What motives would Teresa's contemporaries have to denounce her to the Inquisition? Llamas Martínez attributes the accusations to the machinations of a handful of detractors, nearly all mentally unbalanced. Indeed, he sees no connection between Teresa's problems with the Inquisition and similar trials of the same period.[113] His concern for Teresa's reputation for holiness makes his analysis of her case unreliable. If Teresa's works are viewed in their historical context, the challenges she encountered follow naturally from the climate of suspicion surrounding women's spiritual experiences.

Teresa's works were also caught in the cross fire of rival religious orders and of factions within the Carmelite order itself. Though Teresa sought confessors in many religious orders and advocated consultation with educated *letrados*, as a woman and as a theologian she was firmly planted in the school of *espirituales*. The theological disputes between these two parties, essentially represented by the Dominicans and Jesuits, respectively, exacerbated the controversy aroused by Teresa and her reform movement.

111. See the testimony of Ana de Jesús (Lobera) in *BMC* 18:479: "Durante su vida no sabía lo que opinaba el Santo Oficio sobre la *Vida*."
112. Teresa's companion Ana de Jesús was extremely influential in extracting the confiscated works from the Inquisition. She negotiated with the inquisitor general and eventually received the manuscripts, but it was not an easy process. For more details, see Silverio de Santa Teresa, "Preliminares," in *BMC* 1:lxxxii–lxxxiv.
113. Llamas, p. 389. Llamas characterizes María del Corro, for example, as a "semihysterical" and "frustrated religious" (pp. 70, 66).

Jerónimo Gracián testifies to the resentment Teresa and the discalced movement aroused in nuns who were content to observe the old Carmelite rule. As we have seen, Gracián, too, was accused before the Inquisition. He attributes the problems in Seville to the interference of the Calced Carmelites, who did not welcome the arrival of the Discalced to Andalusia. Teresa's reforms were implicitly critical of the religious life of the Calced Carmelites, and the monks at the Carmelite monastery in Seville saw Gracián's arrival there in 1573 as a condemnation of them. Apparently the monastery had joined the Discalced reform, but the monks were not living by the Discalced rule. "We had to leave [Pastrana] to go to Seville," Gracián relates, "to dissolve a monastery of Discalced Carmelites that had been established on a bad foundation, some Calced who, not to be outdone by the others, had turned themselves into Discalced and taken over a monastery at San Juan del Puerto."[114] Gracián came with papal briefs authorizing the reform of this monastery, and the monks fought back by accusing him before the Inquisition of "very abominable things, stupid and ugly." In the end, the monks had their way: Gracián was sentenced to do penance and live as a recluse in the Discalced monastery of Alcalá de Henares.[115]

Gracián's account throws further light on the Discalced Carmelites in Seville: they were involved in a competition of sorts among religious orders for the attention and support of the faithful. The reputation of the Discalced for dedication to a life of prayer and its manifestations in mystical phenomena gained them great prestige. Their reforms put pressure on other religious orders, the Calced Carmelites in particular, to raise their monastic standards. It is not surprising that those who wanted to maintain the status quo used the most effective means at hand to block the reformers. The interference of the Inquisition in questions of internal monastic reform reveals how easily the tribunals could be manipulated to investigate matters that had nothing to do with "heretics."[116]

114. Jerónimo de la Madre de Dios Gracián, *Peregrinación de Anastasio*, in *BMC* 17:83: ". . . sería necesario para evitar inconvenientes ausentarnos e ir a Sevilla a deshacer un convento de Carmelitas Descalzos que se había fundado con mal fundamento, de unos Calzados que por emulación de otros se habían hecho Descalzos y tomándoles un convento en San Juan del Puerto."

115. See ibid., p. 93: "Sentencióme el Nuncio a privado de voz y lugar, recluso en el colegio de los Carmelitas Descalzos de Alcalá con no sé qué ayunos, disciplinas y oraciones, atento que la sentencia no era por haberle impedido a él su jurisdicción, que fué lo que él sintió; pero como el Rey acudió al Papa que le limitó sus poderes, no podía dar a la sentencia esta causa, sino por los procesos que le habían enviado los Calzados de Andalucía, que aunque eran de cosas muy abominables, torpes y feas, por no haber oído mi descargo no era razón ser más pesada."

116. For further discussion of the relationship between the "troubles" in Seville and the tensions between the Calced and the Discalced, see the testimony of Beatriz de Jesús in *BMC* 18:117; Julián de Avila, *La Vida de la Santa Madre Teresa de Jesús*, ed. Vicente de La Fuente (Madrid, 1881), pp. 302–5; María de San José, "Historia de las Fundaciones," and Diego de Yepes, "Carta a Luis de León," both in Teresa, *Escritos de Santa Teresa*, pp. 556–57, 567.

Several people had reason to denounce Teresa to the Inquisition, and institutional officials had good reason of their own to suspect her orthodoxy. Her visionary experiences appeared similar to those of women suspected of *alumbradismo*. The contemplative orientation of Teresa's reforms led to practices that went against the contemporary emphasis on vocal prayer. Indeed, Teresa's life and works raised serious questions about the role of revelation in the religious life at a time when the institutional church was determined to monitor and control access to God. The Inquisition wanted a clear statement from Teresa about her allegiance and obedience to the institutional church and its representatives. Though the inquisitors never stopped either Teresa's reforms or her writing career, her encounters with them significantly affected the expression of her religious experience, both in style and in content. The textual survival strategies she adopted enabled her to continue her vocation.

3

The Right to Write: Authority
and Rhetorical Strategy
in Teresa's Works

Through writing Teresa accomplished many things: she defended the legitimacy of her religious experience; she articulated her vision for the reform of the Carmelite order (and, implicitly, for the church at large); and, most important, she established herself as a teacher of mystical doctrine. At issue was the public role she assumed as a teacher, a proposition fraught with tensions for anyone writing after the appearance of the Valdés Index, but especially for a woman.

Teresa appeared suspect to her contemporaries for many reasons: she was a *conversa* and was often linked socially with other *conversos*; she was accused of being troublesome and unstable, a gadabout when she should be praying in her monastic cell;[1] she led a sometimes unpopular reform movement; she was a woman, with no formal theological education, but she dared to teach mystical theology; she wrote about mysticism at a time when the Valdés Index proscribed such books; and she spoke about such problematic subjects as visions and religious experiences that manifested themselves physically.

Teresa's struggle to claim some sort of authority for her teachings appears throughout her works and takes many forms. The most critical kind of authority Teresa lacked was doctrinal authority. In this arena she faced the most serious challenges, because the mechanisms of the institutional church worked so hard to control teaching authority. At a time when experiential authority was rapidly eroding, Teresa had no other weapon in her arsenal to defend herself from attacks on the credibility of her teachings. Thus her self-representation was the most critical element in her efforts to establish her authority as a teacher.

Teresa realized the shakiness of her position as a mystical theologian and repeatedly acknowledged her limitations as an unlettered woman in her efforts to disarm hostile readers with her humility and lack of pretentious-

---

1. Literally, "inquieta y andariega." Teresa's repeated absences from her religious community to found convents were blatant infractions of the claustration rule decreed by the Council of Trent for contemplative nuns.

ness.[2] At the same time, Teresa was well aware of the value of her teachings, and she lamented her lack of ecclesiastical and theological authority: "I wish I had great authority so people would believe this. I beg the Lord to give it to me."[3]

How was a woman, deprived of a university education and any institutional title beyond prioress—a title she avoided as much as possible—to work around the limitations imposed upon her by the institutional church? The key to Teresa's survival and success as a writer was the use of rhetorical strategies that defined and justified her role in the church. These strategies extended in various directions, answering and anticipating criticism, but they were not simply reactive. Teresa was engaged in a process of self-construction which was an active attempt to forge a new definition of religious authority for women at the same time that it responded to the inhospitable climate for women in sixteenth-century Spain.

Teresa's construction of herself took two major forms. First, she attempted to dissociate herself from her own will with elaborate demonstrations of humility and obedience. These protestations were at least as persuasive for generations of Teresian commentators as they were for Teresa's contemporaries. Once she established her willingness to conform to her superiors' commands, however, Teresa could represent herself in ways that many of her contemporaries would otherwise have rejected outright. Second, she affirmed her role as an intercessor before God, continuing the medieval tradition of quasi-sacerdotal expression and establishing herself as a teacher and transmitter of divine wisdom.

The Strategy of Subordination

Alison Weber was among the first to characterize Teresa's humility as a rhetorical strategy designed to present herself in a nonthreatening way: "Teresa's rhetoric of feminine subordination—all the paradoxes, the self-deprecation, the feigned ignorance and incompetence, the deliberate obfuscation and ironic humor—produced the desired perlocutionary effect."[4] The force of Teresa's personality and her reputation for audacity and unconventionality could be mitigated by the doubts and inner vacillations on which she harped. J. Mary Luti describes this dynamic well: "Teresa made everyone aware that she was aware how singular her activity was; as long as they

2. See Weber, *Teresa of Avila and the Rhetoric of Femininity*, pp. 35–50, 72–76.
3. *Vida* 19:4: "Yo quisiera aquí tener gran autoridad para que se me creyera esto. Al Señor suplico Su Majestad la dé." Although Teresa was aware of the legacy of medieval women mystics, as we know from the list of books she read, she never appealed to this tradition to justify her teaching authority.
4. Weber, *Teresa of Avila*, p. 159.

could point to her avowed discomfort, she became the exception which confirmed the rule."[5]

Ultimately, the survival of Teresa's works depended to some extent on the success of this rhetoric of humility. Teresa had to achieve a difficult and delicate balance: it is true that no woman was ever punished for excessive humility, yet one could not gain recognition for holiness if one were too humble. "Christian saints," Aviad Kleinberg points out,

> were expected to play an impossible role. They were denied the right to advertise themselves too explicitly, for one of the most important attributes of the true saint was humility. But total humility—a complete refusal to co-operate with potential admirers—would result in anonymity. . . . If the saint was to play a social role in the church militant, his or her sanctity had to be seen and socially recognized. Saints needed, therefore, to advertise both their claim and their proof without seeming too assertive.[6]

For Teresa the tensions were especially acute, for female humility often reinforced patriarchal structures and stereotypes. She did not accept the view that women were incapable of spiritual discernment, but her critique of it had to be quite circumspect. Too, it was increasingly difficult for women to achieve a significant role in church reform. Rather than attack these strictures outright, Teresa had to appear to be a hesitant public figure, willing to serve under obedience but reluctant to attract attention to herself.

In her writings Teresa adopted several strategies to underscore her humility. First, her colloquial style suggested that she was conversing rather than teaching. Second, she portrayed herself as a woman who was writing only because she had been ordered to do so. Finally, she repeated her willingness to submit her doctrine to the judgment of trained theologians. For male and female readers alike, Teresa's humility underscored her sincerity. Convincing her readers of her sincerity was very important, because it separated her from the *alumbrados*, who deceived others and were themselves deceived. For Jerónimo Gracián, her simple but compelling style was also a sign of divine grace:

> The same lack of artifice found in these books of Mother Teresa de Jesús reveals that it was not her own invention, but doctrine given by the spirit, which does not depend on human work to enter the heart. And in using this style she demonstrates the truth plainly, without adornments, rhetoric, or artifice; although if one looks carefully, the style is superb for convincing and bringing forth fruit. . . .[7]

5. Luti, "Teresa of Avila," p. 71.
6. Kleinberg, *Prophets in Their Own Country*, p. 112.
7. Gracián, *Dilucidario*, in *BMC* 15:17: "Y esta misma falta de artificio que llevan estos libros de la madre Teresa de Jesús, descubre no ser invención suya, sino doctrina, dada del es-

The natural, unaffected ring of Teresa's style was part of her ingenuous appeal and was tied to her desire to provoke a response in her reader. According to her Carmelite contemporaries, the similarity between the speaking and the written Teresa was what made her books recognizable.[8] This intentional resemblance represents Teresa's attempt to prolong, expand, and develop the colloquies of instruction she offered her religious sisters. She was setting down on paper the norms she taught by word and example as prioress at San José in Ávila and later as founder of her other convents. She knew that her works would be read not only in private but aloud to groups of people, during recreation and in the refectory—at the times she herself put to use to continue the education of her nuns. Teresa's colloquial style is in sharp contrast to the profundity of the content of her works. In this sense, the simplicity of her style best serves Teresa's pedagogical purpose; her approachable style made God more approachable.

Teresa was careful to identify her audience as the circle of nuns in the Carmelite reform movement. Clearly the influence of her books extended far beyond the walls of Carmelite convents, but this, she could claim with all due modesty, was not her intent. As she discovered her own niche within a patriarchal literary tradition, Teresa used the rhetoric of humility to defend her vocation as a teacher, in the domain of learned men. In the *Camino de perfección* she argued that her condition as a woman gave her a distinct advantage over male theologians in the spiritual preparation of other religious women, because "the *letrados*, since they have more important things to do and are manly men, don't take so much notice of things that in themselves seem trivial."[9] Ironically, Teresa discovered, humility could win her greater influence in the church.

Partly in recognition of her lack of theological training and authority and partly to protect herself against accusations of heterodoxy, Teresa often qualified points she thought would be controversial by adding, "it seems to me." With this phrase she underscored her willingness to modify her mystical doctrine if university-trained theologians showed her that she had erred. In the *Moradas* Teresa explained this literary strategy:

---

píritu, que no aguarda al artificio humano para entrar en el corazón. Y en ir en aquel estilo muestra con llaneza la verdad, sin composturas, retóricas, ni artificios; aunque, si bien se mira, el estilo es altísimo para persuadir y hacer fruto. . . ."

8. See, e.g., the testimony of Mariana de la Cruz and Beatriz del Espíritu Santo in *BMC* 18:435–42.

9. *CV*, Prologue:2–3: "Pienso poner algunos remedios para tentaciones de religiosas [que pone el demonio] . . . a que las almas de mis hermanas vayan muy adelante en el servicio del Señor. . . . [L]os letrados, por tener otras ocupaciones más importantes y ser varones fuertes, no hacen tanto caso de las cosas que en sí no parecen nada. . . ."

In difficult things, even though it seems to me that I understand them and speak the truth, I always use this language of "it seems to me," because if I am mistaken, I tend strongly to believe what well-educated people say; because even if they haven't experienced these things, educated people have a something, I don't know what it is, so that, since God considers them the light of his Church, when something is true, it makes them accept it; and if they are true servants of God, they are never shocked by the great things He does, for they understand that God can do much more than that.[10]

Teresa uses this strategy often. In the *Vida*, for instance, when she describes the role of the understanding in the mystical suspension of the soul—a delicate point because of the controversy surrounding the *alumbrados*—Teresa writes: "The soul is suspended so that it seems outside itself; the will loves; memory seems almost lost; the understanding doesn't reason— it seems to me—but it's not lost. . . ."[11] In the same way Teresa backed away from her observations on the role of grace in mystical experience, because this, too, was a controversial issue: "It's impossible, given our nature—it seems to me—to have the courage to do great things unless one understands it's by God's help."[12]

To humility Teresa added repeated submission of her doctrine to the judgment of representatives of the institutional church. In the conclusion of the *Moradas*, for example, she incorporated multiple protests of humility, begging for her readers' prayers and establishing her subjection to the Roman Catholic church: "If anything should be wrong [here], it's because I fail to understand, and in everything I defer to what the holy Roman Catholic Church holds, for in this I live and affirm and promise to live and die."[13] And in the *Vida* she addresses her confessor García de Toledo: "My work would be blessed if I happened to say something that only once

10. *Moradas* 5:1:7: "Siempre en cosas dificultosas, aunque me parece que lo entiendo y que digo verdad, voy con este lenguaje de que 'me parece', porque si me engañare, estoy muy aparejada a creer lo que dijeren los que tienen letras muchas; porque, aunque no hayan pasado por estas cosas, tienen un no sé qué grandes letrados que, como Dios los tiene para luz de su Iglesia, cuando es una verdad, dásela para que se admita; y, si no son derramados sino siervos de Dios, nunca se espantan de sus grandezas, que tienen bien entendido que puede mucho más y más."

11. *Vida* 10:1: "Suspende el alma de suerte, que toda parecía estar fuera de sí; ama la voluntad; la memoria me parece está casi perdida; el entendimiento no discurre—a mi parecer— mas no se pierde. . . ."

12. *Vida* 10:6: "Es imposible, conforme a nuestra naturaleza—a mi parecer—tener ánimo para cosas grandes quien no entiende está favorecido de Dios." For other examples of Teresa's use of "a mi parecer," see *Vida* 15:3, 25:5.

13. *Moradas*, Conclusion:4: "Y si algo estuviere en error, es por más no lo entender, y en todo me sujeto a lo que tiene la santa Iglesia Católica Romana, que en esto vivo, y protesto, y prometo vivir y morir."

caused the Lord to be praised; with this I would be well satisfied, even if later you burned it."[14] Teresa's humble dissociation of herself from her doctrine seemed further proof both of her virtue and of divine inspiration. Recognition of the authority of the institutional church and conformity with the standards of humility considered to be appropriate for women were critical to the survival of Teresa's ideas.

Obedience, another traditional Christian virtue, also proved to be quite pliable for Teresa. It confirmed her humility while to some extent protecting her from criticism as a woman in a public role. In many complex ways, Teresa enshrouded her activities in obedience. The rhetoric of obedience went a long way toward establishing Teresa's goodwill toward institutional figures. She portrayed herself as in all ways obedient—to her confessors, to theologians, and to representatives of the hierarchical church—and her writing and reform activities as undertaken in obedience to God.

Because women could not openly take it upon themselves to be teachers, Teresa had to attribute her works to the commands of her confessors. All writers, but women in particular, encountered strong resistance to the circulation of their spiritual works. Although Teresa always appeared to take on the task of writing with surprisingly good grace, she rarely admitted on paper that the idea of recording and transmitting her ideas was her own. Instead, she wrote of obedience and the influence of others on her decision to take up the pen. This strategy protected her against accusations of arrogantly violating the biblical order that women should not teach.[15] Here Teresa's rhetoric has been so successful that she has been misinterpreted by nearly all literary critics, who understand her motivation to write solely as obedience to her confessors; thus the abundance of comments such as "She writes not with any literary purpose or by her own initiative, but under obedience to her confessors or at the request of her nuns."[16] Although mistaken, this interpretation is exactly what Teresa meant her readers to assume, so she would not be accused of taking pride in her religious

14. *Vida* 40:23: "Más dichoso sería el trabajo si he acertado a decir algo que sola una vez se alabe por ello el Señor, que con esto me daría por pagada, aunque vuestra merced luego lo queme."

15. See 1 Tim. 2:11–12. Many sixteenth-century women were criticized for daring to teach, and Alonso de la Fuente made much of Teresa's audacity in presuming to do so, as we shall see.

16. R. Lapesa, *Historia de la lengua española* (Madrid, 1981), p. 316. Even Víctor García de la Concha, who provides many novel insights into Teresa's style, does not question the assumption that Teresa wrote under obedience. For some recent reflections on the importance of obedience in Teresa's literary vocation, see his *Arte literario de Santa Teresa*, pp. 91–92; and Enrique Llamas Martínez, "Introducción al 'Libro de la Vida,'" in Barrientos, *Introducción a la lectura de Santa Teresa*, pp. 208–10.

experiences.[17] In accepting this premise, however, critics have denied Teresa the creative initiative in her work and have also fallen into the trap of its logical corollary, the idea that Teresa's work, lacking in literary motivation, must then also lack intentionality of style and content.

Rosa Rossi, the first scholar to explore Teresa's rhetorical use of obedience, argues that when Teresa uses the word, she means "with leave" or "under precept."[18] The approval of a known theologian lent credibility to Teresa's enterprise and demonstrated her affiliation with the institutional church. Yet Rossi does not analyze the historical context that required justification to write mystical treatises, so she reveals only one of the rhetorical functions of the word "obedience" in Teresa's works.

"Obedience" also established Teresa's theological credentials, her right to write, despite her lack of a university education. She mentioned obedience in the prologues to all her major works: the *Vida*, the *Camino de perfección*, the *Meditations on the Song of Songs*, the *Libro de las fundaciones*, and the *Moradas*. The context of each of these works helps to explain the variations in Teresa's use of the word "obedience." As the *Vida* was Teresa's first major work, one would expect its prologue to supply the strongest justification of her literary vocation and thus to make the greatest rhetorical use of "obedience." Instead, Teresa limited herself to declaring humbly that those people whom she must obey have limited her artistic license: "They have ordered me and given me great liberty to write about my method of prayer and the mercies the Lord has given me, and I wish they had given me [the same liberty] to tell clearly and in detail about my great sins and wayward life."[19] Here Teresa cloaked the genesis of her work in the order she received to "write about my method of prayer," thus protecting herself against accusations of novelty, but she gave no real details about this order. Who ordered her to write? When? Why?[20] The Inquisition's intense scrutiny of the book and its refusal to release it for circulation must have persuaded Teresa to adopt different strategies to justify her forays into the literary world.

---

17. We saw in chapter 2, in the case of the *alumbrada* María de Zuñiga, how women who cherished visions and other gifts they claimed had been granted them by God were punished for their pride.

18. See Rosa Rossi, "Teresa de Jesús: La mujer y la palabra," *mientras tanto* 15 (1983): 40.

19. *Vida* 1:1:"Quisiera yo que, como me han mandado y dado larga licencia para que escriba el modo de oración y las mercedes que el Señor me ha hecho, me la dieran para que muy por menudo y con claridad dijera mis grandes pecados y ruín vida." Clearly the emphasis is on liberty, which appears a second time in the sentence in the word "la," rather than on the act of command and Teresa's response to it.

20. Sprinkled throughout the *Vida* are various hints as to who the first recipients of the book were. See, e.g., 10:7–8.

Teresa's next book, the *Camino de perfección*, explicitly addressed the spiritual needs of her nuns, teaching them the Carmelite vocation in mental prayer. Here Teresa dispensed with the notion of obedience to her religious superiors; she mentioned that she had received permission from her confessor, Domingo Báñez, but said she was really yielding to the importunities of the Discalced Carmelite nuns of San José in Avila. She made this notion of obedience to her fellow sisters more explicit in the second version of the *Camino*:

> Since the sisters of this convent of San José know I have permission from Father Domingo Báñes [sic], of the order of the glorious Saint Dominic, who is now my confessor, to write some things about prayer in which it seems I may hit upon the truth because I have spoken with many spiritual and holy people, they have begged me so eagerly to tell them something about it that I have decided to obey them. . . .[21]

In the first version, Teresa wrote "I have decided to do it" rather than "I have decided to obey them."[22] Teresa deliberately restricted the audience and content of the *Camino*, hoping that this move would protect her from outside interference. Indeed, because it avoided the most difficult doctrinal questions and was organized around the Lord's Prayer, the *Camino* was in many ways the least controversial of Teresa's mystical trilogy.

After finishing the *Camino de perfección*, Teresa began a commentary on some verses of the Song of Songs. This was a somewhat risky project because of the Valdés Index's prohibition of reading the Bible in the vernacular. Teresa's major exposure to the Song of Songs was in liturgical scripture readings, but apparently she had also read parts of it, probably in quotation in devotional books. She wrote in the Prologue to the *Meditations on the Song of Songs*: "Every time I hear or read some words from the Songs of Solomon . . . [even] without understanding the splendor of the Latin in Spanish, it sweeps me up and moves my soul more than the pious books I understand."[23] This prologue reflects the old idea of "obedience" as "liberty": "Now with the advice [*parecer*] of persons I am obliged to obey, I will

21. *CV* 1:1: "Sabiendo las hermanas de este monasterio de San José cómo tenía licencia del padre presentado fray Domingo Bañes, de la orden del glorioso Santo Domingo, que al presente es mi confesor, para escribir algunas cosas de oración en que parece podré atinar por haber tratado con muchas personas espirituales y santas, me han tanto importunado les diga algo de ella que me he determinado a las obedecer. . . ."

22. *CE* 1:1: ". . . ha sido tanto el deseo que las he visto y la importunación, que me he determinado a hacerlo. . . ."

23. *Meditaciones sobre los cantares*, Prologue:2: "Cada vez que oigo o leo algunas palabras de los *Cantares* de Salomón . . . sin entender la claridad del latín en romance, me recogía más y movía mi alma que los libros muy devotos que entiendo."

write something of what God has given me to understand"; and in a somewhat self-protective move she declares that she has her confessor's permission to write the book.[24] Under any other circumstances, of course, the book would have been immediately suspect. Like the *Exclamations of the Soul to God*, a mystical meditation on communion written sometime during 1569, and Teresa's poetry, the *Meditations* are an intimate expression of Teresa's understanding of God and her longing for permanent union with Him. Teresa wrote two versions of the *Meditations*, the first in 1566–67, the second sometime between 1572 and 1575. Domingo Báñez approved the second version on August 10, 1575.

Neither of the original manuscripts survives, because about 1580 one of Teresa's confessors ordered her to burn them. She never recorded a word about the incident, but María de San José (Gracián) described it during her testimony in the Proceso de Madrid in 1595 as an instance of Teresa's obedience: "Diego de Yanguas told this witness that the said Mother [Teresa] had written a book about the Songs of Solomon, and as it didn't seem right to him that a woman should write about the Scriptures, he told her so, and she was so quick to yield to her confessor's opinion that she burned it immediately."[25] It is only because some Carmelites had copied the text before the order was given that we know what Teresa wrote.[26]

The *Foundations* and the *Moradas* are special cases; here "obedience" serves a different rhetorical function. These books were written after Teresa had had encounters with the Inquisition, and the *Vida* had been collected for continued study. Since what she had already written had provoked suspicions, Teresa was hardly in a position to continue writing. In this case, her obligation to obey orders was her only excuse. In these two works she described in detail who had ordered her to write and when she received the order. The suspicion that shadowed her works was also reflected in her repeated assurances that she adhered to the doctrine of the "Holy Roman

---

24. Ibid., 3: "Ahora, con parecer de personas a quien yo estoy obligada a obedecer, escribiré alguna cosa de lo que el Señor me da a entender."

25. *BMC* 18:320: "Y el padre fray Diego de Yanguas dijo a esta testigo, que la dicha Madre había escrito un libro sobre los *Cantares*, y él pareciéndole que no era justo que mujer escribiese sobre la Escritura, se lo dijo, y ella fué tan pronta en la obediencia y parecer de su confesor que lo quemó al punto."

26. The survival of several copies of Teresa's commentaries on the Song of Songs is a matter of interesting speculation. Although María de San José attributed the virtue of obedience to Teresa, it seems too great a coincidence that several copies of *both* versions of the commentaries are extant. It is certainly possible that Teresa knew about these copies and, since they received the approval of the censor Domingo Báñez in 1575, allowed them to circulate with her blessing. Other commentators insist that Teresa ordered all copies of the book burned, and thus agreed with the judgment of Diego de Yanguas. See, e.g., Daniel de Pablo Maroto, "Meditaciones sobre los Cantares," in Barrientos, *Introducción a la lectura de Santa Teresa*, p. 386.

Church" and the censorship of its theologians. This formulaic submission to the institutional church is not found in her other prologues.[27]

The great similarity of the two prologues confirms that Teresa was employing a new formula in these two works—strong evidence for the new rhetorical function of the word "obedience." In the *Moradas* Teresa wrote:

> Few things that obedience has obliged me to do have been so difficult for me as writing now about prayer; first, because the Lord seems to give me neither the spirit nor the desire to do it; second, because for the past three months my head has been so filled with clamor and weakness that it's difficult for me to write even what I must to take care of business. But I understand that the force of obedience tends to make things that seem impossible easy, so I have resolved to do it gladly, though it seems to go against my natural inclination.[28]

In the *Foundations*, she wrote:

> Because it seemed impossible to me [to finish the work I agreed to do] (because of the many tasks—letters and other obligations that my superiors have ordered me to do), I was praying to God [about it] and rather troubled (because I was so fainthearted and in such poor health, and even without this burden the work sometimes seemed unbearable because of my weak nature), [and] the Lord said to me: "Daughter, obedience gives strength."[29]

When Teresa proclaimed her obedience to her superiors, she was proclaiming her allegiance to the institutional church. With the *Foundations* and the *Moradas*, some symbol of this allegiance was critical because of the accusations that had been raised against her to the Inquisition. Thus in stating her obedience to her superiors, Teresa was distinguishing herself from both the *alumbrados* and the *luteranos*, many of whom were punished not only for their beliefs or practices but for the tenacity with which they clung to them.

There is, of course, other evidence that obedience was not the essential motivation for Teresa's literary vocation. First, Teresa's contemporaries describe thick notebooks that she carried about so she could record her reli-

27. See *Foundations*, Prologue:6, and *Moradas*, Prologue:3.

28. *Moradas*, Prologue:1: "Pocas cosas que me ha mandado la obediencia se me han hecho tan dificultosas como escribir ahora cosas de oración: lo uno, porque no me parece me da el Señor espíritu para hacerlo ni deseo; lo otro, por tener la cabeza, tres meses ha, con un ruido y flaqueza tan grande que aún los negocios forzosos escribo con pena. Mas, entendiendo que la fuerza de la obediencia suele allanar cosas que parecen imposibles, la voluntad se determina a hacerlo muy de buena gana aunque el natural parece que se aflige mucho."

29. *Foundations*, Prologue:2: "Pareciéndome a mí ser imposible (a causa de los mucho negocios, así de cartas como de otras ocupaciones forzosas, por ser en cosas mandadas por los prelados), me estaba encomendando a Dios, y algo apretada (por ser yo para tan poco y con tan mala salud, que, aún sin esto, muchas veces, me parecía no se poder sufrir el trabajo conforme a mi bajo natural), me dijo el Señor: 'Hija, la obediencia da fuerzas.'"

gious experiences whenever they occurred. In her testimony from Lisbon, where she was prioress of the Discalced convent, María de San José Salazar declared: "For a long time this witness had some notebooks in her possession, written in the hand of the said Mother [Teresa], which contained many revelations. . . ."[30] Most likely parts of these notebooks served as the first drafts of her mystical works or notes for them. Second, her works contain writing in some genres that are scarcely subject to external command. Her poetry, for instance, is a direct response of praise and thanksgiving for the spiritual gifts she experienced.[31]

Teresa's vast correspondence is also telling; a person of few words who wrote only under obedience would write no more letters than she had to, and they would be no longer than necessary to serve the purpose at hand. Teresa's letters—more than 450 of them are extant—throw much light on the woman, her relations with others, her diplomatic capacities as founder and administrator, the context of her reforms, and the problems she encountered. In sum, they constitute another written expression of herself. The abundance of material that no one could command her to write is a reflection of Teresa's literary gifts and her strong desire to express her ideas in writing. In print, however, Teresa never expressed such a desire.

The idea that Teresa wrote with great care and of her own initiative goes against much of the literary criticism of her works, which has emphasized her "spontaneous style."[32] The fact that most scholars have interpreted Teresa's style in this fashion merely underscores the impressive success of her rhetoric. One of the leading representatives of this school of criticism was Ramón Menéndez Pidal, who suggested Teresa wrote in inspired fits of genius, too absorbed in her work to be bothered with questions of rhetoric.

> [One] factor in Teresa's indomitable spontaneity is improvisation taken to its extreme. As the Carmelite reformer writes, she is always carried along by the rapid flow of her ideas. . . . The stylistic motto of Juan de Valdés and other sixteenth-century writers is: I write as I speak; but Saint Teresa doesn't really write, she talks on paper; so the vigor of the emotional syntax is always greater than the ordinary channels of grammar.[33]

---

30. *BMC* 18:492–93: "Esta testigo tuvo mucho tiempo algunos cuadernos en su poder, escritos de la letra de la dicha Madre, en que se contenían muchas revelaciones. . . ." See also the testimony of Beatriz de Mendoza ibid., p. 398.

31. Other works in this category include her *Exclamaciones del alma a Dios* and the *Desafío espiritual*.

32. Some of the problems inherent in this line of interpretation are discussed in Weber, *Teresa of Avila*, pp. 5–16.

33. Ramón Menéndez Pidal, "El Estilo de Santa Teresa," in *La lengua de Cristóbal Colón: El estilo de Santa Teresa y otros estudios sobre el siglo XVI* (Madrid, 1958), pp. 124–25.

Underlying Menéndez Pidal's interpretation—and that of many other analysts before and since—is the image of Teresa writing while in ecstasy. Both Teresa's contemporaries and later commentators understood her uncomplicated style to be indicative of direct inspiration from God. Descriptions of Teresa writing while in ecstasy abound in the testimonies of the Carmelite nuns during the canonization process. María del Nacimiento, who was in Teresa's cell as she was writing the *Moradas*, described how Teresa sat down to work on the book only when she had just received communion:

> When she wrote it was with great speed and with such great beauty in her face that it caused this witness to admire her, and she was so absorbed in what she was writing that if there were any noise it never disturbed her; so this witness understood that everything she wrote was written while she was in [a state of] prayer.[34]

For many of Teresa's male contemporaries, the theory of divine inspiration was the only way to account for the fact that a woman could explain such exalted doctrine. As J. Mary Luti noted, "Teresa's writings become examples of the miraculous, and the miracle they represent is then greatly to be admired."[35]

Spontaneous inspiration, however, did not stop Teresa from fussing over minutiae. María del Nacimiento also testified:

> One night [Teresa] was writing in the monastery of Toledo until sometime past midnight, and with a bad headache. Because a word in one of her letters didn't seem right to her, she didn't want to leave it as it was, though her companion told her it wasn't very important; and even though the letter was very long and it was so late, and she with a bad headache, she wanted to write the letter over again, to take out that one word she didn't think was quite right.[36]

---

34. *BMC* 18:315: "Cuando escribía era con gran velocidad y con tan gran hermosura en el rostro, que a esta testigo le admiraba, y estaba tan embebida en lo que escribía, que, aunque allí junto se hiciese algún ruido, no la estorbaba; por lo cual entendía esta testigo que todo aquello que escribía y el tiempo que estaba en ello estaba en oración." The fact that this anecdote was common knowledge among Teresa's contemporaries is reflected by the fact that other witnesses, without going into the same details that María gave, testified that "the Holy Spirit was present and helping [her] as she wrote her books" ("El Espíritu Santo asistía y estaba presente cuando los escribía"): testimony of María Coronel, *BMC* 19:375; see also that of Ana María de Jesús, *BMC* 19:446.

35. Luti, "Teresa of Avila," p. 74.

36. *BMC* 18:308: "Una noche estuvo escribiendo en el monasterio de Toledo hasta más de las doce y teniendo muy mala la cabeza; porque le pareció que en una carta iba una palabra no muy cierta, no la quiso pasar, aunque su compañera le decía no era de mucha importancia; y con ser la carta muy larga y tan tarde, y ella con gran dolor de cabeza, quiso más tornar a trasladar la carta, que no fuese en ella aquella palabra que no podía decirse con mucha certeza."

As the critic Víctor García de la Concha points out, if Teresa paid this much attention to the details of a letter, "we can easily guess what must have occurred in larger works and especially in her mystical works."[37]

The tone of sincerity in Teresa's prose is at first striking, but it is far too calculated to be taken at face value. We must balance it both with Teresa's desire to achieve a specific purpose in the reader's religous life and with the contemporary restrictions on women's religious expression. Teresa's artistic license took many forms: portraying herself in the *Vida* as a terrible sinner, worse than all her sisters in religion; fudging the details of her family background; and feigning ignorance of the term "mystical theology," which might have seemed inappropriately technical for an unlettered nun.[38] Ironically, we can see that Teresa employed much artifice to convince readers of her sincerity.

The idea that Teresa wrote out of dutiful obedience to her confessors can no longer be defended. It shifts her literary motivation and creativity to her confessors and attributes the genius of her works to the direct inspiration of the Holy Spirit.[39] "These interpretations," as Rosa Rossi points out, "all have in common the tendency to deny the autonomy of the 'word' of this woman: it was always someone else who spoke—God, or the will of her male confessor, or her instinct—never her *persona*."[40] The best explanation for Teresa's work is that she wanted to write, partly to respond to the Valdés Index's censorship of manuals on mystical prayer, partly to continue her re-

---

37. García de la Concha, *El arte literario*, pp. 100–101. Indeed, there is much evidence that Teresa was extremely protective of her prose. Any change in wording made by a copyist exasperated her. In the canonization process Ana de Jesús (Lobera) testified that when Teresa spotted changes made in a copy of one of her manuscripts, she said, " 'God forgive my confessors for giving away what they order me to write, and the others for keeping it, copying it, and changing some words. This isn't mine, or this [indicating passages].' And later she would scratch them out and write between the lines in her own hand to correct their changes" ("Cuando venían a sus manos, decía: Dios los perdone a mis confesores que dan lo que me mandan escribir; y ellos por quedarse con ello trasládanlo y truecan algunas palabras, que ésta y ésta no es mía, y luego las borraba y ponía entre renglones de su letra, lo que le habían mudado"): *BMC* 18:484–85.

38. See *Vida* 10:1. Teresa's *converso* background is completely hidden behind descriptions of her devout parents. See *Vida* 1–6. See also her discussion of her father, Alonso de Cepeda, in *Vida* 1:1–2, 7:10–16. She portrays him in glowing terms, but his debts caused Teresa years of legal problems after his death.

39. Even Joseph Chorpenning, who demonstrates the deliberate narrative theological structure of Teresa's works, still refuses to give Teresa credit for creativity. "Neither Teresa's natural intelligence nor readings nor consultation with theologians suffice to explain from where she derives her elevated doctrine. . . . Just as Ignatius Loyola was taught by God himself at Manresa, Teresa was instructed by Christ himself": *The Divine Romance: Teresa of Avila's Narrative Theology* (Chicago, 1992), pp. 16–17.

40. Rossi, "Teresa de Jesús: La mujer y la palabra," p. 42.

form efforts and offer the new Carmelites their own tradition of religious literature, and partly because she was a born writer.

The Strategy of Instrumental Authority

Teresa laid great stress on her special access to God. Anyone who has direct communication with God has authority. By claiming to be divinely inspired, Teresa replaced her humbly admitted lack of theological credentials ("it seems to me") with the most authoritative words of all—the words of God. Teresa's mystical doctrine—as well as her ability to promulgate it—was thus justified by its divine origin.

Teresa's claim of special access to God took a variety of forms. Because of her role as a teacher of mystical doctrine, many of them revolved around the ways in which God had revealed mystical truths to her, or had approved her statements about the mystical way. Teresa often relied on the visionary mode to establish her special connection with God: her visions came to her as she prayed or when she received the sacraments. Finally, particularly in the *Vida*, she stressed the efficacy of her intercessory prayers, suggesting that she had indeed found favor with God.

Sometimes Teresa combined humility with authority. In this strategy she set herself up as merely a transmitter, "like the birds they teach to speak [who] know nothing but what they demonstrate to them or what they hear, and repeat it over and over."[41] Although she was not learned, her doctrine was worthy of consideration because it was not her own: "This is excellent doctrine and not mine, but taught by God."[42]

The *Vida*, Teresa says elsewhere, is a mixture of direct revelation and her own insight.

> Many of the things I write here are not from my own head, but my heavenly Teacher told them to me, so on the points where I say clearly "This I understood" or "The Lord told me," I am very careful not to add or omit a single syllable; so when I don't remember everything perfectly right away, it comes from me, because some things will be [my own doctrine]. I don't call what's good mine, for I know there is nothing [good] in me except what the Lord has given me without meriting it; rather I say "it comes from me" to mean it was not given to me in revelation.[43]

41. *Moradas*, Prologue:2: "Así como los pájaros que enseñan a hablar no saben más de lo que les muestran u oyen y esto repiten muchas veces . . ."
42. *Vida* 19:14: "Es excelente doctrina ésta y no mía, sino enseñada de Dios."
43. *Vida* 39:8: ". . . muchas cosas de las que aquí escribo no son de mi cabeza, sino que me las decía este mi Maestro celestial; y porque en las cosas que yo señaladamente digo: 'esto entendí', o 'me dijo el Señor', se me hace escrúpulo grande poner o quitar una sola sílaba que sea; así cuando puntualmente no se me acuerda bien todo, va dicho como de mí, o porque algunas cosas también lo serán. No llamo mío lo que es bueno, que ya sé no hay cosa en mí, sino lo que

As she concluded the *Vida*, Teresa reiterated her role as a voice for God, suggesting that her readers would have to acknowledge the divine source of her doctrine. "If my work is well done," she wrote, "they are good and learned people, [and] I know they will see where it comes from and will praise the one who has spoken through me."[44] This need to legitimize the female vocation to theological discourse is common to many women mystics.[45]

By referring to things she claims God actually said to her, Teresa also used divine authority to justify her words. Whether paraphrased or quoted directly, God's words lent a more authoritative appearance to both her doctrine and her vision of the reformed Carmelite order. Thus when Teresa groped for a way to explain what happens to the soul in the prayer of union, she wrote:

> I was thinking when I wanted to write this—having just received communion and being in this same [state of] prayer that I write about [here]—[about] what exactly the soul does in that time. The Lord said these words to me: "It completely disintegrates, daughter, to become more a part of me: it's no longer it that lives, but I. . . ."[46]

God provided Teresa with the explanation she sought—an explanation that was all the more authoritative for its echo of Scripture.[47]

Teresa used God's words also to justify her vocation as a reformer, even making veiled threats against anyone who would stand in the way of her founding new monasteries. In describing her struggles to found the first Discalced convent of San José, Teresa wrote:

> One day, having just received communion, the Lord ordered me to do everything I could to arrange it [the new convent], making me great promises about

---

tan sin merecerlo me ha dado el Señor; sino llamo 'dicho de mí', no ser dado a entender en revelación."

44. *Vida* 40:24: "Si va bien, son buenos y letrados, sé que verán de dónde viene y alabarán a quien lo ha dicho por mí." The "good and learned people" to whom Teresa refers were three men who were to inspect her book, probably Domingo Báñez, Gaspar Daza, and perhaps Juan de Avila.

45. For a discussion of this phenomenon in the works of Hildegard of Bingen, see Barbara Newman, "Hildegard of Bingen: Visions and Validation," *Church History* 52 (June 1985): 163–75; and Gillian T. W. Ahlgren, "Visions and Rhetorical Strategy in the Letters of Hildegard of Bingen," in *Dear Sister: The Letters of Medieval Women* (Philadelphia, 1992), pp. 46–63.

46. *Vida* 18:14: "Estaba yo pensando cuando quise escribir esto—acabando de comulgar y de estar en esta misma oración que escribo—qué hacía el alma en aquel tiempo. Díjome el Señor estas palabras: Deshácese toda, hija, para ponerse más en Mí; ya no es ella la que vive, sino Yo. . . ." After her death, as we shall see, some of Teresa's critics objected strongly to her using words she claimed God had spoken to her, arguing that by doing so she compounded her error.

47. See Gal. 2:20; cf. *Vida* 6:9.

how the convent would not fail to be established, and how He would be greatly served in it, and how it would be called San José . . . and that I should tell my confessor all this that He was ordering me to do, and that He was begging him not to go against [the idea] or hinder me in it.[48]

God's approval of Teresa's vocation and the way she made day-to-day decisions seems to have placed quite a burden on her. Toward the end of her *Vida* she went so far as to suggest that God wanted her to take on a public voice in order to make known the graces she had experienced: "And since the Lord wanted these mercies that He gives me to be known publicly, as He told me several years ago they had to be, I've been tired out, and so far I've gone through a lot . . . for each person understands it in his own way."[49]

Teresa also used a kind of instrumental authority, which accentuated the orthodoxy and trustworthiness of her doctrine because she was acting only as an instrument for the actual communication of God. This strategy is most apparent in the metaphors she claimed God revealed to her as she attempted to put her mystical experiences into words: "Today, having just received communion, the Lord . . . offered me these comparisons and taught me the way to explain it [the prayer of quiet], and what the soul must do here; and sure enough, I was amazed and understood everything at once."[50] Teresa's God spoke in metaphors, which could then be given directly or indirectly to the mystic to express a hidden reality.

Not all of Teresa's metaphors were divinely inspired, but at various points she suggested that God approved them. In fact, God actually complimented her on her use of metaphor to understand the transformation of the soul in rapture as a preparation for union:

> It seems that [this fire] consumes the old person with his faults and negligence and misery, and in the same way as the phoenix—so I have read—and from the ash itself, after it has burned, another is born, just so the soul is transformed into something else afterward, with different desires and great fortitude. It doesn't seem to be the same one it was before, but rather it sets out with new purity on the pathway of the Lord. I asked His Majesty if this was the way it was, and if it began to serve Him once more, and He said: "You have made a good compari-

---

48. *Vida* 32:11: "Habiendo un día comulgado, mandóme mucho Su Majestad lo procurase con todas mis fuerzas, haciéndome grandes promesas de que no se dejaría de hacer el monasterio, y que se serviría mucho en él, y que se llamase San José . . . que dijese a mi confesor esto que me mandaba y que le rogaba El que no fuese contra ello ni me lo estorbase."

49. *Vida* 40:21: "Y con haber querido el Señor se sepan en público estas mercedes que Su Majestad me hace—como me lo dijo algunos años ha, que le habían de ser, que me fatigué yo harto, y hasta ahora no he pasado poco . . . porque cada uno lo toma como le parece."

50. *Vida* 16:2: "El Señor hoy, acabando de comulgar . . . me puso estas comparaciones y enseñó la manera de decirlo, y lo que ha de hacer aquí el alma; que, cierto, yo me espanté y entendí en un punto."

son; see that you don't forget it, so you'll always manage to go on improving yourself."[51]

In many other ways Teresa received confirmation of divine favor. In the *Vida* she recounted several instances of her ability to intercede on behalf of the dead. On one occasion she pleaded with Christ to release a former Carmelite provincial from purgatory:

> As I was begging the Lord for this as best I could, it seemed that he [the provincial] came out of the depths of the earth at my right side, and I saw him ascend to the heavens with great joy. He was quite old, but I saw him as thirty—even younger, it seemed to me—and with splendor in his face.[52]

Through such visions Teresa saw several of her Carmelite sisters as well as many Jesuits ascend to heaven. Indeed, Teresa's claims to divine favor were so bold that in another vision Christ appeared to her and promised he would do anything she asked. "He promised me there was nothing I asked of him he wouldn't do; that He already knew I would ask for nothing that wasn't consistent with his glory, so he would do what I was asking now."[53]

Teresa's contemporaries saw evidence of her spiritual powers through such concrete signs as levitation, ecstasy, and prophecy. Many of them accepted Teresa's claims to special access to God because they were accompanied by virtuous behavior and their expression was punctuated by evidence of humility, subordination, and incompetence (which underscored the divine origin of such favors). Teresa's own behavior reinforced others' beliefs that her spiritual powers were a grace from God.

The Success of Paradoxical Self-Representation

Teresa's rhetorical strategies were complex, interconnected, and effective because they appealed to the central paradox of Christianity: God upholds the lowly. In constructing herself as a humble and obedient woman, Teresa disarmed many of her critics and carved out a unique place for herself in the Christian mystical tradition. Such rhetorical strategies were critical in her

51. *Vida* 39:23: "Parece que consume el hombre viejo de faltas y tibieza y miseria; y a manera de como hace el ave fénix—según he leído—, y de la misma ceniza, después que se quema, sale otra, así queda hecha otra el alma después con diferentes deseos y fortaleza grande. No parece es la que antes, sino que comienza con nueva puridad el camino del Señor. Suplicando yo a Su Majestad fuese así, y que de nuevo comenzase a servirle, me dijo: Buena comparación has hecho; mira no se te olvide para procurar mejorarte siempre."

52. *Vida* 38:27: "Estando pidiendo esto al Señor lo mejor que yo podía, parecióme salía del profundo de la tierra a mi lado derecho y vile subir al cielo con grandísima alegría. El era ya bien viejo, mas vile de edad de treinta años—y aun menos me pareció—y con resplandor en el rostro."

53. *Vida* 39:1: "El me prometía que ninguna cosa le pidiese que no la hiciese; que ya sabía El que yo no pediría sino conforme a su gloria, y que así haría esto que ahora pedía."

ability to overcome the strictures of her day, which would have prevented her (as they did most women) from a public religious role, particularly any role that involved teaching. Teresa's apparently simple and sincere style, coupled with her rhetoric of obedience, dissociated her from heterodox writers. Together with her protestations of unworthiness, they allowed her to hold a position of singular influence. Her works gained in authority over time because of the influence they had on their readers.

Teresa's rhetoric is a response to the climate of suspicion that surrounded women's mystical experience in her day. Her straightforward style, her lack of pretension—in short, the "natural" flow of her prose—was designed to be nonoffensive in a time and culture that found esoteric religious experience threatening and that firmly denied that a woman could embody such religious authority. At all costs, Teresa could not appear to take public ownership of her own will. Whether the obedience she professed was to her religious superiors or to God, Teresa had humbly to dissociate her teachings from her self in order to conform to contemporary understandings of a woman's proper role.

Lest we forget, the external controls to which Teresa submitted on one level were not effective enough to curtail the scope of her influence. Teresa adopted the strategies she did in order to take on roles that were increasingly being limited to men. She became an intercessor before God for the laity and the religious alike, she played a large part in the pastoral care of her religious communities, and she was a teacher of mystical doctrine. The account she gave of her life in the *Vida* allowed her to become part of the hagiographical tradition she had loved, as Luti explains:

> . . . [T]he story stood permanently as a complex exemplum, a handbook of do's and don't's for seekers and guides alike; and, by showing Teresa's heroic humility and obedience throughout her time of trial, her association with and unqualified approval by a few universally recognized good, learned and holy men, and her divinely-initiated and supported triumph over demons, it testified to the saintly character of the one who so frankly reported the events of her "wretched" existence, all to God's greater glory. In short, it helped establish Teresa's personal credibility as a locus of the holy, a receiver of extraordinary gifts, a woman with a claim on the divine.[54]

Teresa's life demonstrates that it was not unacceptable for a woman to wield spiritual power in sixteenth-century Spain—so long as she used her power in ways that men determined were orthodox and were dedicated to the service of others. Other women, too, were struggling to pursue holiness and virtue. Teresa was determined to help them.

54. Luti, "Teresa of Avila," pp. 174–75.

4

Apología por la Mística Femenina: Teresa's Theological Agenda

As Teresa's mystical and reforming vocation evolved, she began to address more forcefully the misogynist and antimystical biases of her day. The three most controversial aspects of Teresa's doctrine were her defense of women's right to mental prayer and spiritual autonomy, her criticism of the climate produced by the Inquisition's censorship, and her teachings on visions and mystical union. These concerns constitute the core of Teresa's agenda as a writer: to provide guidance and to empower women and men to achieve a meaningful relationship with God.

At the same time, her critique of the Inquisition, her struggles to achieve a place for women in the Counter-Reformation, and her teachings on visions and mystical union provoked deep concern among inquisitional officials. Teresa's bid for women's spiritual autonomy and authority was difficult to reconcile with the trend toward increased clericalization and a more catechetical approach to piety. Further, her teachings on visions and union were controversial not because of their novelty but because, in the face of numerous challenges to Rome's authority, they demonstrated forcefully the importance of continued revelation in the Christian tradition, implicitly arguing that access to God cannot ultimately be controlled by the institutional church.

Our examination of Teresa's doctrine can help us determine its orthodoxy and thus to assess the posthumous criticisms of her works. If Teresa's doctrine is found to be orthodox, then we can dismiss the explanation that her works were censored because they were incorrect or unorthodox, and we must determine why some theologians attempted to repress her ideas. Another reason to analyze Teresa's doctrine of visions and mystical union is to fit it into the tradition of Christian mysticism, for this is the major strategy of those who defend her orthodoxy. In fact, as will become apparent, Teresa herself took pains to locate her doctrine within the larger mystical tradition of Western Christendom. This strategy became more pronounced over time, indicating her growing need to establish her authority and orthodoxy in the face of the Inquisition's accusations against her.

As we have seen, Teresa's claims to authority were rooted in experience. According to Teresa, God had given her a new understanding of herself and the monastic vocation, and she had embarked on the reform of the Carmelite order. God had given her profound experiences of prayer, and she shared them with her contemporaries. God had given her the vocabulary and images to use in her mystical works, and Teresa acted as an instrument of divine revelation. Thus her task as a writer and theologian was to explain how God reveals God's self to the individual and to the world.

In effect, Teresa did this in the *Vida*, the *Camino*, and the *Moradas*, showing how the soul's growth toward union with God was the human response to God's gradual self-revelation. The *Moradas* makes the notion of revelation an integral part of the context for union: each level of the interior castle reveals God's presence in the soul more clearly. For Teresa this journey in revelation began with the understanding of ourselves in relation to God. Although revelation is possible for all Christians, Teresa lamented the fact that so few Christians received revelation in a contemplative manner: "It's a great shame and quite distressing that, by our own fault, we don't understand ourselves, or know who we are."[1]

Growth in the knowledge of God, revealed gradually to the soul, was a lifelong journey for Teresa. The crux of her vocation, then, was to teach Christians how to approach divine wisdom. In the *Moradas* she described how, as the soul approaches its inner mansion, it experiences visions and ultimately union with God. Both visions and mystical union are revelatory. Teresa's visions give her glimpses of God that are later confirmed in the true vision of God discovered in union. Mystical union is then a "breaking through" of fragmented visions of God to an actual living in the Trinity. The knowledge of God experienced in mystical union is an experiential epistemology, in which God is a reality lived within oneself, not an Otherness perceived from the outside. This experience can never be limited to any class of Christians, nor can it be completely mediated by the institutional church. Teresa's mystical doctrine was clearly consistent with the orthodox Christian tradition, yet polemical debates in sixteenth-century Spain made it difficult to express such truths, particularly when they were designed to encourage women's spiritual growth.

Women and Prayer

The defense of women's experience of prayer was the major motivating force behind the construction of Teresa's *Camino de perfección*, a defense that had become less specific and personal than in the *Vida*. The *Camino* is pri-

---

1. *Moradas* 1:1.2: "No es pequeña lástima y confusión que, por nuestra culpa, no entendamos a nosotros mismos, ni sepamos quién somos."

marily a treatise on mental prayer; after defending the validity and importance of this form of prayer, it proceeds to explain what it is and to teach readers how to advance in prayer by offering the concrete example of contemplation on the Lord's Prayer.

The value and role of mental prayer in the life of the church was a controversial issue in Teresa's day. In 1555 Juan de la Cruz (OP) published his treatise *Diálogo sobre la necesidad de la oración vocal*, expressing his concern that the pursuit of mental prayer would discourage Christians from traditional practices of virtue. Mental prayer was superfluous, he argued, as it ought to be a part of one's vocal prayers, and even dangerous, because it could become a distraction from traditional morality. Teresa was sensitive to her contemporaries' suspicions and addressed their fears repeatedly.[2]

For Teresa, the value of mental prayer was ultimately proved by the good works performed by those who engaged in it. Thus a clear teaching on mental prayer would inspire her readers to achieve it, and eventually would demonstrate its validity and importance.[3] Her contemporaries were so suspicious, however, that Teresa had to produce two more versions of the *Camino* in efforts to allay their fears. The survival of all three versions provides us with a unique perspective on the challenges Teresa faced as an author of mystical texts.[4]

Her role as a teacher and defender of mystical doctrine was quite tenuous, so her first task was to justify her enterprise. To this end, Teresa pointed to her office as prioress and her pastoral responsibilities toward the nuns in her care. In the first (Escorial) text she wrote: "What I want to counsel you and I could even say teach you (because as mother I now have this responsibility) . . ." In the second (Valladolid) version her justification was even more insistent: "What I want to counsel you now, and I can even say teach you (because, as mother, with the office of prioress that I have, it is permissible) . . ."

Teresa's *Way of Perfection* addressed the problem of contemporary prejudice against women on several occasions. Her argument for a stronger ec-

---

2. E.g., *CV* 21:7 and *CE* 36:3.

3. See, e.g., *CV* 21:9: "Si dicen que hay peligro en la oración, procura se entienda cuán buena es la oración, si no por palabras, por obras."

4. The first version, written in 1565–66, is known as the Escorial text. The second version, written in 1566–67, is called the Valladolid version. About 1579 Teresa wrote a third version, now known as the Toledo text. The changes in this third text are not so extensive as the ones she made in the second version, and the Toledo version is frequently used to confirm changes made in the Valladolid text. A modern copy of the Toledo text is available in *BMC* 3:359–491. A modern reproduction of the Escorial manuscript, with a transcription, is found in *Reproducción fotolitográfica y fieles traslados impresos del "Camino de perfección" y el "Modo de visitar los conventos," escritos por Santa Teresa de Jesús, que se veneran en El Escorial y algunos autógrafos inéditos*, ed. Francisco Herrero Bayona (Madrid, 1883). Teresa's *Obras completas* note most of the censor's comments.

clesiastical role for women was one of the first passages that the censor García de Toledo marked for excision. Teresa argued in chapter 4 of the Escorial version that deprecation of women for their "moral inferiority" was not an accurate representation of God's views. The church's need for reform, Teresa argued, made all Christians valuable. Indeed, there was "no reason to reject virtuous and noble souls, even if they are women." Teresa complained of the poor treatment women of goodwill had received in their pastoral work:

> Isn't it enough, Lord, that the world keeps us silenced and incapable of doing anything of value for You in public and we don't dare speak of truths we bewail in secret, but you won't hear our rightful petition? I don't believe it of such a good and just lord; you are a just judge, not like the world's judges, who, since they are sons of Adam, and are, in short, all men, there is no female virtue they don't view as suspect.[5]

Teresa complained again about the difficulties faced by women who wanted to pursue a life of prayer, particularly the belittlement and discouragement offered by men:

> Now, turning to those who want to follow it [the way of perfection] and not stop till they have reached the end, which is to drink of the water of life . . . I say it's very important—all-important—[to have] a very resolute determination not to stop till you've reached it, come what may . . . even if it seems you haven't the courage to face the hardships along the way . . . as often happens when they tell us: "It's dangerous," "So-and-so lost her way here," "Someone else made a mistake," "That one who prayed a lot went wrong," "It's bad for virtue," "It's not for women—they can be deluded," "They'd better stick to their spinning," "Those subtleties aren't necessary," "The Our Father and the Hail Mary are quite enough."[6]

---

5. *CE* 4:1: "No basta, Señor, que nos tiene el mundo acorraladas e incapaces para que no hagamos cosa que valga nada por Vos en público ni osemos hablar algunas verdades que lloramos en secreto, sino que no nos habiais de oír petición tan justa? No lo creo yo, Señor, de vuestra bondad y justicia, que sois justo juez, y no como los jueces del mundo, que como son hijos de Adán y, en fin, todos varones, no hay virtud de mujer que no tengan por sospechosa."

6. *CV* 21:2: "Ahora, tornando a los que quieren ir por él y no parar hasta el fin, que es llegar a beber de esta agua de vida . . . digo que importa mucho, y el todo, una grande y muy determinada determinación de no parar hasta llegar a ella, venga lo que viniere . . . siquiera . . . no tenga corazón para los trabajos que hay en él . . . como muchas veces acaece con decirnos: 'hay peligros', 'fulana por aquí se perdió', 'el otro se engañó', 'el otro, que rezaba mucho, cayó', 'hacen daño a la virtud', 'no es para mujeres, que les podrán venir ilusiones', 'mejor será que hilen', 'no han menester esas delicadezas', 'basta el Paternóster y Avemaría'." Daniel de Pablo Maroto calls these phrases "historical relics" and claims that Teresa either heard or read them during the course of her life. See Teresa's *Obras completas*, p. 670, n. 3. Llamas attributes one of these comments to Bartolomé de Medina, who preached publicly against Teresa, saying: "Es de mujercillas andarse de lugar en lugar y que mejor estuvieran en sus casas rezando e hilando." See Llamas, p. 18.

Thus Teresa warned her fellow Carmelites to expect resistance to their vocation in mental prayer, partly because it was under suspicion and partly because women were considered less capable of it than men.

In several other passages Teresa criticized prejudice against religious women, masking her bitterness with a veil of irony that was thick enough to protect her views from further excision. In chapter 15 of the Valladolid text Teresa observed that even if women were forbidden to preach in church, they were called to be "preachers" in their deeds: "Well, we all must try to be preachers in works, since the Apostle and our inadequacy won't let us be [preachers] in words."[7] Elsewhere, as she described the "palace of great richness" within the soul, Teresa questioned the supposed "mental handicap" women suffered because of their lack of familiarity with Latin: "Since we women don't have Latin, all this [explanation] is necessary so we can truly understand that we have something else more precious, beyond compare, within us. . . . And pray God women are the only ones to behave so heedlessly."[8] In echoing her contemporaries' disrespect for women, Teresa appeared to the censor to be accepting their judgments, but clearly she meant the exact opposite of what she said.[9]

As we saw in chapter 2, Teresa expressed great concern over the appearance of the Valdés Index in 1559. By the time she wrote the *Camino*, however, her concern had turned to criticism of what she considered the dearth of resources necessary for advancement in the mystical life. Teresa criticized the Valdés Index in four passages of the *Camino de perfección*, but not in so many words. Rather than condemn the Index itself, she reassured her Carmelite readers that if they could learn to do without spiritual books and content themselves with the most basic props of Christian spirituality, they could be reasonably sure that these, at least, would not be taken from them. In fact, Teresa extended this ironic commentary on censorship even to God: "Praise God, who is mighty above everyone and whom they cannot take away from you."[10] Teresa herself removed this sentence when she prepared the second version of the *Camino*. Her criticisms were not lost on the censor, who deleted "they won't take the Our Father and the Hail Mary away from you," and noted in the margin, "She seems to be reproving the In-

---

7. *CV* 15:6: "Pues todas hemos de procurar de ser predicadoras de obras, pues el Apóstol y nuestra inhabilidad nos quita que lo seamos en las palabras." Cf. *CE* 23:1. Note the use of the feminine ending of both "todas" and "predicadoras," signaling that Teresa's "we" are women.
8. *CV* 28:10: "Como no tenemos letras las mujeres, todo esto es menester para que entendamos con verdad que hay otra cosa más preciosa, sin ninguna comparación, dentro de nosotras. . . . Y plega a Dios sean solas mujeres las que andan con este descuido. . . ." Cf. *CE* 48:2.
9. On this point see Weber, *Teresa of Avila*, pp. 91–96.
10. *CE* 38:2: "Alabad a Dios, que es poderoso sobre todos y que no os lo pueden quitar."

quisitors for prohibiting books on prayer."[11] The censor did not recognize all of Teresa's ironic comments, for he left untouched a similar passage earlier and Teresa's deeper criticisms at the end of the book: "It seems the Lord wants us to understand, sisters, the great comfort that's contained here, and that when they take books away from us, they can't take away this book [the Lord's Prayer], which is spoken from the mouth of Truth itself, so it cannot err."[12]

The censors could not countenance criticism of the Index and of restrictions on women's role in the church, but these passages were an essential part of Teresa's argument. To her the Index had provoked a void in books on contemplation, which then led to a lack of spiritual formation among the clergy, poor spiritual direction, and a general decline in the standards of mental prayer in the monastic life. She wrote the *Camino* to remedy this problem. Further, she believed that religious women, since they were barred from all clerical and teaching activities, had a special vocation to engage in mental prayer on behalf of the church. In view of the suspicion surrounding the experiences of spiritual women, however, she had to defend and justify this vocation.

Changes in the second draft of the *Camino* responded not only to the censor's comments but to prejudice against contemplation. In the first version Teresa had written that suspicion of mental prayer was actually a trick of the devil to encourage a lukewarm attitude among religious. To counter this tendency Teresa called her readers to their vocation:

> This is the duty of [professed] religious. Whoever tells you this is dangerous, hold him to be just as dangerous, and flee from him, and don't forget, because you may well need this counsel; the danger is not to have humility and other virtues; but for the way of prayer to be a way of danger—God never wanted that. The devil seems to have invented these fears.[13]

---

11. See Herrera Bayona, *Reproducción foto-litográfica*, fol. 72v: "Haced bien, hijas, que no os quitarán el Paternóster y el Avemaría." The censor comments: "Parece que reprehende a los Inquisidores que prohiben libros de oración."

12. *CE* 73:4: "Parece ha querido el Señor entendamos, hermanas, la gran consolación que aquí está encerrada y que cuando nos quitaren libros no nos pueden quitar este libro, que es dicho por la boca de la misma Verdad, que no puede errar." Although there is no indication of censorship, this passage does not appear in the Valladolid version. The earlier passage that was not censored appears in *CE* 35:4: "Y no os podrán quitar libro, que no os quede tan buen libro, que si sois estudiosas con humildad, no habéis menester otra cosa." This passage passed into the Valladolid version (21:3) with some minor changes: "Y no os podrán quitar libros, que si sois estudiosas, y teniendo humildad, no habéis menester otra cosa."

13. *CE* 36:3: "Este es el oficio de los religiosos. Quien os dijere que éste es peligro, tenedle a él por el mismo peligro, y huid de él, y no se os olvide, porque por ventura habréis menester este consejo; peligro será no tener humildad y otras virtudes; mas camino de oración camino de peligro, nunca Dios tal quiera. El demonio parece ha inventado poner estos miedos."

Teresa set out to provide the Carmelites with strategies to use against anyone who railed about the "danger" of mental prayer:

> Daughters, forget these fears; in such things pay no attention to what people
> think. Note that these are not the times to be believing everyone, only those you
> see act in accordance with the life of Christ. Try . . . to believe firmly what our
> Mother the Holy Church holds, and you'll know you're on the right path. . . . If
> anyone tries to scare you, humbly explain the way to them. Say you have a
> [monastic] rule that requires you to pray without ceasing, that this is what it or-
> dains, and you must abide by it. If they tell you that this must mean [praying]
> aloud, ask whether your understanding and heart must be in what you say; if
> they say yes (and they can hardly say anything else), right there you see they're ac-
> knowledging that by sheer necessity you have to have mental prayer and con-
> templation if God bestows it on you.[14]

Teresa's advice here is three-pronged. First, she counsels her readers to pro-
fess clearly their allegiance to the church. Second, she suggests that they defend their practice of mental prayer by employing a rhetoric of obedience to
their monastic rule and profession. Finally, she proposes that the nuns challenge the distinctions between mental and vocal prayer by showing first that
mindless vocal prayers do not constitute true devotion and then that vocal
prayer accompanied by mental devotion is the same as mental prayer.[15]

Teresa shifts strategies in the second (Valladolid) text, replacing her biting
criticism of her critics with more technical advice aimed at allaying the fear
of mental prayer. Here she notes with some irony that an error by one spiritual person causes more scandal than the combined sins of the multitudes;
and she neatly turns this prejudice on its head, declaring that if a real contemplative were to fall into error, it would truly be a cause for wonder:

> How strange it is, as if the devil didn't tempt those who don't follow the way of
> prayer! And everyone marvels more over one who approaches perfection and
> then falls than a hundred thousand who are steeped in fraud and public sin. . . .
> Truth to tell, they're right, because so few of those the devil fools pray the Our
> Father that the novelty of the thing surprises everyone. It's very human to ignore

---

14. *CE* 36:6: "Hijas, dejaos de estos miedos; nunca hagáis caso en cosas semejantes de la
opinión del vulgo. Mirad que no son tiempos de creer a todos, sino a los que vierdes van conforme a la vida de Cristo. Procurad . . . creer firmemente lo que tiene la Madre Santa Iglesia, y
a buen seguro que vais buen camino. Dejaos de temores adonde no hay que temer; si alguno
os lo pusiere, con humildad declaradle el camino. Decid que Regla tenéis que os manda orar
sin cesar, que ansí lo manda, y que la havéis de guardar. Si os dijere que será vocalmente, apu-
rad si ha de estar el entendimiento y corazón en lo que decís; que si os dice que sí (que no
podrá decir otra cosa), veis ahí donde os confiesa havéis por fuerza de tener oración mental y
contemplación si os la diere Dios."

15. One is tempted to guess that Teresa employed a strategy similar to this one in her ap-
pearances before the Inquisition's tribunals and in arguments with her confessors.

what one sees all the time and to marvel at what happens very rarely or almost never; indeed, the demons themselves marvel at it.[16]

We see that Teresa has also modified her statement about the possibility of being tricked by the devil in prayer: in the Escorial version she claimed it "never" happened.[17] This fear of being tricked by the devil is experienced mainly by outside observers, she says now, because mental prayer brings virtuous rewards, including increased self-knowledge and an understanding of our insignificance before God.[18]

Teresa attributed the prejudice against mental prayer to fear of the unknown, so her primary task was to describe and define it, and so to dispel mistaken notions of what it involved. Teresa honed her definition of mental prayer as she revised the *Camino*, spelling out in more detail the role of the faculties in a state of suspension and in union with God. In the first version Teresa defined perfect contemplation as a state in which "the soul's Teacher works in it, not its own faculties."[19] In the Valladolid text Teresa explained further:

> This divine Master is teaching it, suspending its faculties, because they would harm rather than benefit [the soul] if they were to function. They delight without understanding how; the soul is on fire with love, and doesn't understand how it loves; it knows it delights in what it loves, and doesn't know how it delights; it does understand that it's not delight that the understanding attains by wanting it; the will embraces it without understanding how; and if it can understand anything, it sees that this joy cannot be merited by all the trials it goes through to win it here on earth.[20]

---

16. *CV* 39:7:"Cosa extraña es ésta, como si para los que no van por camino de oración no tentase el demonio, y que se espanten más todos de uno que engaña de los que van más llegados a perfección, que de cien mil que ven en engaños y pecados públicos. . . . A la verdad, tienen razón, porque son tan poquísimos a los que engaña el demonio de los que rezaren el *Paternóster* como queda dicho, que, como cosa nueva y no usada, da admiración; que es cosa muy de los mortales pasar fácilmente por lo continuo que ven y espantarse mucho de lo que es muy pocas veces o casi ninguna; y los mismos demonios los hacen espantar."

17. Thus *CE* 68:4: "lo que nunca ha sido."

18. See *CV* 39:5. No parallel in *CE*.

19. *CE* 41:2: "Entiende que, sin ruido de palabras, obra en su alma su Maestro y que no obran las potencias de ella, que ella entienda. Esto es contemplación perfecta."

20. *CV* 25:2: "Entiende que, sin ruido de palabras, le está enseñando este Maestro divino, suspendiendo las potencias, porque entonces antes dañarían que aprovecharían si obrasen. Gozan sin entender cómo gozan; está el alma abrasándose en amor, y no entiende cómo ama; conoce que goza de lo que ama, y no sabe cómo lo goza; bien entiende que no es gozo que alcanza el entendimiento a desearle; abrázale la voluntad sin entender cómo; mas en pudiendo entender algo, ve que no es este bien que se puede merecer con todos los trabajos que se pasasen juntos por ganarle en la tierra." See also the more detailed treatment of the soul's experience of the prayer of quiet in *CV* 31:4–8 as compared to *CE* 53:4.

She also provided more details on the prayer of union in the second version. First, in introducing the term, Teresa specified that "union" here meant "when all of the soul is united with God," whereas she left the term rather ambiguous in the Escorial text.[21] Second, Teresa deleted any commentary that did not clarify her definition of union. In the Escorial text she had written: "Anyone who had this prayer, if they look at it carefully, will understand what I mean after reading this, and should see what it amounts to; if not, it [what I have written] seems nonsense."[22] This passage is gone from the Valladolid text, which continues its commentary on the experience of the prayer of union: "What torments the soul is the understanding, which is not the case when all three faculties [memory, understanding, and will] are united, because the One that created them suspends them, for the delight He gives them takes complete possession of them, though they don't know and can't understand it."[23]

Teresa also described the effects of contemplation in much more detail in the Valladolid version: souls who have experienced true contemplation are bothered by the respect and esteem in which others hold them, they value hardship more than comfort in their daily lives, and they do not enjoy the benefits of wealth if their riches do not help them serve God.[24] Teresa may have provided these details to enable her readers to distinguish between people who had experienced true and false revelation—or to distinguish herself from people who were confused on this point.

In the second version of the *Camino* Teresa's theological descriptions of mystical union had grown more conservative: instead of desiring to "appear like You in something," Teresa contented herself with "imitating You in something."[25] She removed her consideration of the relationship of God and the soul—"The Lord is within us and there we can be with Him"—from her second version, perhaps suspecting it would prove theologically troublesome.[26]

Teresa realized that claiming enlightenment from God on a particular issue was not always the most prudent or most effective way to prove her

---

21. Compare *CV* 31:10: "esta oración, de cuando está toda el alma unida con Dios . . ." with *CE* 53:6: "esta oración de unión . . ."

22. *CE* 53:6: "Quien tuviere esta oración entenderá claro lo que digo—si lo mira con advertencia—después de haber leído esto, y mire que importa; si no, parece algarabía."

23. *CV* 31:10: "Quien la atormenta, es el entendimiento; lo que no hace cuando es unión de todas tres potencias, porque las suspende el que las crió, porque con el gozo que da, todas las ocupa sin saber ellas cómo, ni poderlo entender."

24. See *CV* 36:8–10. Cf. *CE* 65:1.

25. "Por parecerme a Vos en algo" (*CE* 42:6) vs. "por imitaros en algo" (*CV* 26:6).

26. The sentence "Mirad que os va mucho tener entendida esta verdad: que está el Señor dentro de nosotras y que allí nos estemos con El" is found in 46:3 of the Escorial text, but is absent from the parallel Valladolid text (28:3).

point. This was the case in her argument that the nuns should be free to search for the right confessor without having to settle for whatever chaplain was at hand. For Teresa, a good relationship with an experienced and educated confessor was essential to spiritual advancement.[27] In the Escorial manuscript she based her position on the fact that she had reached it "after much prayer by many people and my own, miserable though it be, and in consultation with very educated people of great understanding and prayer; so I hope in the Lord that it's the most appropriate."[28] In the Valladolid text she backed away from the authority of prayer to place the practice of her Carmelite nuns on firmer ground:

> And this is what is done now, and not because it's my idea alone; because the bishop we have now, and under whom we serve—since for many reasons we are not under the jurisdiction of the order—who encourages all religion and saintliness and is a great servant of God—his name is Alvaro de Mendoza, of noble lineage and very keen on favoring this convent in every way—brought together people of learning, spirituality, and experience to discuss this point, and this is what was decided.[29]

The move to deflect responsibililty for her reform decisions to hierarchical officials was precisely the sort of defense Teresa had to employ to prevent accusations of *alumbradismo*. Reliance on her mystical experiences for authority left Teresa vulnerable to the charge that she misunderstood the message transmitted to her in prayer, or, worse yet, might not have had any such divine experience at all.

On other points the changes Teresa made in the second version of the *Camino* reflect a deepening of her convictions and a refusal to repeat what could be found in other spiritual treatises. She deleted many of her deprecatory references to herself and to other women. In the Escorial manuscript she described the potential uncertainties of prayer, reminding the nuns that obedience to their religious superior ensured that they would not stray from the path of perfection. These uncertainties arose mainly in souls who took more pleasure in prayer than in embracing the cross, as Teresa explained:

27. On this point, see *CE* 8:2 and *CV* 5:2.

28. *CE* 8:6: "Esto se determinó después de harta oración de muchas personas y mía, aunque miserable, y entre personas de grandes letras y entendimiento y oración; y así espero en el Señor es lo más acertado."

29. *CV* 5:7: "Y esto es lo que se hace ahora, y no por sólo mi parecer; porque el obispo que ahora tenemos, debajo de cuya obediencia estamos, que, por causas muchas que hubo, no se dio la obediencia a la orden, que es persona amiga de toda religión y santidad y gran siervo de Dios—llámase don Alvaro de Mendoza, de gran nobleza de linaje y muy aficionado a favorecer esta casa de todas maneras—, hizo juntar personas de letras y espíritu y experiencia para este punto, y se vino a determinar esto."

I have decided that, these [monastic] virtues [obedience, etc.] are what I want you to have, my daughters, and what you should cultivate and righteously long for—not these other devotions [the delights of prayer]: they are quite doubtful. Perhaps in someone else they will come from God, and in you His Majesty will allow them to be a delusion from the devil, and he will trick you as he has done to so many; in women this is a dangerous thing.[30]

The Valladolid text remains substantially the same, but the last phrase is gone. The censor had deleted her eloquent defense of women in chapter 4, but she could at least refuse to cooperate in denigrating them.

In fact, Teresa's representation of herself changed. She no longer referred to her "rudeness and imperfection,"[31] or to the fact that "for her sins she deserves the demons' scorn."[32] She no longer protested her incapacity to write ("How confusedly I write, just like someone who doesn't know what he's doing").[33] These belittling comments were so close to the misogynist criticisms of women's spiritual experience that they could not have helped Teresa's case for her own authority.

Aware that their confessors might doubt the genuineness of her nuns' spiritual experience, Teresa gave much practical advice on the discernment of true virtues, pointing out that often what at first glance seems virtuous may well be temptation that leads away from God. False humility, in particular, was potentially confusing to the soul, which might recognize humility as a virtue but could become overwhelmed by its own sin and begin to despair of God's mercy. True humility, Teresa noted, would not disturb or overpower the soul's peace in God:

> Although one understands clearly, seeing one's own wretchedness, that one deserves to be in hell, and grieves, and it seems right that all should abhor one,

---

30. *CE* 29:7: "Concluyo que estas virtudes son las que yo deseo tengáis, hijas mías, y las que procuréis, y las que santamente envidiéis. Esotras devociones en ninguna manera; es cosa incierta. Por ventura en la otra será Dios, y en vos permitirá Su Majestad sea ilusión del demonio y que os engañe como ha hecho a muchas, que en mujeres es cosa peligrosa." My interpretation of "esotras devociones" as the delights of prayer differs significantly from that of Daniel de Pablo Maroto, who claims that Teresa refers to mystical contemplation in general. This interpretation he sees as consistent with the argument Teresa has been making in the two preceding chapters. It is not, however, consistent with Teresa's general arguments. The reference is most likely to the material Teresa has been discussing in the same chapter—that is, the importance of applying discipline to every part of the mystical life. This reading is confirmed by the later Toledo manuscript, which has "Beware of being upset by not having delights" ("De tener pena por no tener gustos os guardad"). See *Obras completas*, p. 646, n. 13. For Teresa's emphasis on virtue rather than spiritual delight, see *CV* 5:2 and 20:3.

31. *CE* 13:4: "aun con mi rudeza e imperfección." Cf. *CV* 9:4.

32. *CE* 19:3: "una como yo, que por sus pecados tiene merecido la hiciesen abajar y despreciar los demonios." Cf. *CV* 13:3. See also *CE* 21:3; *CV* 14:3.

33. *CE* 22:1: "Qué desconcertado escribo, bien como quien no sabe qué hace." Cf. *CV* 15:1.

and one almost doesn't dare ask for mercy, if one has true humility, this pain comes with its own sweetness and joy, and we wouldn't want to be without it. It doesn't agitate or oppress the soul, but rather it expands it and makes it more capable of serving God. This other pain disturbs and agitates the soul and turns it upside down, and it's very painful. I think the devil tries to make us think that we have humility, and on the other hand—if he could—that we don't trust God.[34]

Here Teresa provided her readers with the inner resources to discern their own spiritual progress—self-knowledge and an ability to focus on the inner spiritual peace that the mystical experience should provide—so they would not have to depend too heavily on their confessors for reinforcement.

Because their experiences of mental prayer and visions were the sources of women's spiritual authority in the church, both phenomena had to be defended in general and as a legitimate part of a woman's spiritual formation. Teresa's recovery of their legitimacy was an essential part of her reform efforts because her own authority stemmed in part from such experiences. If Teresa's prayer and visions were not judged to be authentic, then neither her mystical doctrine nor her reform could be valid either.

The overall production of the *Way of Perfection* involved much critical reflection on the doctrine the book propounded as well as on its expression. Teresa followed two strategies in the revision process, sometimes expanding her treatment of issues considered problematic, sometimes dropping them altogether. In the second version Teresa had more to say about such topics as the practice of mental prayer, the discernment of spirits and spiritual urges, and the various facets of mystical experience, particularly mystical union. Her expanded treatment of these issues reflects her concern that her readers should have a "balanced" spirituality, firmly rooted in the traditional monastic virtues of humility and obedience and yet open to the inner movements of God within the soul. Receptivity to God could be achieved only through the disciplining of personal desires—thus Teresa's insistence that the soul not value the delights God gives it on the way to mystical union—and a discerning self-knowledge that could recognize and reject any internal tendencies that were inconsistent with the fullest expression of love of God and love of one another.

---

34. *CV* 39:2: "Aunque uno, de verse ruin, entienda claramente merece estar en el infierno y se aflige y le parece con justicia todos le habían de aborrecer, y que no osa casi pedir misericordia, si es buena humildad, esta pena viene con una suavidad en sí y contento, que no querríamos vernos sin ella. No alborota ni aprieta el alma, antes la dilata y hace hábil para servir más a Dios. Estotra pena todo lo turba, todo lo alborota, toda el alma revuelve, es muy penosa. Creo pretende el demonio que pensemos tenemos humildad, y—si pudiese—a vueltas, que desconfiásemos de Dios."

The passages Teresa ultimately rejected were those that might have harmed her credibility as a teacher of mystical doctrine or antagonized the censors. Many of the things she ultimately deleted seemed to get in the way of her message and even threatened her readers' access to it. Here again we see the struggle between the desire to teach what her experience had taught her and her frustration with the need to justify it.

Visions

The discernment of spirits and the origin of religious visions were among the most controversial issues of Teresa's day. They struck at the heart of the institutional church's role in mediating the presence of God to Christians. The increasingly clericalized orientation of the post-Tridentine Spanish church—its emphasis on proper catechetical doctrine disseminated through priests, the reiteration of the sacramentality of confession, and the upsurge in editions of confessional manuals—was at once an attempt to establish and regularize Catholic religious practice and an effort to promote a particular ecclesiology. Visionary theology, a way of constructing and expressing a worldview on the basis of divine revelation, did not necessarily disagree with the first orientation but it implicitly established an ecclesiology that at times would come into conflict with structures of ecclesiastical authority.

The conflicts could have multiple origins. Visions took many forms and their meanings were not always immediately apparent. Often their interpretation required a sensitivity confessors did not have. The theological implications of visions often did not become clear until they were put into practice. The visionary might receive a revelation that she believed called her to a state of religious life or to a religious function not sanctioned by the institutional church. The revelation could have doctrinal or practical applications that challenged the prevailing orthodoxy or the perspective of her confessor.

A woman's visions formed the crux of her validation as a woman, as a teacher, as a moral agent, and as a Christian with a unique contribution to make to her society and her church. Visions, as Elizabeth Alvilda Petroff explains, served a variety of functions, even for the same person:

> Visions led women to the acquisition of power in the world while affirming their knowledge of themselves as women. Visions were a socially sanctioned activity that freed a woman from conventional female roles by identifying her as a genuine religious figure. They brought her to the attention of others, giving her a public language she could use to teach and learn. Her visions gave her the strength to grow internally and to change the world, to build convents, found hospitals, preach, attack injustice and greed, even within the church. Visions also provided her with the content for teaching although education had been denied

her. She could be an exemplar for other women, and out of her own experience she could lead them to fuller self-development.[35]

Precisely because visions empowered religious women in so many ways, most sixteenth-century theologians argued that female visionaries had to be subjected to a series of controls, particularly by their confessors.

Theological literature designed to control women's visions by having men probe their origins, interpret them, and test the religious practices and virtue of the visionary emerged in the fifteenth century with the writings of Jean Gerson. In his *De probatione spirituum* (1415) Gerson established standards of rigor that would plague women through the next century:

> Therefore, if you listen to or give advice to such a [visionary] person, be on your guard, so that you do not applaud her, praise her, or look upon her as a saint worthy of revelations and miracles. Better still, contradict her, scold her severely, ridicule her as one whose heart is proud and her eyes lofty and who deals with matters too great and wonderful for her.[36]

Gerson's advice was followed by many of Teresa's contemporaries, including her colleague John of the Cross. One Carmelite nun, he wrote, "has too much confidence and too little caution about erring internally . . . which is not the sign of a good spirit, but on the contrary makes people take it lightly and belittle it."[37] The nun's lack of humility convinced John of the Cross that her mystical experience was not genuine, and he recommended that her confessor and community humble her to teach her true virtue. "What I would suggest is that they . . . belittle it and put it down; and they should test her harshly in the exercise of virtues, primarily in self-contempt, humility, and obedience . . . and the tests must be good ones, because there is no devil who will not suffer anything for the sake of his honor."[38]

---

35. Petroff, *Medieval Women's Visionary Literature*, p. 6.

36. Paschal Boland, *The Concept of Discretio Spirituum in John Gerson's "De Probatione Spirituum" and "De Distinctione Verarum Visionum a Falsis"* (Washington, D.C., 1959), pp. 32–33. By speaking specifically of women here, Gerson implies that discernment of spirits is more important in their case than in that of male visionaries, because women are much more susceptible to the devil's wiles. This bias was shared by many other writers. See, e.g., ibid., pp. 36–37, and "Memorial en defensa de la doctrina y de los libros de la Madre Teresa de Jesús," in Llamas, p. 427. Gerson's continuing influence in Spain is reflected in the citation of *De probatione spirituum* in the condemnation of Francisca de Austria in 1602. See AHN, Inq., leg. 104, no. 5.

37. Juan de la Cruz, "Censura y parecer que dio el beato Padre sobre el espíritu y modo de proceder en la oración de una religiosa de nuestra Orden, y es como sigue," in his *Obras completas*, ed. Jucinio Ruano de la Iglesia (Madrid, 1982), p. 896: "Tiene demasiada seguridad y poco recelo por errar interiormente . . . la cual no tiene el verdadero espíritu, sino, por el contrario, gana que lo tengan en poco y se lo desprecien."

38. Ibid.: "Lo que yo diría es que no le manden ni dejen escribir nada desto, ni le dé muestra el confesor de oírselo de buena gana, sino para desestimarlo y deshacerlo; y pruébenla en el ejercicio de las virtudes a secas, mayormente en el desprecio, humildad y obediencia; y en el

In more general terms, John of the Cross reflected the distrust of many people when he warned against blind acceptance of a revelation: "A readiness to accept them [revelations] opens the door to the devil so he can trick the soul in other ways that seem to be good, for he knows very well how to dissemble and disguise himself; as the Apostle says, he can transform himself into an angel of light."[39] Theological manuals advised priests to examine the character of the visionary carefully and probe his or her motivation for divulging the visions.

Teresa had constantly to defend the trustworthiness of her visions and the insights they inspired. To empower other women in their struggle to express their visionary experiences, Teresa tried to establish norms for the discernment of spirits which were more sympathetic both to religious experience and to women. Teresa's visionary theology evolved over time and changed considerably between the *Vida* and the *Moradas*. In the *Vida* she related many visions and described their influence on her mystical development. She wrote quite freely about her visionary experience, taking it for granted that her readers—most of whom knew her personally—would not doubt their validity. Her defense of the orthodoxy of her visions was implicit rather than explicit: by contrasting visions given to her by God with visions inspired by the devil, Teresa indicated that she was well aware of the differences between the two kinds of visions, leaving the reader to infer that, unless she indicated otherwise, the visions she described were all divinely inspired.

As she struggled to describe visions of Christ in chapter 28 of the *Vida*, the language available to her hardly seemed adequate to the task:

> Sometimes it seemed to me I was seeing an image, but many other times it seemed like Christ himself, depending on how clearly he deigned to show himself to me. Sometimes it was so indistinct that it seemed to be an image, not like drawings, even the most accomplished kind, and I've seen many good ones. . . . If it's an image, it's a living image; not a dead man but the living Christ. . . . And sometimes he comes with such great majesty that no one can doubt that it's the Lord Himself, especially after receiving communion, for we know he is there, as our faith tells us.[40]

---

sonido del toque saldrá la blandura del alma en que han causado tantas mercedes, y las pruebas han de ser buenas porque no hay demonio que por su honra no sufra algo."

39. Juan de la Cruz, "Subida del Monte Carmelo," in his *Obras completas*, pp. 154–55. ". . . en quererlas admitir [las revelaciones] abre puerta al demonio para que la engañe en otras semejantes, las cuales sabe él muy bien disimular y disfrazar de manera que parezcan a las buenas; pues puede, como dice el Apóstol, transfigurarse en ángel de luz."

40. *Vida* 28:7–8: "Bien me parecía en algunas cosas que era imagen lo que veía, mas por otras muchas no, sino que era el mismo Cristo, conforme a la claridad con que era servido mostrárseme. Unas veces era tan en confuso, que me parecía imagen, no como los dibujos de acá, por muy perfectos que sean, que hartos he visto buenos. . . . Si es imagen, es imagen viva; no hombre muerto, sino Cristo vivo. . . . Y viene a veces tan grande majestad, que no hay quien pueda dudar, sino que es el mismo Señor, en especial en acabando de comulgar, que ya sabemos que está allí, que nos lo dice la fe."

Such visions literally imprint the presence of God in the soul, transforming and preparing it for a deeper and more lasting union:

> The majesty and beauty [of Christ] remain so imprinted that there is no way to forget it, unless the Lord wants the soul to endure the great loneliness and aridity that I will describe later; then it seems to forget even God. The soul becomes another, continually enraptured; a new, living love of God seems to begin.[41]

Because of the deep, positive effects of these visions, Teresa claims, there is "no peril" in them; indeed, their effects are to "show that the devil has no real power here." For Teresa, visions inspired by the devil are easy to distinguish from her divinely inspired visions, for the devil "makes images in order to dispel the true vision that the soul has seen; but it [the soul] resists them spontaneously; it becomes troubled, tormented and restless, so that it loses its devoutness and the joy it had before, and is unable to pray."[42] Each soul, then, provides all the signs needed to distinguish true visions; the trick is to learn to read them, but discernment is easy for anyone who proceeds "with humility and simplicity." Teresa reinforces this confidence by adding that "if one has experience, it seems to me, the devil can do no harm."[43]

Teresa also denies absolutely that visions are products of the imagination, for the experience of them and their effects on the soul go beyond human ability to contrive. "Why, without remembering it or ever having thought it, to see in an instant things the imagination couldn't contrive in a vast amount of time—because, as I have said, it far transcends what we can understand on earth—that's impossible."[44]

The visions she describes range from general to quite specific. The visions of Christ in chapter 28 seem integral to the mystical experience, but others seem peripheral to the journey toward union with God. In chapter 32 Teresa describes visions that helped her decide to reform the Carmelite order. A vision of hell persuaded her not to relax the monastic rule. A vision received after communion confirmed Teresa's plans to found San José in Avila, and even provided its name. A vision in the church of Santo Tomás in Avila con-

41. *Vida* 28:9: "Tan imprimida queda aquella majestad y hermosura, que no hay poderlo olvidar, si no es cuando quiere el Señor que padezca el alma una sequedad y soledad grande que diré adelante, que aun entonces de Dios parece se olvida. Queda el alma otra, siempre embebida: parécele comienza de nuevo amor vivo de Dios en muy alto grado."

42. *Vida* 28:10: "Hace representaciones para deshacer la verdadera visión que ha visto el alma; mas así la resiste de sí, y se alborota, y se desabre e inquieta, que pierde la devoción y gusto que antes tenía y queda sin ninguna oración."

43. Ibid.: "No me parece la engañará si anda con humildad y simplicidad. . . . Así que, adonde hay experiencia, a mi parecer, no podrá el demonio hacer daño."

44. *Vida* 28:11: "Pues sin acordarnos de ello, ni haberlo jamás pensado, ver en un punto presentes cosas que en gran tiempo no pudieran concertarse con la imaginación, porque va muy más alto, como ya he dicho, lo que acá podemos comprender; así que esto es imposible."

firmed the project, despite the townspeople's resistance to it.[45] Teresa also had several visions of souls ascending to heaven.[46] In the final chapter her vision that "in the time to come this order will flourish and will have many martyrs" sounds like a prophecy about the Discalced reforms.[47] As we have seen, Teresa's many visions—particularly the one about martyrs—raised significant questions about the orthodoxy of her mystical experience.[48]

Although Teresa's visionary theology evolved over time, even in the *Vida* she indicated her awareness of the Augustinian tradition of visionary theology.[49] Describing a spiritual vision of Christ, Teresa writes:

> Although this vision is imaginary, I never saw it or any other vision with my bodily eyes, but with the eyes of the soul. Those who know better than I say the [intellectual] kind I described earlier is more accurate than this one, and this kind much more so than those seen with the physical eyes. They say that is the lowest kind, the one in which the devil can appear more often in disguise, though I couldn't understand this then. . . .[50]

By the time she described her visions in the *Moradas*, she had become quite comfortable with the distinctions between imaginary and intellectual visions,[51] and she focused less on visions themselves than on ways to confirm their divine source.

The most basic test was to examine the effects of a vision on the person's life.

> Even the devil could never reveal things that leave the soul with such effects and peace and calm and growth, particularly three things of the highest order: First,

45. This vision includes details that struck some readers as trivial or even arrogant. Teresa saw herself clothed in a white garment by Mary and Joseph, which she understood to mean that she was cleansed of her sins. Then she received a large jeweled cross from Mary. See *Vida* 29:7. Other visions are described in 36:20 and 38:6 and 9.

46. See, e.g., *Vida* 34:19 (her sister María) and 36:20 (Peter of Alcántara).

47. *Vida* 40:13: "En los tiempos advenideros florecerá esta orden; habrá muchos mártires."

48. From 1574 on, Teresa's *Vida* was known as a book of visions and prophecies.

49. Augustine creates the framework for a visionary epistemology in bk. 12 of *De Genesi ad litteram*, in which he identifies three types of vision: corporeal, spiritual, and intellectual. The corporeal vision is perceived by the body and the senses; the spiritual vision includes a "spiritual image," as in 1 Cor. 15:44; and the intellectual vision takes place within the mind. The intellectual vision is the most reliable; according to Augustine, an intellectual vision does not err (bk. 12, chap. 14, sec. 29). *De Genesi ad litteram* is available in J. P. Migne, *Patrologia Latina* (Paris, 1887), 34:245–486.

50. *Vida* 28:4: "Esta visión, aunque es imaginaria, nunca la vi con los ojos corporales, ni ninguna, sino con los ojos del alma. Dicen los que lo saben mejor que yo, que es más perfecta la pasada que ésta, y ésta más mucho que las que se ven con los ojos corporales. Esta dicen que es la más baja y adonde más ilusiones puede hacer el demonio, aunque entonces no podía yo entender tal. . . ."

51. See her discussion in *Moradas* 6:4.3–9.

knowledge of God's greatness, for the more things we see flow from it, the more we come to appreciate it. Second, self-knowledge and humility at seeing how such a lowly thing, in comparison with the Creator of such wonders, has dared to offend God and dares to look to Him. Third, lack of esteem for worldly things, other than those that can be put to the service of such a great God.[52]

These effects, Teresa implies, should be readily apparent in the way the person lives, and certainly obvious to that person's confessor. Not all confessors, however, will be able to read these signs, so Teresa also gives practical advice to readers whose visions have been dismissed as fantasies or the devil's tricks. They must enlist the help of a learned and spiritual confessor.

> If they say [your vision] is a fancy, don't let it trouble you, for a fancy can do your soul little harm or good; pray to the divine Majesty that He won't let you be deceived. If they tell you it's the devil, that's more of a problem, though no truly learned person will say that if you display the effects I have described. But, when they do say that, I know the Lord Himself is with you, and He will comfort and protect you, and will give the confessor light, so he can give it to you.[53]

For Teresa the reluctance of theologians and confessors to accept visionary experience as an authentic way to know God is a sign of their own lack of spiritual development, indeed their lack of true wisdom, for no "truly learned" person would have difficulty recognizing an authentic visionary experience.

The problems of authority discussed in chapter 3 are amply reflected in Teresa's discussion of her visionary experience. She describes an encounter with a confessor who did not believe her visions: "I knew they were telling him to be on his guard with me, not to let the devil trick him by believing a word I told him; they gave him examples of other people. All this wore me out. I was afraid there'd be no one to confess me, that they'd all shun me."[54]

---

52. Ibid., 6:5.10: "Es imposible ni el demonio podría representar cosas que tanta operación y paz y sosiego y aprovechamiento dejan en el alma, en especial tres cosas muy en subido grado: conocimiento de la grandeza de Dios, porque mientras más cosas viéramos de ella, más se nos da a entender. Segunda razón: propio conocimiento y humildad de ver cómo cosa tan baja, en comparación del Criador de tantas grandezas, la ha osado ofender, ni osa mirarle. La tercera, tener en muy poco todas las cosas de la tierra, si no fueren las que pueden aplicar para servicio de tan gran Dios."

53. Ibid., 6:8.8: "Y si os dijeren que es antojo, no se os dé nada, que el antojo poco mal ni bien puede hacer a vuestra alma; encomendaos a la divina Majestad, que no consienta seáis engañadas. Si os dijeren es demonio, será más trabajo; aunque no dirá, si es buen letrado, y hay los efectos dichos; mas cuando lo diga yo sé que el mismo Señor, que anda con vos, os consolará y asegurará, y a él le irá dando luz, para que os la dé."

54. *Vida* 28:14: "Supe que le decían que se guardase de mí, no le engañase el demonio con creerme algo de lo que le decía; traíanle ejemplos de otras personas. Todo esto me fatigaba a mí. Temía que no había de haber con quien me confesar, sino que todos habían de huír de mí."

Though at times Teresa paid lip service to the belief that women were less able than men to distinguish between good and evil spirits, her mystical theology operated on the opposite presumption: for her, visions were a source of theological authority. Her works were not just an apology for visionary phenomena in general; they were an attempt to recover the legitimacy and authority of the female visionary experience. In the *Vida* Teresa reviewed her criteria for the discernment of visions, which included consistency with the Scriptures and church teachings.

> I believe revelation to be true if it does not go against what is [written] in the Sacred Scriptures or against the laws of the Church, which we are obliged to follow; because, although it [my revelation regarding the reform of the Carmelite order] truly seemed to me to be from God, if that learned man had told me that we couldn't do it [live without an income] without offending [God], and that we were going against conscience, I think I would have backed off immediately, or I would have looked for another way; but the Lord gave me no other [way] but this.[55]

Teresa allowed for some guidance from a confessor, but she ultimately felt compelled to remain true to her visions, seeing them as the Lord's command or "way"; and the way for the Discalced Carmelites was to live in poverty. "All the prophecies I told about this house [San José], and others I'll tell about it and about other things, all have come to pass . . . the Lord told them to me."[56] The fulfillment of her prophecies added to her notion of discernment: visions were shown to be from God when what they prophesied came to pass.

Thus, without directly applying the norms explained in treatises on the discernment of spirits,[57] Teresa presented a strong case for the legitimacy of her visions. Besides, she presented her visions as growing out of orthopraxy: they were often triggered by moments of intense petition or by reception of the Eucharist.[58] In addition to reinforcing her allegiance to the sacramental life of the church, she implied that in the orthodox experience of visions there was no tension between charisma and institution.

---

55. *Vida* 32:17: "Creo ser verdadera la revelación como no vaya contra lo que está en la Sagrada Escritura o contra las leyes de la Iglesia que somos obligados a hacer; porque, aunque a mí verdaderamente me parecía era de Dios, si aquel letrado me dijera que no lo podíamos hacer sin ofenderle, y que íbamos contra conciencia, paréceme luego me apartara de ello, o buscara otro medio; mas a mí no me daba el Señor sino éste."

56. *Vida* 34:18: "De todas las que he dicho de profecías de esta casa, y otras que diré de ella y de otras cosas, todas se han cumplido . . . me las decía el Señor."

57. There is no evidence one way or the other that Teresa had read any of these treatises, but through her confessors she certainly experienced some of the tests they outlined.

58. See, e.g., *Vida* 28:1 and 3.

An experience with her confessors demonstrated her allegiance to the institutional church. When they suspected that her visions were the devil's work, they ordered her to resist them by making a sign of disrespect with her hand.

> Making the sign of contempt when I saw a vision of the Lord gave me great pain; because when I saw him present, if they had tortured me I couldn't have believed it was the devil. . . . I begged Him to forgive me, since I did it only out of obedience. . . . He told me not to be concerned, that I did well to obey, and that He would make sure the truth was known.[59]

In this case Teresa's obedience went against her conscience, for she had no doubt that her visions were of divine origin. In submitting to her confessors, however, Teresa showed her allegiance to the institutional church, demonstrated that she did not value her visions (or her own authority) more than the authority of her religious superiors, and protected herself in a terrain that had already proved rocky for many other spiritual women.[60]

Mystical Union

The doctrine of mystical union is usually among the most difficult aspects of any mystic's thought. Understanding Teresa's use of the word "union" is complicated by the fact that she wrote about union in a variety of contexts and in several organizational systems. In the *Vida* she describes the "prayer of union" in words very similar to those she uses to describe union in the seventh *moradas*. In the *Vida* union is the culmination of a journey upward through various levels of prayer. Her description of rapture beyond this ex-

---

59. *Vida* 29:6: "Dábame este dar higas grandísima pena cuando veía esta visión del Señor; porque cuando yo le veía presente, si me hicieran pedazos, no pudiera yo creer que era demonio. . . . Suplicábale me perdonase; pues yo lo hacía por obedecer. . . . Decíame que no se me diese nada, que bien hacía en obedecer, mas que El haría que se entendiese la verdad."

60. Many women mystics and visionaries who did not state plainly their allegiance to the institutional church were officially condemned and even executed. This was the case with both Marguerite Porete and Joan of Arc, who refused to submit to the church and deny their own experiences. To some extent, the problems Teresa faced in realizing her literary vocation were experienced by all writers of late sixteenth-century spiritual treatises. Melquíades Andrés notes that language became the focus of attention in the effort to combat the Protestant heresy in the 1550s, as witness the Inquisition's order that Bibles be revised in 1554, the tensions that rent the Dominicans and Jesuits, and the issuance of the Valdés Index in 1559. See Andrés Martín, "Pensamiento teológico y vivencia religiosa," in García-Villoslada, *La Iglesia en la España*, p. 357. Andrés does not apply his comments to Teresa's works, but he does indicate the direction of research necessary to understand her literary style: "When we have a better understanding of the inner workings of the era's spirituality, we will understand the intentionality and import of many of its expressions" (p. 358). He does note (p. 357) that the Index obliged Teresa to reflect more seriously on her experience and to consult with theologians in an effort to understand and describe it accurately.

perience of prayer, however, implies that the prayer of union is not the soul's ultimate goal, but one more step along the way. In the *Moradas* the journey toward union with God is inward rather than upward. Here Teresa presents her most developed statements on mystical union.

Indeed, in the *Moradas* visions are more clearly integrated into the entire mystical experience, so that they are not a stage in spiritual growth, but represent the soul's evolving knowledge of God. In describing how God's wisdom is revealed and imprinted in the soul, Teresa expresses clearly the idea that visions involve the continued revelation of divine wisdom:

> Here is this soul that God has made utterly foolish, the better to impress true wisdom upon it. . . . God implants Himself inside that soul so that when it returns to itself, it can't possibly doubt that it was in God, and God in it. So firmly does this truth remain within it that even though years go by and God never again grants it that favor, it can neither forget it nor doubt it happened (and this quite apart from the effects that linger in it; I'll speak about those later). This [certainty of the soul] is the important thing.[61]

Ultimately, union with God is intimately related to the visionary experience, for the vision and understanding of the Trinity are what signal the soul's entrance into the seventh *moradas*.

The union Teresa describes in chapters 18 and 19 of the *Vida* is not identified as "the prayer of union" until chapter 25,[62] but the description she offers in the earlier chapters is very similar to the one found in the fifth *moradas*, in which she also discusses the "prayer of union." The major characteristic of union as she describes it in the *Vida* is the soul's experience of great delight in God without understanding exactly what it delights in. All of its faculties are absorbed in delight in God, and it can neither do nor think of anything else.[63]

In the *Vida* Teresa is explicit about the fullness of this union: "We all know what 'union' means: it's two separate things becoming one."[64] This

---

61. *Moradas* 5:1.9: "Pues tornando a la señal que digo es la verdadera, ya veis esta alma que la ha hecho Dios boba del todo para imprimir mejor en ella la verdadera sabiduría. . . . Fija Dios a sí mismo en lo interior de aquel alma de manera que, cuando torna en sí, en ninguna manera puede dudar que estuvo en Dios, y Dios en ella. Con tanta firmeza le queda esta verdad, que aunque pase años sin tornarle Dios a hacer aquella merced, ni se le olvida, ni puede dudar que estuvo. Aún dejamos por los efectos con que queda, que éstos diré después. Esto es lo que hace mucho al caso."

62. See *Vida* 25:11.

63. *Vida* 18:1: "Acá no hay sentir, sino gozar sin entender lo que se goza. Entiéndese que se goza de un bien, adonde junto se encierran todos los bienes; más no comprende este bien. Ocúpanse todos los sentidos en este gozo, de manera que no queda ninguno desocupado para poder en otra cosa exterior ni interiormente."

64. *Vida* 18:3: "Lo que es unión ya se está entendido, que es dos cosas divisas hacerse una."

union is temporary and fleeting: an experience of union lasting more than half an hour would be remarkable. Indeed, the soul may not even recognize this type of union at the time. Its effects in the soul, however, are the best indication of its presence after the fact.[65]

Teresa distinguishes union from ecstasy, in which God lifts the soul to new heights of knowledge and understanding.[66] E. W. Trueman Dicken argues that the three experiences of God—the prayer of union, ecstasy, and full mystical union—are in fact the same but are experienced differently.[67] The critical distinctions between ecstasy and final union lie in intensity, participation, and permanence. In this sense, the experiences of the prayer of union, ecstasy, and union form a kind of continuum in which mystical experience grows progressively more intense, more inclusive, and more permanent.[68] Each level of experience depends on the previous level: rapture does not come until the soul has experienced the prayer of union.[69] Full union with God does not come until the soul has been prepared for it by ecstatic experience.

Though these experiences seem to be the same root experience gradually intensified, the dynamics of the soul's experience of them vary considerably: the soul cannot resist ecstasy, but it can resist the prayer of union. In ecstasy, Teresa says: "there is no way to resist, but in union, since we are in our own sphere, there is; though it takes pain and force, one can nearly always resist."[70] Ecstasy demonstrates the power of God and fills the soul with a

---

65. *Vida* 18:12: "Verdad es que a los principios pasa en tan breve tiempo—al menos a mí así me acaecía—, que en estas señales exteriores ni en la falta de los sentidos no se da tanto a entender cuando pasa con brevedad. Más bien se entiende en la sobra de las mercedes, que ha sido grande la claridad del sol que ha estado allí, pues así la ha derretido. Y nótese esto, que—a mi parecer—por largo que sea el espacio de estar el alma en esta suspensión de todas las potencias, es bien breve. Cuando estuviese media hora, es muy mucho."

66. *Vida* 20:2: "Coge el Señor el alma, digamos ahora a manera que las nubes cogen los vapores de la tierra, y levántala toda ella—helo oído así esto, de que cogen las nubes los vapores o el sol—y sube la nube al cielo y llévala consigo, y comiénzala a mostrar cosas del reino que le tiene aparejado. No sé si la comparación cuadra; mas en hecho de verdad ello pasa así."

67. E. W. Trueman Dicken, *The Crucible of Love* (New York, 1963), p. 424: "The *nature* of the union is the same in all three of the highest mansions: in each case the soul and God are indistinguishably intermingled, in a manner more akin to mechanical mixture than to chemical combination."

68. Trueman Dicken argues that permanency and intensity are the major distinguishing characteristics of these experiences. "The difference between the three stages lies mainly, even perhaps solely, in the degree of permanency of that union, which only in the *Seventh Mansion* becomes indissoluble. It is possible, but not certain, that there may be also a difference of intensity in the union of the three stages, the last being more intense than the earlier ones, or in a sense more complete" (ibid.). This assessment seems to leave out the changing role of the soul in this experience.

69. See *Vida* 25:11.

70. *Vida* 20:3: "Aquí no hay ningún remedio de resistir; que en la unión, como estamos en nuestra tierra, remedio hay; aunque con pena y fuerza, resistir se puede casi siempre."

deeper experience of a transcendent God, so it creates a new humility in the soul.[71] Implicit in Teresa's description is the idea that ecstatic experience may form a part of the journey toward union with God, and certainly it has a role in the further development of the soul, but it does not constitute full union with God.[72]

In both the prayer of union and ecstasy the soul's faculties are suspended. Teresa's description of this aspect of the prayer of union in the fifth *morada* is remarkably similar to that of chapter 18 of the *Vida*.[73] In both cases the experience of union with God is fleeting, but it leaves the soul with the certainty that "it was in God, and God in it." The soul experiences such a union as being "dead to the world in order to live in God," a physical state in which no movement is possible.[74] Teresa likens it to fainting. In this state the soul is not disturbed by distracting thoughts because its memory, imagination, and understanding are suspended. In fact, Teresa explains, the soul "neither sees nor hears nor understands."[75]

> Here the faculties of the soul are absent; they are suspended, so that in no way, as I have said, can one believe they are functioning. So this importunate little butterfly of the memory gets its wings burned here; it can no longer flit about. The will should be totally occupied in loving, but it doesn't understand how it loves. The understanding, if it understands at all, doesn't understand how it understands; at least it grasps nothing of what it understands.[76]

---

71. *Vida* 20:7: "Muéstrase el gran poder del Señor, y cómo no somos parte, cuando Su Majestad quiere, de detener tampoco el cuerpo como el alma, ni somos señores de ello; sino que—mal que nos pese—vemos que hay superior y que estas mercedes son dadas de El, y que de nosotros no podemos en nada, nada, e imprímese mucha humildad."

72. On this point see Tomás de la Cruz, "L'extase chez Sainte Thérèse d'Avila," in *Dictionnaire de spiritualité, ascetique et mystique, doctrine et histoire*, ed. Marcel Viller, 11 vols. to date (Paris, 1932–), 4:2153–2158.

73. Particularly noteworthy in this respect is the repetition of the confusion Teresa experienced regarding the presence of God in all things. Cf. *Vida* 18:16 and *Moradas* 5:1.10. In the *Moradas* text this anecdote is in the third person rather than the first.

74. *Moradas* 5:1.9: "El tiempo que está así, que siempre es breve"; "en ninguna manera pueda dudar que estuvo en Dios, y Dios en ella"; ibid., 5:1.4: "ha muerto al mundo para vivir más en Dios."

75. Ibid., 5:1.9: "Ni ve, ni oye, ni entiende."

76. *Vida* 18:14–15: "Aquí faltan todas las potencias, y se suspenden de manera que en ninguna manera—como he dicho—se entiende que obran. . . . Así que a esta mariposilla importuna de la memoria aquí se le queman las alas; ya no puede más bullir. La voluntad debe estar bien ocupada en amar, mas no entiende cómo ama. El entendimiento, si entiende, no se entiende cómo entiende; al menos no puede comprender nada de lo que entiende." For the primary role of the will in this union, see *Vida* 18:12: "La voluntad es la que mantiene la tela, mas las otras dos potencias presto tornan a importunar. Como la voluntad está queda, tórnalas a suspender y están otro poco y tornan a vivir."

Because the faculties remain suspended and the soul has no power of imagination,[77] the prayer of union is necessarily brief.

The suspension in God is a suspension not only of the soul's faculties but also of its ability to function, even sinfully:

> And I will dare to contend that if it's truly union with God, the devil can neither enter nor do any harm, because His Majesty is so closely united to the essence of the soul that he won't dare approach; nor should he even understand this secret. . . . Oh, great boon, the state where the evil one can't harm us![78]

Teresa appears to be identifying a state in which the soul is immune to temptation, but note that she attributes this immunity not to the soul's own righteousness but to its direct association with God. Since union is such a fleeting experience, immunity must also be temporary, and Teresa urges her readers to be constant in the pursuit of virtue:

> The duty that seemed most evident to me—after asking God ceaselessly in prayer to hold us in his hand and thinking continually how, if He forsakes us, we'll land right in the pit, and that's the truth, and never to depend on ourselves, for that would be madness—is to behave with great care and caution, watching how we progress in virtue.[79]

This passage balances and qualifies Teresa's discussion of freedom from temptation: a soul free from sin would have no need to be concerned about its progress in virtue.

In rapture, too, the soul's faculties are temporarily suspended, inhibited from their natural functions and "so tied up that they're left without any freedom."[80] If the rapture is particularly strong, the soul's faculties remain so spellbound that they can hardly function for one, two, even three days afterward.[81] Indeed, after several experiences of rapture, the soul begins to feel frustrated by its inability to delight in God thoroughly. Teresa

---

77. *Vida* 18:13: "sin ninguna imaginación en nada."

78. *Moradas* 5:1.5: "Y osaré afirmar que, si verdaderamente es unión de Dios, que no puede entrar el demonio ni hacer ningún daño, porque está su Majestad tan junto y unido con la esencia del alma, que no osará llegar, ni aun debe entender este secreto. . . . Oh gran bien, estado adonde este maldito no nos hace mal!"

79. Ibid., 5:4.9: "La diligencia que a mí se me ofrece más cierta—después de pedir siempre a Dios en la oración que nos tenga de su mano y pensar muy continuo cómo, si El nos deja, seremos luego en el profundo, como es verdad, y jamás estar confiadas en nosotras, pues será desatino estarlo—es andar con particular cuidado y aviso mirando cómo vamos en las virtudes."

80. Ibid., 6:11.2: "En un punto ata las potencias de manera que no quedan con ninguna libertad."

81. *Vida* 20:21: "Después que torna en sí, si ha sido grande el arrobamiento, acaece andar un día o dos, y aun tres, tan absortas las potencias, o como embobecida [el alma], que no parece anda en sí"; 25:5: ". . . quedan las potencias de manera que, aunque no están perdidas, casi nada obran."

lamented: "When, my God, will I manage to see my soul united in your glory, when all my faculties will delight in you?"[82]

Tomás de la Cruz has noted a pattern in Teresa's experience of ecstasy: it followed an imaginary or intellectual vision, it was brief, and it produced lingering effects.[83] These observations locate Teresa within an orthodox, Augustinian framework of visionary theology, providing her with some form of validation at a time when ecstatic experience was suspect.

The fragmented experience of union is somewhat resolved when the soul finally arrives at the seventh *moradas*. Here the faculties are "awakened" and conscious of God's presence, but still "they don't function; it's as though they're in a state of shock."[84] Now the soul's faculties experience delight or awe in the union with God.[85] This union is a realization and completion of all the temporary states of union the soul has experienced in the "prayer of union" and in rapture. In rapture the soul experiences a new closeness to God, but does not have the use of its faculties to understand the closeness. The soul in rapture experiences God in its "superior part," but not at its center.[86] For union to occur, "God must have a place in the soul where only His Majesty dwells, let's call it 'another heaven.' "[87] This dwelling place is the "center" of the soul,[88] in which the soul receives a peace that overcomes any distractions or problems of daily life. Since the soul has overcome its own passions, in union it achieves a peace in God that cannot be disturbed.[89]

---

82. *Vida* 30:16: "¿Cuando, Dios mío, acabaré ya de ver mi alma junta en vuestra alabanza, que os gocen todas las potencias?"

83. Tomás de la Cruz, "L'extase chez Sainte Thérèse d'Avila," 4:2158.

84. *Moradas* 7:3.8: "Este movimiento interior procede del centro del alma y despierta las potencias"; 7:3.11: "A mi parecer, aquí no se pierden las potencias, más no obran, sino están como espantadas."

85. The soul's ability to experience union with God without losing its faculties is absent from Teresa's description of mystical experience in the *Vida*—a major difference between the *Vida* and the *Moradas*.

86. See ibid., 7:1.5: "Yo bien creo que la ha metido [Dios] en estos arrobamientos, que yo bien creo que la une consigo entonces y en la oración que queda dicho de unión, aunque no le parece al alma que es tanta llamada para entrar en su centro, como aquí en esta morada, sino a la parte superior. En esto va poco: sea de una manera o de otra, el Señor la junta consigo; mas es haciéndola ciega y muda, como lo quedó San Pablo en su conversión, y quitándola el sentir cómo o de qué manera es aquella merced que goza; porque el gran deleite que entonces siente el alma es de verse cerca de Dios. Más, cuando la junta consigo, ninguna cosa entiende, que las potencias todas se pierden."

87. Ibid., 7:1.3: "Así como la tiene en el cielo, debe tener en el alma una estancia adonde solo su Majestad mora, y digamos: otro cielo."

88. Ibid., 7:2.9: "En metiendo el Señor al alma en esta morada suya, que es el centro de la misma alma . . ."

89. See ibid., 7:2.11.

This state of peace does not guarantee that the soul will not fall into temptation and sin, however.

> It may seem as though I mean that when God grants the soul this mercy, it's certain of its salvation and of not falling [into sin] again; I say no such thing, and whenever I seem to suggest that the soul is safe, I mean so long as the divine Majesty has it in his hand and it doesn't displease him. At least I know for certain that even if it's been in this state for many years, it never takes anything for granted, in fact it's more apprehensive than before in guarding against any little offense against God, and extremely eager to serve him.[90]

At some level, then, the soul is in a protected state, but "this great gift [of union] cannot be fully realized in this life, because if we were to draw away from God, this supreme good would be lost."[91] Thus Teresa accepted separation from God through sin as part of the human condition and never guaranteed that union would deliver the soul from sin. She made sure that she could not reasonably be accused, as the early *alumbrados* had been, of believing that the soul in prayer was sinless.

The soul's entrance into its center, the dwelling place of God, begins with an intellectual vision of the Trinity, and the new perception of this internal presence never entirely leaves it, though the intensity of the soul's perception of this presence is constantly changing.[92] The purpose of this vision of the Trinity is to prepare the soul for further advancement toward perfection.[93] The soul then receives a vision of the Sacred Humanity of Christ. This vision has a different quality from earlier visions the soul may have experienced because it is designed to reveal the special quality of the gift of

90. Ibid., 7:2.9: "Parece que quiero decir que, llegando el alma a hacerla Dios esta merced, está segura de su salvación y de no tornar a caer; no digo tal, y en cuantas partes tratare de esta manera, que parece está el alma en seguridad, se entienda: mientras la divina Majestad la tuviere así de su mano y ella no le ofendiere. Al menos sé cierto que, aunque se ve en este estado y le ha durado años, que no se tiene por segura, sino que anda con mucho más temor que antes en guardarse de cualquiera pequeña ofensa de Dios, y con grandes deseos de servirle."

91. See ibid., 7:2.1: "Esta gran merced no debe cumplirse con perfección mientras vivimos, pues si nos apartásemos de Dios, se perdería este tan gran bien."

92. See ibid., 7:1.7: "Y cada día se espanta más esta alma, porque nunca más le parece se fueron de con ella, sino que notoriamente ve, de la manera que queda dicho, que están en lo interior de su alma, en lo muy, muy interior, en una cosa muy honda, que no sabe decir cómo es, porque no tiene letras, siente en sí esta divina compañía." See also 7:1.9: "El traer esta presencia entiéndese que no es tan enteramente, digo tan claramente, como se le manifiesta la primera vez y otras algunas que quiere Dios hacerle este regalo; porque, si esto fuese, era imposible entender en otra cosa ni aun vivir entre la gente; más, aunque no es con esta tan clara luz, siempre que advierte se halla con esta compañía."

93. See ibid., 7:1.9: "Parece que quiere aquí la divina Majestad disponer el alma para más con esta admirable compañía, porque está claro que será bien ayudada para en todo ir adelante en la perfección."

union which the soul is about to experience. "The first time God bestows this gift [of union], His Majesty wishes to appear to the soul through an imaginary vision of His Most Sacred Humanity so that [the soul] really understands it and is not unaware that it's receiving such a sovereign gift."[94] The intellectual vision given to the soul in union marks the authenticity of the experience.

Further indications of the validity of mystical experience are the effects of union on the soul. The soul feels utter disregard for itself, for it realizes that everything it can do on its own amounts to very little in God's eyes; nonetheless, it would not fail to do everything it could to serve God "for anything in the world."[95]

The second effect of union on the soul is its desire to suffer and a secret happiness in persecution.[96] Further, the soul has a great desire to be alone or to be occupied in things that may benefit other souls. It finds itself in a state of continual withdrawal. Even in this state, however, the soul should remain humble and practice virtue, for "whoever does not grow, shrinks."[97]

Though Teresa incorporated visions in her description of union in a way that was new to the mystical tradition, she was careful to place them in an Augustinian framework. She was also careful to characterize mystical union as one of spirits, citing a key Pauline text: "Perhaps this is what Saint Paul says: He who is joined to God becomes one spirit with Him, referring to this sovereign marriage, which presumes that His Majesty has arrived in the soul through union."[98] This use of 1 Corinthians 6:17 locates Teresa in a tradition of mystics such as Bernard of Clairvaux, William of Saint-Thierry, and Richard of Saint Victor, all of whom use the same biblical text and teach the *unitas spiritus*.[99] The consistency of Teresa's position with the traditional teachings on mystical union was a key reason that theologians could defend her views of union in the posthumous debate over her orthodoxy.

---

94. Ibid., 7:2.1: "La primera vez que Dios hace esta merced quiere su Majestad mostrarse al alma por visión imaginaria de su Sacratísima Humanidad para que lo entienda bien y no esté ignorante de que recibe tan soberano don."

95. Ibid., 7:3.2: "Es su pena ver que es nada lo que ya pueden sus fuerzas. En todo lo que puede y entiende que es servicio de nuestro Señor no lo dejaría de hacer por cosa de la tierra."

96. Ibid., 7:3.4–5.

97. Ibid., 7:4.9: "Quien no crece, descrece."

98. Ibid., 7:2.5: "Quizá es esto lo que dice San Pablo: el que se arrima y allega a Dios, hácese un espíritu con El, tocando este soberano matrimonio, que presupone haber llegado su Majestad al alma por unión."

99. For a review of this tradition, see Bernard McGinn, "Love, Knowledge, and *Unio Mystica* in the Western Christian Tradition," in *Mystical Union and Monotheistic Faith: An Ecumenical Dialogue*, ed. Moshe Idel and McGinn (New York, 1989), pp. 59–86. Teresa's doctrine, McGinn writes, "adds little that is new to the main line of theological understanding of union" (p. 82).

Teresa and the Christian Mystical Tradition

We have seen Teresa's thought evolve on several key points. She broke new ground when she treated visions sympathetically, provided a set of standards to enable suspicious contemporaries to accept them, and integrated them into the mystical journey. In her discussion of mystical union Teresa entered into dialogue with the authors of the mystical treatises she had once read. Her teachings on the role of the faculties of the soul, her characterization of mystical union as one of spirits, and her incorporation of intellectual visions in this union indicate that by the time she wrote the *Moradas*, Teresa had synthesized her own experience enough to describe to her readers what to expect when they, too, proceeded along the path of prayer. Her careful preparation of both her texts and the mystical doctrine they propound reveal her appreciation of contemporary circumstances and the need for a detailed, practical manual of mystical theology.

Teresa de Jesús has often been seen as an important synthesizer of the mystical tradition, since she pulls its elements together in a way that makes them coherent and approachable. I suggest that Teresa's synthesis can be understood in a more specific way: she makes clear the interdependence of the visionary and mystical traditions. The integration of visions with mystical union is Teresa's way of affirming the visionary epistemology so challenged during her day.

The vision of the Trinity that heralds entry into mystical union with God is Teresa's contribution to mystical thought, and it is symbolic of the large role that visions play in her mystical theology. Teresa experiences a visual knowledge of God that moves her to a deeper love of God. Her conversion before the statue of Christ marks the beginning of this journey toward uncovering the seen (and thus known and lived) God within herself. Once revealed, the knowledge of God cannot be taken away from the soul, because it has been seen and thus stored inside the memory.[100] Because God is revealed directly to the soul, there is no way for an outsider to control access to God or to monitor the soul's progress toward union with God unless the person who has the experience reveals the process to someone else. Teresa's doctrine thus encourages spiritual autonomy and open access to God; her major message, which she modeled in her own life, is that the discovery of God's presence in the soul is a spiritual imperative for all people.

Because access to revelation was such a keenly debated issue in the sixteenth century, Teresa provided a list of the effects of both visions and mystical union to help her readers recognize them. She encouraged her nuns to have a good working relationship with their confessors, and she attempted

---

100. This notion of a permanent perception of God was what so troubled some of her readers.

to do so in her own relationships with learned theologians. Yet nothing Teresa did could guarantee her the spiritual autonomy she sought, for the inquisitors remained suspicious and both her detractors and her supporters tried to control access to her books by refusing to publish them.

Despite Teresa's careful preparation of her mystical works, they were criticized severely after their publication in 1588. At root, theologians' objections focused on the potential for religious dissent in Teresa's heavy dependence on revelation, and they questioned both her authority and her orthodoxy. The objections they raised in various *memoriales* submitted to the Inquisition help us understand more clearly the restrictions placed on Teresa by her historical circumstances.

5

Preter Naturam?
Posthumous Debates
on Teresa's Orthodoxy

The publication of Teresa's complete works was accomplished by the diligent work of many disciples.[1] One of the main forces behind this effort was Ana de Jesús, who in 1586 was in Madrid, arranging for the establishment of a new Discalced convent there. As prioress, she established a rapport with the Augustinian biblical scholar Luis de León, a professor at the esteemed University of Salamanca. Both Jerónimo Gracián and Ana de Jesús favored Luis de León as the editor of Teresa's works. León secured a commission from the Consejo Real to review her manuscripts and prepare them for publication. His introduction to Teresa's *Obras completas* was a formal approbation of her doctrine. The posthumous publication of Teresa's collected works in Salamanca in 1588 expanded their influence. The reservations about the circulation of Teresa's manuscripts expressed by Domingo Báñez, Juan de Avila, and other theologians during Teresa's lifetime appeared again in a second and sharper wave of criticisms. Various *memoriales*, or briefs, solicited and unsolicited, found their way to the Consejo de la Suprema y General Inquisición (Suprema), the council that oversaw the inquisitional tribunals.[2] In general, the posthumous criticisms were much more specific and their accusations harsher, perhaps because many of these readers had not known Teresa personally.[3] To read the documents that record the Inquisition's posthumous procedure against Teresa is to have access to internal debate about theological issues of considerable contemporary importance:

1. For more details on the recovery of Teresa's manuscripts and the preparation of the 1588 edition, see Llamas, pp. 282–95.

2. For more information on the role of the Suprema and its relationship with the inquisitor general, see Henry Kamen, *Inquisition and Society in Spain in the Sixteenth and Seventeenth Centuries* (Bloomington, Ill., 1985), pp. 33, 134–45.

3. Teresa's involvement with Bartolomé de Medina (1527–80) demonstrates that even her critics had been disarmed by her charisma. A Dominican and professor in Salamanca, Medina had heard about Teresa's visions and had serious doubts about their validity. When Teresa learned of Medina's criticisms (in 1574), she went to him regularly to talk about his reservations and to convince him of her sincerity and orthodoxy. In the end he became her staunch supporter.

the possibility of mystical union, anthropology and human potentiality, and the nature of revelation and its role in the church.

The objections raised in the review of Teresa's published works took on different themes from those we observed during her lifetime. After her death there was little doubt about her moral fiber and the good her reform efforts had done. Indeed, time was proving Teresa's sanctity. The second procedure raised fewer questions about her character and even her sincerity. Detractors generally claimed that she was deluded, not that she intended to mislead others. They disputed her teaching authority and accused her of subverting the natural order by teaching men. They pointed to the risk that her works might lead their readers, particularly women, to follow Teresa's spiritual path, only to be misled as she had been. They claimed that her mystical doctrine was both unprecedented and false. They linked Teresa to the *alumbrado* movement and attempted to establish a connection between her mystical practices and those of earlier heretical groups. Finally, they tried to discredit the mystical tradition itself by implying that all mystical experience led to rejection of ecclesiastical authority and therefore to heresy. Teresa's apologists defended her right to teach and maintained the validity of both the mystical tradition and the role of revelation in Christianity.

Commentators and Issues

Despite extensive theological review during Teresa's lifetime, her works had to endure the scrutiny of more *calificadores*, university-trained theologians who reviewed books as consultants for the Inquisition.[4] The cast of characters in this five-year debate appears to be split between the Dominicans, who had the most objections to Teresa's works, and the Augustinians, who defended them. Alonso de la Fuente (1533–94) was the major instigator of the procedures against Teresa's published works.[5] A Dominican preacher, Alonso submitted five *memoriales* to the Consejo between 1589 and 1591.[6] He became involved with the Inquisition after his experiences on the preaching circuit led him to identify what he believed to be a contemporary spiritual danger in the *alumbrados*. Throughout the 1570s and 1580s

4. For more information on the *calificador* and other inquisitional offices, see Kamen, *Inquisition and Society*, pp. 134–60.

5. For more information on Alonso de la Fuente, see Huerga, *Historia de los alumbrados*, 1:49–97, 315–473; idem, *Predicadores, alumbrados e inquisición en el siglo XVI* (Madrid, 1973), pp. 39–63; Llamas, pp. 308–40, 345–51; Mir and Cuervo, "Los alumbrados de Extremadura"; and Luis Sala Balust, "En torno al grupo de alumbrados de Llerena," in his *Corrientes espirituales en la España del siglo XVI* (Madrid, 1963), pp. 509–23.

6. AHN, Inq., leg. 4442, no. 43, and 2076. Modern transcriptions of these *memoriales* and other documents in leg. 4442 used in the citations below are found in Llamas, pp. 395–485.

Alonso wrote many *memoriales* against this group, addressed to both ecclesiastical and civil authorities. Few people escaped Alonso's notice: in these
memoriales are *beatas* and priests, books and authors, even archbishops.[7]
Alonso's continued submission of unsolicited *memoriales* to the Consejo
reflects his concern that Teresa's doctrines fomented the very phenomenon
he had dedicated his life to fight. Alonso had seen the results of unorthodox
prayer practices, and he believed his experience enabled him to identify and
condemn the "bad seed" in Teresa's works. This is how he presented himself
in the first *memorial*:

> The business [of *alumbrados*] is one the Inquisition has identified and tackled.
> And I in particular, in the company of the inquisitor Montoya, saw with my
> own eyes the practice of all this theory and experienced the sense and signifi-
> cance of every bit of it. And I ought to be believed in this matter as an eyewit-
> ness, just as all historians are believed in those things they saw and examined as
> eyewitnesses, especially since my observations are credible and well founded
> and stand to reason.[8]

Alonso is not a particularly sympathetic character. Both his contemporaries and modern historians paint a portrait of an intolerant man with an
inflated ego dedicated to the eradication of heretical practice, which he
alone fully understood.[9] Indeed, Alonso was so dedicated to the elimination of the *alumbrados* that he came to see heresy in any form of prayer that
differed in any way from the norm. According to Enrique Llamas, his unbalanced criticisms cost him the favor of the authorities, especially in his
later years. Llamas does concede, however, that Alonso's experience gave
him a "special ability" to make clear the recurring theological problems of
the *alumbrados*.[10] Whatever his personal shortcomings may have been,

---

7. See Huerga, *Predicadores, alumbrados e inquisición*, p. 46.

8. "Memoriales de Alonso de la Fuente," in Llamas, p. 399: "Y es negocio que lo ha tentado
y manijado la Inquisición. Y yo en particular, en compañía del inquisidor Montoya, vi por vista
de ojos la práctica de toda esta theórica y supe el sentido y significación de cada cosa. Y será
razón que sea creído en esta materia como testigo ocular, como son creídos todos los histori-
adores en aquellas cosas que vieron y tentaron como testigos de vista, especialmente quando
mis notaciones son verisímiles y bien fundadas y llegadas a razón. . . ."

9. Alvaro Huerga, however, says that although Alonso does give this impression, he was
not always convinced he was right; and when he had banished his doubts, he blamed himself
for not knowing how to make the truth clear, or the "old and sickly" inquisitors for their refusal to see it. See Huerga, *Historia de los alumbrados*, 4:91.

10. Llamas, pp. 308–9. In line with Llamas's apologetic purpose, however, he does not
grant Alonso much theological merit. Alonso's "special ability" enabled him to "clarify those
dark and dissembling practices of the *alumbrados*," who disguised their "mystical Witches' Sabbath" as "an exalted life of prayer and union with God," but "on occasion abandoned themselves to the brutal satisfaction of the lowest instincts."

Alonso de la Fuente's criticisms of Teresa posed a series of theological questions that other critics and apologists had to address, and his repeated letters to the Inquisition spurred them to open a formal investigation of Teresa's works.

Perhaps even before it received Alonso's first *memorial*, the Consejo received an anonymous "Defense of the Doctrine and Books of Mother Teresa de Jesús" in response to it. After answering the general criticisms of "vanity" and "strangeness," the author challenged Alonso to argue more directly from Teresa's texts and less generally from his understanding of *alumbrado* doctrine.[11] The "Defense" responded to the objections Alonso had raised to both Teresa's doctrine and her character.

In 1589, when he realized the book he had edited had provoked some controversy, Luis de León wrote another "Apología," more extensive than the one that had served as a prologue for Teresa's *Complete Works*. Addressing himself to unknown detractors of Teresa's works, Luis declared: "Regarding the books of the Holy Mother Teresa de Jesús, which were printed last year and distributed throughout Spain, some—or so I have heard—either because they know no better, or to appear to be knowledgeable, or for other reasons, have spoken of them with less respect than they should have."[12] Although Luis claimed that he had only "heard" these criticisms, it is possible that he read them—though not in Alonso's first *memorial*, because the criticisms there are quite specific and do not match Luis's description.[13] Luis de León wrote his "Apología" to respond to three points of criticism:

> They object . . . for three reasons: first, because they [the books] teach a prayer they [the critics] call "union," which they say it is not right to teach; they don't say why. Second, because they include some recondite things, so that everyone

11. Ibid., p. 430: "[El autor] poniendo por fundamento que la doctrina deste libro es toda de Taulero y de los alumbrados, refiriendo algunas cosas, que dice son heregías y doctrina nueva; mas no cita lugar ninguno de Teresa de Jesús, donde tales errores tenga, sino como está persuadido que su doctrina es mala, antójasele que dice lo que nunca dixo y que siente lo que [sintieron] Taulero y los alumbrados. Al presente no se trata de Taulero ni de alumbrados, sino del libro de Teresa de Jesús, en el qual no se halla ni la sentencia, ni las palabras que la impone, ni otras equivalentes, como se verá respondiendo en particular." Llamas speculates that the author is Pedro Martínez de Muro. He discusses the date of the defense on pp. 321–22.

12. Luis de León, *Obras completas*, 2 vols. (Madrid, 1957), 1:915: "De los libros de la santa Madre Teresa de Jesús, que el año pasado se imprimieron y extendieron por toda España, algunos, según he oído, por no saber más, o por parecer que saben, o por otros respetos de emulación, han hablado menos bien que debían."

13. Granted, Luis's description of the substance of the criticisms is quite vague, but Alonso does not discuss the nature of Teresa's revelations in his first *memorial*. The crux of Alonso's comments concern the locus of union.

may understand them. Third, because the holy Mother Teresa tells of many revelations she had.[14]

The first criticisms of the Dominican Juan de Orellana, dated April 22, 1591, were solicited by the Consejo in Madrid as part of their evaluation of Teresa's works. Orellana, who had known Teresa personally,[15] spoke well of her character, though he still rejected her doctrine. He declared that he found her to be "a Christian and religious woman, who searched for the truth; because I know she searched often for confessors to whom to communicate her conscience who were so educated and good that she could follow their advice with confidence."[16]

Antonio de Quevedo, another Augustinian, wrote a defense in direct response to Alonso de la Fuente and Juan de Orellana. This document was submitted to the Inquisition on June 18, 1591. According to Enrique Llamas, Quevedo's response was probably commissioned by the Inquisition, who found Orellana's comments too brief to be of much help to them in their evaluation of the books' theological contents.[17] Quevedo clearly had studied Alonso's *memoriales*, as his comments addressed nearly all of Alonso's criticisms, point by point.

Finally, the Dominican Juan de Lorenzana submitted a condemnatory *memorial* to the Consejo on June 25, 1593.[18] Lorenzana affirmed Alonso's criticisms and added some substance to them. Lorenzana attempted to associate Teresa with a tradition of heterodox mysticism, arguing in particular against her visionary experiences.

Teresa's Teaching Authority and Gender Ideology

The arguments assembled by Teresa's critics make it clear that Teresa was well aware of the hostility toward women who dared to teach. Her many rhetorical strategies were not universally effective. Some critics considered her appeals to direct revelation too bold. Her Dominican critics both de-

---

14. Luis de León, *Obras completas*, 1:915: "Sólo ponen inconvenientes en su lección por tres títulos y razones. Una, porque enseñan la oración que llaman de *unión*, que dicen no es bien enseñarla, y no dicen por qué. Otra, porque tienen algunas cosas oscuras, para ser entendidas generalmente de todos. La tercera, porque la santa Madre Teresa cuenta en ellos muchas revelaciones que tuvo."

15. Llamas identifies him as the Orellana to whom Teresa refers in her letter at the end of September 1574 to María Bautista. See Teresa's *Obras completas*, p. 1335.

16. "A la Madre Teresa de Jesús yo la tuve por mujer cristiana y religiosa, y amiga de acertar; porque sé que buscó veces para comunicar su conciencia religiosos tan doctos y tan buenos, que pudo seguramente seguir su parecer": Llamas, p. 354. Orellana's more extensive *memorial* dated August 24, 1593, is ibid., pp. 470–85.

17. Ibid., p. 359. Antonio de Quevedo's original appraisal of Teresa's works is in AHN, Inq., leg. 2072, no. 43. Llamas transcribes Quevedo's comments on pp. 435–44.

18. See AHN, Inq., leg. 2072, no. 43. The piece is transcribed in Llamas, pp. 444–69.

nied Teresa's ability to instruct others and rejected her claims to divine revelation. They considered it inappropriate for a woman to teach in any case, but her claim that God had called her to write, and in some instances had actually given her the words to use, was dangerous and subversive.

Teresa's critics noted first that her works were written in the vernacular, and thus were addressed particularly to women.[19] Many of her critics and even some of her defenders were concerned about this issue. Juan de Orellana believed that the circulation of Teresa's works "provided an opportunity for many people, especially women, to be tricked by the devil disguised as an angel of light."[20] The danger lay in the many *alumbrados*. These were times, he explained, like those Paul described, in which people "turn from the truth they have heard to [their own] fantasies."[21] Thus, although Orellana did not think Teresa was intentionally trying to deceive others, her works had to be prohibited or they would lead many people astray.[22] Indeed, Orellana was so concerned about the popularity of Teresa's cult that he advocated exhuming her body to show that it had decomposed. He realized that the faithful would be scandalized, but he thought the step was necessary to discredit Teresa and prevent the circulation of heretical doctrine.[23]

Other assumptions about women emerged during the posthumous inquiry. Alonso de la Fuente, for instance, denied women's capacity to have legitimate mystical experiences and to write about them. In a letter to the Consejo that accompanied his first *memorial* Alonso expressed his doubts that Teresa—or any other woman, for that matter—could have written the *Vida*; it would be "*preter naturam* and something taught by an angel, because it exceeds the capacity of a woman." Since the books contained false doctrine, however, Teresa must have been taught "by the evil angel, the one who misled Mohammed and Luther and all the other heresiarchs."[24] Alonso also found unacceptable the idea that clerics—Dominicans in particular—

19. Llamas, p. 396.

20. Ibid., p. 355: "Demás desto, es ocasionada esta doctrina para que a muchos, señaladamente mujeres, los engañe el diablo transfigurado en ángel de luz."

21. Ibid., p. 480: "Porque estamos en el tiempo de que dixo san Pablo: 'a veritate quidem auditum avertent [sic] ad fabulas autem convertentur.'" Cf. 2 Tim. 4:3–4: "The time is sure to come when, far from being content with sound teaching, people will be avid for the latest novelty and collect themselves a whole series of teachers according to their own tastes; and then, instead of listening to the truth, they will turn to myths" (Jerusalem Bible).

22. Llamas, p. 482: "Como yo creo que le acontecía a la Madre Teresa que, sin ninguna duda, la tengo por engañada del diablo, mas no fue de intención y de propósito engañadora. Mas, si ahora no se vedan sus obras y libros serlo an [sic] los libros, aunque no a su cuenta."

23. See ibid., pp. 483–84. Apparently Orellana was not yet aware that Teresa's body had been discovered intact in 1591.

24. Ibid., pp. 396–97: ". . . es negocio *preter naturam* y cosa enseñada por ángel, porque excede la capacidad de muger. Mas, no fue posible ser ángel bueno, sino ángel malo y el mesmo que engañó a Mahoma y Lutero y a los demás heresiarcas."

made spiritual progress when they followed Teresa's suggestions or counsel. This reversal of the natural order "is a strong argument for the unprecedentedness of this doctrine, in which a woman was wise and the educated men who were her followers had little sense; because according to the ancient doctrine of the Church, these wise and educated men know more than any woman."[25]

The idea that Teresa was disrupting the natural order by teaching men was very troublesome for many critics. To Juan de Orellana it was the height of audacity for Teresa, a woman who "certainly grants little to [theological] education,"[26] to have taught the learned theologians who ordered her to write the story of her life. With some sarcasm he noted: "It is very clear that she teaches the well-educated from her greater experience, though they too are experienced." What offended Orellana most was the fact that Teresa "takes the judging of this doctrine away from the ecclesiastical judges, the Holy Office, and its examiners, and bestows it only on those who engage in this perverse [way of] prayer." Such a reversal of authority was "the origin of so many heresies in our times."[27]

Juan de Lorenzana echoed this complaint when he argued that certain issues in Christian theology were reserved for those people who had been named "doctors" by the church. Further, he found unacceptable the idea that Teresa could teach theology to men. Lorenzana noted that Teresa alternately called the confessor to whom the *Vida* was addressed "father" and "son." For a woman to call her confessor "son" was a sign of "arrogance and immodesty and incivility and lack of humility."[28]

Teresa's critics gave several reasons for disputing her authority. First, they understood the teaching office to be denied to women scripturally. Both

25. Ibid., p. 402: "Es argumento de la novedad desta doctrina, en que esta muger era savia, y del poco seso de los hombres doctos que se le subiectaron; porque en la doctrina antigua de la Iglesia más savían estos hombres doctos y graduados, que no una muger."

26. Ibid., p. 472: "Bien poco concede a las letras por cierto." On p. 473, Orellana refers to *Vida* 13:16: "Así que importa mucho ser el maestro avisado—digo de buen entendimiento—y que tenga experiencia; si con esto tiene letras, es grandísimo negocio; mas, si no se pueden hallar estas tres cosas juntas, las dos primeras importan más." See also *Vida* 34:15.

27. Ibid., p. 473: "Bien claro se vee [sic] que enseña ya ella por la mayor experiencia a los grandes letrados, que tienen también experiencia"; p. 475: ". . . quita el juzgar desta doctrina a los jueces eclesiásticos, al santo Oficio, y a sus calificadores, y le remite a solos los que tienen esta perversa oración. . . . Lo qual es principio de quantas heregias hay en nuestros tiempos."

28. Ibid., p. 459: "Mal me parece que . . . llama a su confesor hijo y otras veces padre, porque dice que él se lo pidió que lo hiciese ansí; no lo hubiera de aceotar, porque es arrogancia y poca modestia y inhurbanidad y poca humildad llamar hijo a su confesor." For Teresa's use of "son" and "father," see *Vida* 16:6. According to Llamas, Teresa changed this form of address in the manuscript, but when Luis de León was preparing the first printed edition of the *Vida*, he retained her original wording. See Teresa's *Obras completas*, p. 98, n. 7.

Alonso and Juan de Lorenzana cited 1 Timothy 2:11–12, traditionally understood as Paul's prohibition of teaching for women. Juan de Lorenzana commented: "Teresa of Jesus would do well to take St. Paul's advice."[29] They believed that both the natural limitations on her ability to reason (which she shared with all other women) and her lack of education hindered her comprehension. Though Lorenzana did not dispute that Teresa was "sharp and had a good understanding," he claimed that she meddled in things that were beyond her, so that sometimes she "didn't understand what she was saying."[30]

In effect, the critics were arguing that as soon as Teresa entered the public realm of theological discourse, she overstepped the proper boundaries of the female role. As far as Lorenzana was concerned, Teresa should have stuck with her work as a founder of convents, for that activity had produced "very good results."[31]

For the critics, Teresa's errors were further proof that she had no "instrumental" authority as the recipient of divine revelation. "Contrary to what she claims . . . ," Lorenzana argued, "she never received advice from God, much less a command or divine inspiration from God, because . . . all [her books] are full of falsehoods and bad doctrines."[32] Teresa's strategies did not overcome the critics' prejudices against women's religious experience. Although Juan de Lorenzana granted that some of Teresa's prophecies were divinely inspired, he doubted the genuineness of others and reprehended her for trying to legitimize them by claiming divine inspiration. Lorenzana had known Teresa personally and had believed her to err on a theological question even though she said she had received a vision about it, so he was not impressed by her written justifications either.

> Once when I was with her at the foundation in Valladolid, talking about prayer, especially the soul's rapture and ecstasy, she told me something that I took to be false by the rules of theology and philosophy and not true by experience; and I contradicted her and gave her the reason, according to what I understood of

29. Llamas, p. 452: "Y fuera bueno que Teresa de Jesús tomara este consejo de san Pablo."

30. Ibid., p. 447: "Otras cosas se contienen en estos libros de Teresa de Jesús, que salieron de su propio ingenio, que aunque era aguda y de buen entendimiento, metióse en muchas cosas sin entenderlas, ni saber lo que decía, atropellando las doctrinas buenas y recebidas en la theología y en las demás ciencias, destruyendo cosas certíssimas; . . . y veces ay que ella no entendía lo que decía."

31. See ibid., p. 445: ". . . anse visto muy buenos efectos desta fundación, por la gran observancia y devoción de los religiosos y religiosas della, a los quales soy muy aficionado."

32. Ibid., p. 448: "Aunque ella más diga lo contrario . . . nunca ubo consejo de Dios y menos mandamiento ni instincto de Dios porque . . . están todos llenos de falsedades y malas doctrinas."

Saint Thomas's doctrine. And she smiled and said, "Indeed, it seems you understand something about prayer."[33]

Lorenzana struggled with the idea of visions and questioned Teresa's, arguing that if the doctrine received in the vision was questionable, then the vision could not be divinely inspired.[34] Further, he rejected Teresa's assurances that the soul could not be fooled by the devil, and did not agree that "true corroboration is the testimony of a good conscience."[35] Alonso de la Fuente concurred that no one could trust visions or revelations.[36]

Echoing Alonso and Lorenzana, Juan de Orellana argued that if revelations were divinely inspired, then their entire content must be true and certain; but he believed much of Teresa's mystical doctrine to be erroneous, and he distinguished between "erroneous doctrine that goes against the faith" and "statements that are false but not in themselves against the faith."

> Of those that are errors in faith, it is obvious that they acquire very grave importance, not to mention that God [supposedly] teaches such errors. For if it is a heretical evil to teach heresies invented out of one's own head, or inferred from the Sacred Scripture through one's own thought and reasoning, which is the common way of introducing erroneous doctrine, how much more so and more demoniacal and pernicious to make God Himself, through private revelations, the teacher and author of perverse dogmas. . . . Of the concepts and propositions that are not relevant to the [body of orthodox] belief, but are lies or falsehoods—though of no importance—from the premise that God declared them it follows that God lies (which is a heretical proposition), or says things that are not true.[37]

33. Ibid., "Estando con ella en la fundación de Valladolid, tratando conmigo cosas de la oración, particularmente de los raptos y arrobos del alma, dixome cierta cosa que yo la tube por falsa por reglas de theología y filosofía y no cierto por experiencia; y yo se la contradixe y le di la razón dello, según lo que sabía de la doctrine de santo Thomás. Y ella se sonrió y dixo: en verdad que parece que entiende algo de oración."

34. Thus, for example, Teresa's doctrine on the role of the faculties of the soul in union. Lorenzana was especially incensed by this doctrine because Teresa claimed it was given to her after she had received communion. See ibid., p. 459.

35. Lorenzana (ibid.) included a long passage of Teresa's *Relación* 64, including the section translated here: "La verdadera seguridad es el testimonio de la buena conciencia." Teresa expressed this idea also in *Fundaciones*, Prologue:3 and 4:2.

36. Alonso (ibid., p. 411) cited *Moradas* 5:1.9: "En ninguna manera pueda dudar que estuvo en Dios, y Dios en ella."

37. Ibid., pp. 470–71: "Es principio necesario lo dicho en este número para poder calificar mejor las cosas y proposiciones destos libros, tanto las que son doctrina errónea contra la fee quanto las que son falsas, mas no son en sí contra la fee. De las que son errores en la fee es manifiesto que se las añade una calidad gravíssima, por no decir que Dios enseña tales errores. Porque si es maldad herética enseñar heregías inventándolas de la propia cabeza, o infiriéndolas de la Sagrada Escritura por ingenio y discurso propio, que es el común modo de introducir doctrina errónea, quanto mayor y más endemoniada y perniciosa será hacer al mismo Dios por sí y por particulares revelaciones maestro y autor de perversos dogmas. . . . De las cosas y

Orellana concluded that the identification and correction of such attempts to legitimize false statements by the claim that they were spoken on God's authority, even when the content of the overall message was not heretical, was the direct responsibility of the Inquisition.[38]

The Prayerful Soul: Active or Passive?

After discrediting Teresa's authority to teach, the critics examined specific doctrines and explained why they found them unorthodox. The major criticisms focused on Teresa's description of rapture and mystical union. The critics had already expressed little sympathy for mystical theology in general, associating it with *alumbradismo*, so it is no surprise to see them read Teresa out of context and distort her teachings on prayer and union.

One element in Teresa's doctrine was particularly troublesome: her understanding of the activity of the soul engaged in mental prayer. Alonso de la Fuente associated her descriptions of prayer with the passivity of the *alumbrados* and their practice of *dexamiento*. To Teresa, Alonso explained, prayer was a "supernatural impulse . . . that comes from the center or mind of the soul . . . which only God produces and the person receives, being merely passive in the process."[39] According to Alonso, prayer must involve cooperation between the soul and God.[40] Citing specifically the descriptions of the third and fourth degrees of mental prayer in the *Vida*, Alonso interpreted Teresa to mean that "this prayer of quiet is the work of God alone, in which man must be passive, leaving the faculties half-lost and in a sort of sleep."[41] All the resources of the soul do nothing to help it attain union or understand the knowledge acquired in union: "God makes the soul ignorant so that true wisdom can be imprinted in it."[42]

---

proposiciones que no tocan a la fee, pero son mentiras o falsedades—aunque levísimas—con la premisa que Dios las dixo se infiere por buena consequencia que Dios miente (que es proposición herética), o dice falsedad."

38. Ibid., p. 471: "Y ansí, el conocimiento, corrección y juicio de quien oviere escrito, o dicho las tales cosas o proposiciones por reveladas de Dios pertenece derechamente al santo Officio quando en las tales revelaciones no hubiese mala doctrina expresada ni formalmente asserta."

39. Ibid., p. 417: "Oración mental quiere decir un movimiento sobrenatural que sale del centro, o mente del alma . . . que sólo Dios produce, y el hombre lo rescibe, aviéndose en ello mere pasive."

40. Here Alonso contradicts himself. Whereas earlier he criticized Teresa's evaluation of the various levels of prayer, now he refuses to acknowledge these levels, and seizes upon Teresa's description of a particular moment in the life of prayer to characterize the entire process.

41. Llamas, p.407: "Esta oración de quietud es obra de sólo Dios, en que el hombre se a more [sic] passivo, quedando las potencias medio perdidas y en cierto sueño."

42. Alonso (ibid., p. 410) cites *Moradas* 5:1.9: "Ya veía esta alma que la ha hecho Dios boba del todo para imprimir mejor en ella la verdadera sabiduría —que ni ve, ni oye, ni entiende en el tiempo que está así. . . ."

Other critics agreed that Teresa made the soul too passive in prayer. According to Juan de Orellana, Teresa taught that

> the soul is completely united with God, and the senses and all the faculties of the soul—understanding, memory, and will—stop functioning; and God of his own accord joins with the soul in its center, the faculties remaining rapt and lost. In this union she says the soul has no freedom, and God instructs it and is its teacher; and the soul sees great visions and revelations that cannot be explained, even an intellectual vision—though not with the eyes of the soul—of the Most Holy Trinity and the three distinct persons.[43]

Juan found Teresa's doctrine "contrary not only to the faith but to right reason, because it is insane to say that a totally inactive soul can be involved in prayer and perfect contemplation, and that it has an intellectual vision of God, and not with the eyes of the soul, and that it is not free on this level [of prayer]."[44]

The same problem arose in regard to the receipt of spiritual gifts in prayer. The major difference between Teresa's doctrine and the church's official teaching, Alonso explained was that when Catholics experience some spiritual feeling while they are praying, they

> receive and enjoy it and suspend their prayer or meditation, piously assuming that it comes from God. Then, when the seizure has passed, they continue their prayer. But that does not mean that if they are carrying out some prescribed task, they must leave it to attend to the spiritual seizure and what it inspires in them when it goes against the prescribed task, because that would be to leave the certain for the dubious.[45]

Alumbrados, on the contrary, prayed for the very purpose of experiencing the spiritual seizure and "attending to whatever it inspires in them, even if it

43. Llamas, p. 355: "El argumento es enseñar varios grados de oración, hasta llegar a uno que llama de total unión y perfecta contemplación, en que el alma está unida con Dios, y los sentidos y potencias del alma todas: entendimiento, memoria, voluntad sin ninguna operación; y Dios, por acción suya se junta con el alma en el centro della, absortas y perdidas las potencias. En esta unión dice que no queda libertad al alma, y que Dios la enseña por sí mismo y es su maestro; y ve el alma grandes visiones y revelaciones, que no se pueden decir, hasta ver con visión intelectual, aunque no con los ojos del alma, la Santísima Trinidad y las tres personas distinctas."

44. Ibid., p. 356: "No sólo esta doctrina es contra la fe, sino también contra la buena razón natural, porque manifiesta insania en decir que estando el alma sin ninguna acción, tiene oración y perfecta contemplación, y que tiene visión intelectual de Dios, y no con los ojos del alma, y que no tiene libertad el alma en aquel grado."

45. Ibid., p. 421: "El cathólico que está rezando, o meditando, cuando siente alguna ternura o devoción, o sentimiento espiritual, recíbelo y goza de aquello y suele suspender la oración o meditación, presumiendo piadosamente que aquello es de Dios. Y pasando aquel movimiento torna a proseguir su oración, mas no se entiende por esto que el que está ocupado en alguna obra de precepto [h]a de dexarla por acudir al movimiento espiritual y lo que allí se le inspira, cuando es contrario al precepto, porque sería dexar lo cierto por lo dudoso."

goes against the precepts of God and against rules of prudence and against reason."[46]

According to these definitions, however, Teresa's doctrine fitted the Catholic norms. Far from blindly following where rapture led, for some time she took her confessors' advice and resisted any sort of rapture.[47] Although she stopped resisting upon the advice of Juan de Avila and others, Teresa never taught that "dubious" experiences of divine inspiration should be preferred to more conventional Catholic devotions. In fact, as Teresa understood prayer, it must never be done in the hope of some spiritual gift.[48]

In response to the accusations about the soul's passivity, Antonio de Quevedo explained that the soul united in God is also absorbed in the action of loving, and thus not entirely passive.[49] Further, Quevedo argued, the soul in union was not completely inactive, only inactive to the external world; inwardly it understood and saw. In the sixth *morada*, Quevedo pointed out, Teresa wrote that the state of union "is not like a fainting spell or convulsion, in which it understands nothing inside or out," which Quevedo took to mean that "the soul was never so awakened to the gifts of God, or with such great light and understanding of His Majesty."[50] And when Teresa wrote that at this level the soul's faculty of understanding "is captivated and does not understand," she meant not that it cannot function but that "it cannot comprehend the magnitude of what is presented to it."[51] Quevedo resolved the problem by distinguishing between absolute freedom and temporal freedom. "She does not deny that the soul is absolutely free, but [says] that it does not comprehend its will and freedom."[52]

---

46. Ibid.: "Mas, el alumbrado pónese a rezar esperando de principal intento aquel movimiento que llama sobrenatural, y como le tiene por de Dios, exclusa dubitatione, todo lo que allí se le inspira lo sigue, aunque sea contra los preceptos de Dios y contra las reglas de prudencia y contra buena razón."

47. See *Vida*, chaps. 23 and 24.

48. See *CV*, chap. 17.

49. Here Quevedo cites *Vida* 19:2: "It seems that—even against its will—the door is closed upon the senses so that [the soul] may delight more in the Lord. Alone with Him, what is there to do but love Him? It neither sees nor hears, except by exerting more effort than it would be worth" ("Parece—aunque no quiso—le cerraron la puerta a todos los sentidos para que más pudiese gozar del Señor. Quédase sola con El, qué ha de hacer sino amarle? Ni ve ni oye, si no fuese a fuerza de brazos; poco hay que le agradecer"). See Llamas, p. 435.

50. See *Moradas* 7:4.3: "No es como a quien toma un desmayo, o paroxismo, que ninguna cosa interior ni exterior entiende." Llamas, p. 435. "Lo que yo entiendo en este caso es que el alma nunca estubo tan despierta para las cosas de Dios, ni con tan gran luz ni conocimiento de su Magestad."

51. Llamas, p. 436: "De manera que dice que el entendimiento en aquel punto está absorto y no entiende, no porque no entienda, sino porque no comprehende la grandeza de lo que se le representa."

52. Ibid., p. 437: "No niega que no sea libre el alma absolutamente, sino que no está en su voluntad y libertad."

Teresa's teachings on rapture also raised questions. Alonso de la Fuente, building on his understanding of how passive the soul was in union, interpreted Teresa to mean that in prayer the soul suffered and almost died to the world.[53] "The author claims that the effects of God and the divine presence are the destruction of nature and of natural light, the death of human faculties and actions, and clearly makes God the murderer of those who wish to serve Him."[54] He was probably referring to Teresa's doctrine of rapture in chapter 20 of the *Vida*: "When it's in rapture, the body remains as if dead, often without being able to do anything by itself, and it stays as it was when [the rapture] seized it: whether seated, or with the hands open or closed."[55] She said clearly, though, that in rapture the soul's faculties "slept" rather than died.[56] The other objects of Alonso's wrath are more difficult to locate. Nowhere, for instance, does Teresa say that the divine presence destroys nature or natural light. The only possible parallel is the metaphor of the caterpillar that must "die" to become a butterfly.[57] Here, however, Teresa describes a natural process of metamorphosis rather than death.

Her defenders drew parallels between her teachings and those of earlier mystical theologians. The author of the "Defense of the Doctrine and Books of Mother Teresa de Jesús," for instance, compared Teresa's teachings on rapture to those of Aquinas and to Job 4:15 and Daniel 10:8–9.[58] Antonio de Quevedo pointed out that both Peter and Paul talked about their own experiences of rapture, and that according to Catholic tradition, Mary Magdalene had extraordinary experiences of God in the desert. Quevedo also noted that Teresa's experience of rapture paralleled Thomas Aquinas's description of it.[59]

Mystical Union

For Alonso de la Fuente, the problems with Teresa's mystical doctrine were rooted in her presumption "that the end and fulfillment of the Christian life

53. See *Vida* 16:1: "No me parece que es otra cosa sino un morir casi del todo a las cosas del mundo, y estar gozando de Dios."

54. Llamas, p. 409: "El autor pone de ley común por efectos de Dios y de su presencia la destrucción de la naturaleza y de la lumbre natural, la muerte de las potencias del onbre y de sus actos, y claramente hace a Dios omicida de los que le desean servir." Antonio de Quevedo countered that God is no more a murderer in this case than in that of a person who dies suddenly (ibid., p. 440).

55. *Vida* 20:18: "Pues cuando está en el arrobamiento, el cuerpo queda como muerto, sin poder nada de sí muchas veces, y como le toma se queda siempre: si sentado, si las manos abiertas, si cerradas."

56. See *Vida* 16:1.

57. See *Moradas* 5:2.6 and 3.5.

58. See Llamas, p. 428.

59. Ibid., p. 441. Quevedo cites Thomas Aquinas, *Summa theologiae*, IIa IIae, q. 175, "On Rapture."

is the union of the soul with God."[60] According to Alonso, Teresa's definition of this union was problematic in several ways: (1) it assumed a sensible experience of God in this life; (2) it argued that the soul had a *fondo*, or essential part, where God was more present than in other parts; (3) it implied a process of divinization in this life; (4) it associated the justification of the soul with this union; and, finally, (5) it attributed to the soul a state of sinlessness while it was involved in this union.

A sensible experience of God, Alonso objected, was impossible in this life. He accused Teresa of teaching that

> one of the effects of that union is that the soul feels the presence of God within itself, just as all the *alumbrados* who arrive at that state of contemplation claim to feel it; they say the very God who dwells and is present in the center of their souls manifests and reveals Himself to them, and lets them perceive Him. This doctrine implies the sensible experience of the presence of God, or important supernatural effects on the justification of man. It is a heretical doctrine . . . and goes expressly against the Scriptures, Job 9: "si venerit ad me non videbo eum," and against Paul, 1 Corinthians 4: "nihil mihi conscius est."[61]

But Job and Paul do not prove Alonso's point. Job 9:11 involves a contrast between God and humanity, beginning with the question "How can a person be just before God?" (Job 9:2). After describing God's majesty, Job concludes that it is so difficult for a human being to appreciate the "author of such great works" that "if He passes before me, I do not see Him." The passage from Paul's first epistle to the Corinthians seems at first to support Alonso's point that human consciousness of God is limited or even impossible; but Alonso has misquoted it. 1 Corinthians 4:4 reads "Nihil enim mihi conscius sum." Alonso's translation makes God the speaker when in actuality the speaker is Paul, who declares that the faithfulness of Christ's ministers is judged only by God, "for I know nothing by myself." Alonso clearly felt no compunction about misrepresenting Scripture to build his case against Teresa.

Teresa's teaching that the soul experienced a vision of the Trinity and received infused knowledge was also problematic. In his analysis of this vi-

---

60. Ibid., p. 403: "Presupone esta doctrina que el fin y perfección de la vida cristiana es unirse el alma con Dios."

61. Ibid., p. 404: "Enseña uno de los efectos de aquella unión declarada, que es sentir el alma la presencia de Dios en sí, como la sienten de ley común todos los alumbrados que llegan [a] aquel estado de contemplación; los quales dicen que el mesmo Dios que está dentro de sus almas en aquel fondón por esencia y presencia se les manifiesta y descubre, y se les da a sentir. La cual doctrina pone de ley común sensible experimento de la presencia del mesmo Dios, o effectos serios sobrenaturales en la justificación del hombre. Y es doctrina herética . . . y es expresamente contra la Escritura, Job 9: 'si venerit ad me non videbo eum,' et contra Paulum, 1 Corinthios, 4: 'nihil mihi conscius est'."

sion, Juan de Orellana distinguished between visionary experience and that of Paul in Acts 9:8.

> She does seem to speak of the same kind of vision as Saint Paul, saying, "He joins her with himself, making her blind and mute, as Saint Paul was at the moment of his conversion. . . ." But she is not speaking of the same kind of vision, which, as the same Master says, is passing; the vision the Mother had. . . was . . . permanent and stable.[62]

In Teresa's description of the intellectual vision of the Trinity she claimed that the soul "carries about this presence," "feels within itself this divine company," and understands the mystery of the Triune being.[63] For Orellana, this was arrogance, for "some theologians deny that [even] Christ our Lord had . . . clear knowledge of the Most Holy Trinity. . . . [Yet] this little woman is given to understand not only the "what" but the "how" so clearly that it's astonishing."[64] This sort of vision is impossible in this life, Orellana claims, and he accuses Teresa of the same errors as the groups that appear in other *memoriales*: the Messalians, the Euchytes, and the Beghards.[65]

The second major objection, the locus of mystical union, revolved around the schema of the *Moradas*. Alonso de la Fuente objected to Teresa's understanding of God's presence in the center of the soul: "Insofar as she means that in that core or place God is more especially present than in any other place by presence and power, it's fiction and false, because by the same token God is present in the foot and in the hand and in a tree in essence, presence, and power."[66] Further, when Teresa describes the soul as like a diamond castle, made in the image of God, and so exalted that "it's difficult to understand its great dignity and beauty," she noted with disappointment that some souls do not appreciate this gift of God and make no attempt to enter into themselves and come to know themselves and God better.[67] To

---

62. Ibid., p. 478: "Aunque parece que sí habla [de la manera de visión que se dice tuvo san Pablo], dice: El la junta con sigo, mas haciéndola ciega y muda como lo quedó san Pablo en su conversión. . . . Pero, no habla de esta manera de visión que, como dice el mismo Maestro, es de passo y la Madre . . . tubo . . . permanente y estaria." See Teresa's description in *Moradas* 7:1.5.

63. See *Moradas* 7:1.6–9.

64. Llamas, p. 477: "Algunos teólogos niegan que Cristo nuestro Señor tuviese por la sciencia indita o infusa noticia clara de la Santísima Trinidad. . . . A esta mugercita el qué u el cómo se le da a entender tan claro que se espanta."

65. See ibid., p. 479.

66. Ibid., p. 405: "En quanto quiere significar, que en aquel fondo, o lugar está Dios más particularmente que en otro lugar alguno por presencia y potencia, es fábula y mentira, porque de la mesma manera existe en el pie y en la mano y en el árbol por esencia, presencia y potencia." For Teresa's view on the composition of the soul and the presence of God in it, see the schematic description of the interior castle in *Moradas* 1:2.14.

Alonso, Teresa's lament was ridiculous, because the soul had no such core to enter.[68]

The anonymous author of the "Defense" likened Teresa's encouragement to souls to enter into themselves to a passage in Augustine's *Confessions* (4:12): "He is right inside the heart, but the heart has wandered away from Him. Return, sinners, to your own heart and cling to Him who made you."[69] Antonio de Quevedo also defended the "center" of the soul as the locus for union with God: this idea was not false "but true, and something that is proper to God."[70]

Alonso's disbelief in the union of the soul and God in the center of the soul led him to question the mode of this union. According to Alonso, Teresa said that union occurred

> when the soul naturally, not by the instrumentality of any sort of image or accident or operation on the part of the creature, is joined to the real presence of God which is in the center and depth of the soul, which is its pure essence and spirit . . . and [God] reveals Himself and communicates with the soul and makes it feel His presence, and finally reveals in this life the splendors of His kingdom and His divine essence.[71]

Thus, according to Alonso, Teresa's mystical doctrine taught a union of "presence" with a new understanding of God's "essence." In this union

> the soul is given by grace all that God has by nature, with no condition except that the person remains [physically] a creature, and in all other things is made God; because there it enjoys God's vision and blessedness and in God sees all things and enjoys all the rest of God's privileges, even knowing the secrets of [others'] hearts.[72]

---

67. *Moradas* 1:1.1: "Basta decir su Majestad que es hecha a su imagen para que apenas podamos entender la gran dignidad y hermosura del ánima."

68. Llamas, p. 405: "Reprehende tontamente a los que no se entran en aquel fondón, la qual reprehensión es tonta, disparatada y necia, porque no [h]ay tal fondón en el alma."

69. Ibid., p. 432.

70. Ibid., p. 437: "No es, bien mirado, falso; sino verdad y cosa que pertenece a Dios propiamente."

71. Ibid., p. 403: "Y esto [unirse con Dios] se entiende quando el alma esencialmente y sin medio alguno de imagen, o de accidente, ni operación de parte de la criatura, se junta con la real presencia de Dios que está en el centro y fondón del alma, que es la esencia pura y espíritu puro della . . . y se descubre y comunica al alma y la da a sentir su presencia, y finalmente la descubre en esta vida las riqueças de su reino y su divina esencia."

72. Ibid., p. 412: "Se le da al alma por gracia todo lo que Dios tiene por naturaleza, sin acepción [excepción] alguna mas de que el hombre se queda criatura, quedándose en todo lo demás hecho Dios; porque allí goza de su bisión y su bienaventuranza y allí en el mismo Dios bee todas las cosas y allí goza de todos los demás privilegios, que son propios de Dios, hasta conocer los secretos de los corazones."

This union transforms the soul in such a way that it "is made God and knows as God knows, so that from then on, everything that man does is the work of God, and everything he does, whether they call it good, bad, or absurd, is transformed in God."[73] Alonso's exaggerated interpretation went directly against Teresa's own admonitions that the soul was still in control of its ability to do good or evil.

When Alonso said that the soul's access to infused knowledge in union made it "think like God," he was attributing full divinization to what to Teresa was a moment of insight. Teresa's point was that union with God gave the soul access to a kind of knowledge that it ordinarily would not have. The soul could not control its access to that knowledge, it might not even understand and appreciate it fully, and its way of knowing was not transformed into God's way.

Although Alonso's criticisms may seem opaque, his direction emerges clearly: her orientation to mystical union, unmediated by the institutional church, left little room for the sacramental life or good works. Teresa's understanding of the mystical life, Alonso argued, led her to associate all facets of the Christian life with union, so that this union subsumed "all the good and the purpose of the creature—justification, grace, Christian perfection and good works, mortification and penitence, prayer and contemplation, and the perfect state."[74] If justification and union were so tightly intertwined, then the pathway toward union must resemble the process of justification. Alonso likened Teresa's claim that the "senses harm rather than help the soul in this state of prayer" to Luther's doctrine that "the works of the Christian not only were irrevelant for achieving grace but even bad and offensive and sins."[75] Echoing earlier criticisms of the soul's passivity, Alonso claimed that Teresa encouraged readers to "wait for God to imprint

73. Ibid., p. 416: "El alma que allí llega queda hecha Dios y sabe a naturaleza de Dios, tanto que de allí adelante, todo lo que obra el hombre es obra de solo Dios, y todo lo que hace bueno y malo y absurdo dicen se le convierte en Dios."

74. Ibid., p. 403: "Y en esta unión se incluye todo el bien y aprovechamiento de la criatura, conviene a saver: la justificación, la gracia, la perfección christiana y el bien obrar, la mortificación y penitencia, la oración y contemplación y el estado perfecto." Alonso's understanding of the sensory aspect of Teresa's mystical experience led him to equate the soul's justification with this "sensible presence of God," something Teresa did not assert. See ibid., p. 408: "Va siguiendo en ella [esta doctrina] el autor la heregía calificada en el artículo 7, en el qual puso presencia sensible de Dios en los justificados y aquí pone los grados del aprovechamiento espiritual sensibles, señalando media unión y media mortificación y media perfección, conocida por el medio sueño, y media modorra, y media perdición de las potencias."

75. Ibid., p. 409: "Echa los fundamentos de las heregías y blasfemias de Lutero, en que dixo que las obras del cristiano no solamente eran impertinentes para conseguir la gracia, mas eran malas y nocivas y pecados." See *Vida* 18:10: "Así que de los sentidos no se aprovecha nada si no es para no la acabar de dejar a su placer, y así antes la dañan."

true wisdom in them," and allowed the action of God to "replace human works and cooperation by [the process of] justification and spiritual advancement."[76]

Alonso based his equation of mental prayer and justification on the idea that Teresa understood the life of prayer to be one of continuous movement: thus if one did not move forward, one moved backward. Alonso concluded that in not progressing in the way of prayer—or, worse still, in rejecting mental prayer—the soul rejected the possibility of salvation:

> In the *Moradas* . . . she says in effect: that souls without prayer are like crippled bodies, and that if they do not change, they will be turned into pillars of salt; that is, the soul that does not practice this supernatural prayer has no vital movement, and if it does not change and give itself to prayer, it must condemn itself, which is a concept . . . common to all *alumbrados*.[77]

Juan de Lorenzana agreed that Teresa equated union with salvation and taught Lutheran doctrines, because the soul was passive in union and must also be passive in its justification. Lorenzana first claimed that Teresa taught the necessity of prayer.[78] Second, he argued that Teresa equated merit with prayer and for that reason taught that souls in union with God could be certain of their salvation. Citing the *Camino de perfección*, Lorenzana wrote:

> She says [the soul] "feels great delight in the body and great satisfaction in the soul; that it's happy just to find itself near the fountain [of life], that even without drinking, that's enough; it seems there is nothing left to want before moving forward." Here Teresa speaks of those who have this [kind of] prayer as though they were already blessed. . . .[79]

76. Ibid., p. 411: "Ni oye, ni bee, ni siente; y entonces está dispierta para imprimir Dios en ella su sabiduría. . . . Es quitar la obra y concurso del hombre para su justificación y aprovechamiento espiritual."

77. Ibid., p. 418: "En las *Moradas* . . . dice en sustancia: que las almas sin oración son como unos cuerpos tullidos y que si no se enmiendan se quedarán hechos estatuas de sal, que es decir: el alma que no se exercita en esta oración sobrenatural no tiene movimiento de vida y si no se enmienda, dándose a esta oración, condenarse [h]a, que es concepto . . . que tienen todos los alumbrados." Alonso refers to *Moradas* 1:1.6: "Decíame, poco ha, un gran letrado que son las almas que no tienen oración como un cuerpo con perlesía o tullido que, aunque tiene pies y manos, no los puede mandar, que así son: que hay almas tan enfermas y mostradas a estarse en cosas exteriores que no hay remedio ni parece que pueden entrar dentro de sí, porque ya la costumbre la tiene tal de haber siempre tratado con las sabandijas y bestias que están en el cerco del castillo que ya casi está hecha como ellas; y con ser de natural tan rica y poder tener su conversación con Dios, no hay remedio. Y, si estas almas no procuran entender y remediar su gran miseria, quedarse han hechas estatuas de sal por no volver la cabeza hacia sí, así como lo quedó la mujer de Lot por volverla."

78. Ibid., p. 455: "Y que Teresa de Jesús ponga mérito y agrado a Dios destos amores de la voluntad en la unión siendo necesarios, según ella, en el último punto declararé." Unfortunately, Lorenzana does not return to this subject.

79. Ibid., p. 463: "Dice: 'siente grandíssimo deleite en el cuerpo y gran satisfacción en el alma; está contenta de sólo verse cabe la fuente, que aún sin beber está ya harta; no le parece ay

If the will of the soul in union was a "captive of God," the soul could do nothing to contribute to its own salvation.[80] Though Lorenzana did not cite a particular text, he was almost certainly referring to *Vida* 14:2: "The will is possessed, so that without understanding how, it is held captive. It only gives its consent so that God may imprison it, like someone who knows well what it is to be captive to the one he loves."[81] Here, however, the soul actively relinquishes its will to be held captive, even though, Teresa grants, it may not be quite sure what is in store for it once it gives up its will.

Teresa seems to have been less concerned with the process of justification than with providing a model for sanctification. Her *camino de perfección* was a way to "procure sanctity," in imitation of the great desert hermits who inspired the original Carmelite rule.[82] Indeed, Teresa clearly dissociated salvation from the life of prayer: "It is not necessary for salvation to be a contemplative."[83] Her critics' objections, however, call into question the clarity of her teachings. On the subject of salvation and mystical experience Teresa expressed various opinions. She said, for instance, that if those who entered the third *morada* did not turn back, they were "on a sure path to salvation"; yet she ultimately denied any security in the matter of salvation: "I seem to mean that once the soul has received this mercy from God, it's sure of its salvation. . . . I say no such thing."[84] Such contradictions provided Teresa's critics with ready ammunition.

Even more dangerous than the notion of the security of salvation, Alonso argued, was Teresa's claim in the fifth *morada* that once the soul had achieved union with God in mental prayer, the devil could do it no harm. To suggest that a living soul could ever be sinless or immune to sin, Alonso

---

más que desear antes de pasar adelante.['] Habla aquí Teresa de los que tienen esta oración, como de bienaventurados ya. . . ." See *CV* 31:3.

80. Llamas, p. 463: "La voluntad es aquí la cuativa [sic]—ecce necessitas boluntatis [sic] . . ." Here Lorenzana fails to explain completely the significance of the captivity of the will.

81. "La voluntad se ocupa, de manera que—sin saber cómo—se cautiva; sólo da consentimiento para que la encarcele Dios, como quien bien sabe ser cautivo de quien ama." Nowhere else does Teresa speak of the will as "captive"; elsewhere the captive is the body or the entire soul. See, e.g., *Vida* 8:11, 16:8, 21:6.

82. See *CV* 41:8 ("No dejéis arrinconar vuestra alma, que en lugar de procurar santidad, sacará muchas imperfecciones") and 11:4.

83. *CV* 17:2: "No porque en esta casa todas traten de oración, han de ser todas contemplativas. Es imposible . . . y pues no es necesario para la salvación ni nos lo pide de premio. . . ."

84. *Moradas* 3:1.1: "Pues si no torna atrás, a lo que podemos entender, lleva camino seguro de su salvación"; 7:2.9: "Parece que quiero decir que, llegando el alma a hacerla Dios esta merced, está segura de su salvación . . . no digo tal."

charged, was to commit heretical error; those were the very errors of Johannes Tauler and of the Beghards condemned by Clement V in 1312.[85]

Although Alonso attributed to Teresa the belief that the soul in union could not sin, we have seen that Teresa flatly denied sinlessness to the soul in the seventh *morada*. If Teresa implied that in moments of union the soul did not sin, she did not claim that the soul was sinless by nature, that its particular relation to God at the moment of union made it so: the power of God at the moment of the soul's rapture was too strong to allow any external force to interfere with His communication with the soul.

Juan de Lorenzana argued that Teresa learned much of her doctrine of mystical union from the works of her contemporary Louis de Blois.[86] Her discussion of the vision of the Trinity in the seventh *morada* and her teachings on the passivity of the soul in union, he charged, were copied from Blois. According to Lorenzana, both Teresa and Blois taught that in the prayer of union, "the soul ceases to function, so that the soul prays and loves and sometimes understands without the soul's functioning."[87] Lorenzana's statement of the doctrine he criticized is somewhat obscure, but his point was that the soul in loving and understanding is working, so it must be in possession of its faculties. The idea that the faculties were totally absorbed in God, he claimed, had been condemned throughout the history of the church. Thus Lorenzana followed Alonso in identifying Teresa—and Blois—with the Messalians, the Euchytes, the Beghards, and Tauler.[88]

The Mystical Tradition on Trial

In a letter to the Consejo dated August 26, 1589, Alonso defined from the outset what he saw in Teresa's work:

85. See Llamas, p. 412. Alonso had begun a campaign against Tauler's doctrine as early as 1579, and in 1584 the Consejo ordered the Seville tribunal to investigate his accusations. In a letter to Antonio Matos de Noroña dated September 3, 1586, Alonso complained that Tauler's works were still not prohibited in the Quiroga Index of 1583–84. A Castilian edition of Tauler's sermons had been published in Coimbra in 1551. See Huerga, *Historia de los alumbrados*, 1:74–76.

86. Louis de Blois (1506–66) was the abbot of the Benedictine monastery at Liessies. Several of his treatises on spiritual instruction had been translated into Spanish, perhaps before the index of 1559. Lorenzana laments the fact that Blois's works were available in the vernacular, because they spread false doctrine among female readers. Indeed, he asked the tribunal to prohibit Teresa's works and to expurgate those of Blois and Francisco de Ribera's *Vida de la madre Teresa de Jesús*, which praised Blois. See Llamas, pp. 446 and 469.

87. Llamas, p. 454: "Dicen que cesa toda la operación del alma, de manera que dicen que ora el alma y ama, y a veces entiende sin operación que aya en el alma."

88. Ibid., p. 454, 460–61. Lorenzana referred to Blois's commentary on Tauler, often included as an appendix to his *Spiritual Instruction*. An English translation is available in Ludovico Blosius, *A Book of Spiritual Instruction*, trans. Bertrand A. Wilberforce (Westminster, Md., 1955), pp. 102–27.

> I find written in it [doctrines of] the Messalian sect, with traces of other sects, especially the ecstatic heretics, *alumbrados* and *dejados*. . . . And with this stratagem the heretics spread their sect without anyone realizing it, and by night the wind blows great harm and danger to souls and to the whole kingdom.[89]

The threat Alonso perceived was a contemporary problem of great importance, for "the doctrine taught here is the same that the *alumbrados* of Extremadura taught and that they teach today in the bishopric of Jaén and many others, for they move freely throughout the kingdom."[90] Alonso was doing all he could to establish guilt by association.

Further, Alonso characterized Teresa's experiences as "novel" and "strange": "We must assume that in all this doctrine—I mean in all the spiritual mysteries that are taught here, which appear new, strange, or admirable, there is nothing more than lies or inventions or error or heresy or sect or demonic fantasy, which requires patience to discover. . . ."[91] Alonso cast a wary eye on Teresa's complaint that very few of her confessors understood her experiences. "When she says that in twenty years she found no one to understand her, it makes me strongly suspect that her spirit was strange and different from the spirit of God. . . . And when she says the wise men don't understand her, it confirms the suspicion of an evil spirit."[92] Alonso's judgment was reinforced by the fact that "servants of God who saw the effects of this spirit close up understood them to be evil, and in fact concluded that the spirit was of the devil and his work."[93] For Alonso, the uniqueness of Teresa's experience was further evidence of heterodoxy.

89. Llamas, p. 396: "Hallo en el scripta la secta masiliana con ramarazos de otras sectas, especialmente de los hereges estáticos, alumbrados y dexados. . . . Y con este ardid van los hereges metiendo su secta sin que nadie los entienda, y el viento corre de noche con grandísimo daño y peligro de las almas y de todo el Reino." The Messalians, a heretical group that arose in the second half of the fourth century in Mesopotamia, engaged in a prayer that supposedly purified the body, ridding it of the devil and preparing it for a union with God that had many physical elements. This prayer, rather than baptism, was what cleansed human beings of sin. For a list of Messalian propositions, see George L. Marriott, "The Messalians and the Discovery of Their Ascetic Book," *Harvard Theological Review* 19 (1926): 193–94.

90. Llamas, pp. 398–99: "Esta doctrina que aquí se enseña es la mesma que enseñavan los alumbrados de Extremadura y enseñan oy los del obispado de Jaén y otros muchos, que andan sueltos por el reino."

91. Ibid., p. 399: "Se ha de presuponer que en toda esta doctrina, digo en todos los misterios espirituales que aquí se enseñan, que parecen nuevos, raros y admirables, no hay en ellos cosa que se escape de mentira, o fábula, o horror, o herejía, o secta, o sueño diabólico, para cuya inteligencia es menester paciencia. . . ."

92. Ibid., p. 400: "En quanto dice que en 20 años no halló quien la entendiese, háceme grave sospecha que su espíritu era peregrino y diferente del espíritu de Dios. . . . Y en quanto dice que los savios no la entienden confirma la sospecha del mal espíritu." See *Vida* 28:14–18.

93. Llamas; p. 400: "Los siervos de Dios que vieron desde cerca los effectos deste espíritu lo tuvieron por malo, y determinase en particular [que] el espíritu fue del demonio y obra

The anonymous "Defense of the Doctrine and Books of Mother Teresa de Jesús" responded to depictions of Teresa's "boasting" and "strangeness" by locating Teresa in a line of mystical orthodoxy: "For these ends [the glory of God and the benefit of others] it is not boasting to mention the mercies God bestowed on her, for Saint Paul did so at great length, and Saint Augustine, and Saint Catherine of Siena."[94]

One of the doctrines that caused Alonso to associate Teresa with the *alumbrados* was the irresistible "impetus" she mentioned in her descriptions of mystical rapture. "This clearly reveals the doings of Satan, which are unjust, violent, uncertain, and full of fear and surprise, and in all things contrary to the effects of the Holy Spirit, whose workings are sweet, subtle, mild, certain, and full of security."[95] The fact that some people made intense spiritual progress in a relatively short time also aroused Alonso's suspicions. In describing some of the early Carmelites, Teresa declared that in a few days they made the same progress in prayer that it had taken her many years to achieve.[96] This rapid advancement was, for Alonso, another sign that "it's the work of an evil spirit and a trick of Satan. . . . And it's like a picture of what's happening in Extremadura, where sanctity . . . is achieved in fifteen days. And one of the *alumbrados*, who was called Juan García, bragged that he had disciples who had reached the height of perfection in three days."[97]

Finally, Alonso objected to Teresa's deprecatory attitude toward vocal prayer, which to him was a clear sign of her *alumbrado* orientation.[98]

---

suya." These "servants of God" were two of Teresa's earliest confessors, Gaspar Daza and Francisco de Salcedo, who had seldom been called upon to judge mystical experiences and eventually encouraged Teresa to confess to the newly installed Jesuits in Avila. See *Vida* 23:14.

94. Llamas, p. 426: "Y por estos fines no es vanidad contar las mercedes que Dios la hizo, pues san Pablo lo hace tan a la larga y san Agustín, y santa Catalina de Sena."

95. Ibid., p. 401: "En este . . . se descubre aviertamente la operación de sathanás, que es dura, violenta, incierta y llena de temor y sobresalto, y en todo contraria a los effectos del Espíritu Santo, cuya operación es dulce, subtil, suave, cierta y llena de seguridad." Teresa's descriptions of the "impetus" (not exactly as Alonso portrays them) are found in, e.g., *Vida* 20:3, 20:19, 21:6, 33:8, 38:1.

96. *Vida* 39:11: "Lo que Su Majestad no acabó conmigo en tanta multitud de años, como ha que comencé a tener oración y me comenzó a hacer mercedes, acaba con ellas en tres meses, y aun con alguna en tres días. . . ." Teresa's point was that spiritual improvement could come at any time God chose.

97. Llamas, p. 402: "En ser tan breve este aprovechamiento espiritual y tan crecido hace sospecha grande que es obra de mal espíritu y prestigio de sathanás. . . . Y es un como retrato de lo de Extremadura donde la santidad . . . se conseguía en 15 días. Y uno de los alumbrados, que se decía Juan García, jactaba diciendo que él tenía discípulos que en tres días avían llegado a la suma de perfección."

98. Ibid., p. 405.

Teresa's ordering of stages in prayer, Alonso argued, implied a hierarchy of value, with different stages representing more "advanced" and thus more important techniques of mental prayer. Alonso observed that vocal prayer did not even figure into the scheme, and that "vocal and mental prayer that consists of petitions and works of the soul, even though it may be very pure, very devout and attentive, is prayer of the first level; that is, imperfect and natural and purely human [i.e., without a divine element]."[99] Alonso found many indications that Teresa was an *alumbrada*, one more in the long line of those whom "Satan has inflated with illusions and dreams that they take to be divine revelations."[100] When his zeal to prove Teresa's *alumbradismo* led him to associate her with the *alumbrados* in Extremadura, however, he undermined his case. Although some of her doctrine was ambiguous, Teresa could easily be differentiated from specific communities of *alumbrados*.

Antonio de Quevedo resisted all such accusations of heresy. As for Teresa's supposed affinity with the Messalians and Euchytes,

> their error was not in saying that God was united with the soul, or in saying that the soul became perfect in prayer, or in saying that with God's help the soul could see the future and many mysteries of the faith; because this is not error. . . . Their error was in saying that prayer alone was sufficient, without baptism, and that it cleansed the soul so that it was left with no evil disturbance in the senses and with no need for fasts or other work of penitence . . . which is as different from what the Mother says as light from darkness.[101]

In this sense, the Messalians made much the same error as the *alumbrados*: they equated mental prayer with justification:

> The *alumbrados* put their whole good, justification, and salvation only in mental prayer, as they call it, excluding every other spiritual work of any kind and the holy exercise of the sacraments and good works, etc. It does not occur to Mother Teresa to teach such a thing, in fact she is constantly arguing the opposite: that [in respect to] those who give themselves up to prayer, the more they yield to it,

99. Ibid., p. 417: "La oración vocal y mental que consiste en peticiones y obras del alma, aunque sea oración muy pura, muy devota y atenta, es oración del primer grado conviene a saver: imperfecta y obra natural y puramente del hombre."

100. Ibid., p. 406: "Se les infunde sathanás en el interior del sentido y los hinche de ilusiones y sueños que ellos tienen por revelaciones divinas."

101. Ibid., pp. 437–38: "Quanto a los mesalianos y euchitas su error no estaba en decir que se juntaba Dios con el alma, ni en decir que se perficcionaba [sic] el alma con la oración, ni en decir que el alma ayudada de Dios via lo porvenir y muchos misterios de la fe; porque esto no es error . . . sino el error de aquéllos estubo en decir que sola la oración bastaba, sin el baptismo, y que ella se limpiaba el alma de manera que quedaba sin ningún mal movimiento en los sentidos y sin ninguna necesidad de ayuno ni de otra obra de penitencia . . . que es tan diferente de lo que la Madre dice, como la luz de las tinieblas."

the more they try sometimes to take on the role of Martha and practice the holy works of the active life—mortification, humility, fasts, honesty.[102]

The other error of the *alumbrados*, according to Quevedo, was the doctrine that one must "follow any spasm of the spirit, even if it involved evil things prohibited by God's law, and that their prayer ended in carnal and perverted desires." Teresa, however, "does not teach that one should follow those spasms, nor does she make much of them, in fact she clearly advises the opposite in many places." Further, the effects of mental prayer that Teresa described were not sensual but spiritual: deep humility, love of God, disdain for wordly things, and a desire to carry the cross of Christ, "which are effects the devil never produced, nor can he."[103]

In sum, Quevedo found "no error" in what Teresa wrote. Though her works treated very difficult themes, they were so well written that they could do no harm to their readers:

> I confess that these books of Mother Teresa's have some obscure things in them, though [if] examined carefully—by those who study the spirit—they are clear, because they understand the language [of the spirit], and to those who do not study prayer or the spirit they will do no harm. In short, they can be useful to many and harmful to none, so there is no reason they shouldn't be read, for there is no book so holy and clear that everyone who reads it understands it; in fact, the best and most useful books are the least understood.[104]

Having justified Teresa's doctrine on specific disputed points and in general, Quevedo felt called upon to justify mysticism as part of the doctrine that the Catholic Church had always followed. His discussion of key texts in

102. Ibid., p. 439: "Los alumbrados todo su bien, justificación y salvación ponían en sola la oración mental, que ellos llamaban, excluiendo toda otra qualquiera espiritual y exercicios sanctos de sacramentos y obras buenas, etc. A la Madre Theresa no le pasa por pensamiento enseñar tal cosa, antes por momentos está persuadiendo lo contrario: que los que se dan a la oración, quanto más se dieren más procuren exercitar a veces officio de Martha y obras sanctas de la vida activa, mortificación, humildad, ayunos, honestidad."

103. Ibid., p. 438: "El error de estos estaba en decir que se abía de seguir qualquier movimiento del espíritu, aunque fuese a cosas feas y vedadas por la ley de Dios, y en que oración paraba en movimientos carnales y torpes. . . . Ni enseña seguir esos movimientos, ni los tiene por ley, antes claramente avisa de lo contrario en muchos lugares. Y los effectos que de su oración quedan no son sensuales, o torpes, sino limpieza, sanctidad, humildad profunda, amor de Dios encendido, menosprecio de el mundo, y desasimiento de todas las cosas, deseo de cruz y de trabajos, que son effectos que nunca los hizo ni puede les hacer el demonio."

104. Ibid., p. 441: "Yo confieso que estos libros de la Madre Theresa tienen algunas cosas algo obscuras, aunque bien mirados—para los que tratan de espíritu—son claras, porque entienden el lenguaje, y a los que no tratan de oración ni de espíritu, no les daña. Y pues pueden ser provechosos a muchos y a nadie dañosos, no hay razón por que no se lean, que no hay libro tan sancto y tan claro que le entiendan todos los que le leen; antes los libros mexores y más útiles son entendidos menos."

the medieval mystical tradition reveals a great many books on mystical theology were circulating in Spain. They were available in Latin, and the theologians whom the Inquisition consulted certainly could have had access to them, yet Quevedo was the only one who actually cited any of them. So that the members of the tribunal could compare Teresa's teachings with texts he considered orthodox, Quevedo quoted Pseudo-Dionysius' *Divine Names*—"The most divine knowledge of God, that which comes through unknowing, is achieved in a union far beyond mind, when mind turns away from all things, even from itself, and when it is made one with the dazzling rays, being then and there enlightened by the inscrutable depth of Wisdom"[105]—and went on to quote Richard of St. Victor, Bernard of Clairvaux, and Jean Gerson's discussion of rapture in *De mystica theologia*. He thus situated Teresa in a long line of theologians who taught the possibility of union with God in this life, and claimed that she had earned herself a place among them because "in her way of speaking and teaching she proceeds with as much assurance as if she had studied a thousand years, and chosen and read all the books that treat this material."[106] Indeed, Quevedo argued, if her works had been written in Latin, "with the same elegance and style that they have in the vernacular, they would be without doubt the most widely read and esteemed that the Church has, outside of the divine and Sacred Scriptures and those of the saints."[107]

Luis de León also situated Teresa within a tradition of Christian mysticism which he felt the need to justify. He referred to Bonaventure, Richard of St. Victor, Jean Gerson, and Francisco de Osuna as exemplary teachers of the doctrine of mystical union, and argued that the difficulty of the doctrine was no reason to censor it. If this were the case, the works of Augustine, Pseudo-Dionysius, Duns Scotus, and many scholastics should also be forbidden.[108] Finally, Luis defended the publicizing of revelations:

> Perchance they will say that although [the revelations] may be good and true, they should not be published and written. If they say this, they are saying something new and unheard of in the church; because, as everyone knows, since its be-

105. Ibid., p. 441: "Sapientia est divinissima Dei cognitio per ignorantiam cognita, unitionem supereminenter quando mens ab omnibus aliis recedens postea etiam seipsam dimittens unita est subsplendentibus radiis inscrutabili et profundo sapientiae illuminata." See Pseudo-Dionysius, *The Complete Works*, trans. Colm Luibheid (New York, 1987), p. 109.

106. Ibid., p. 443: "Y en la decir y enseñar procede con tanto tiento como si mil años hubiera estudiado, y escogido y leído los libros todos que desta materia tratan." Here "la" refers to "la doctrina."

107. Ibid., p. 444: "Si estuviera en lengua latina con la elegancia y stylo que está en la vulgar fuera sin duda de la más rescebidas y estimadas que la Iglesia tiene fuera de la divina y Sagrada Scriptura y de los sanctos."

108. Luis de León, "Apología," in his *Obras completas*, 2:917.

ginning God's revelations to people have always been recorded. In the sacred books there are many; in ecclesiastical histories many more; and in the lives of the saints, no end. . . . There is a very large book on the revelations of Saint Brigid, another on those of Saint Gertrude. The life of Saint Catherine of Siena is full of revelations and miracles never seen before. Just yesterday in Valencia they published the *Life* of Brother Luis Beltrán, full of revelations and prophetic sayings. Why should we have to cover up what is good, what reveals God's marvels, what arouses reverence and love, what encourages all sanctity and virtue?[109]

Luis recognized that some people feared the effects of Teresa's mystical doctrine on the unlettered or inexperienced, that "the desire for similar things [visions, revelations, etc.] may open doors in women, who are credulous, so that the devil may trick them with illusions." But in fact Teresa was trying to do just the opposite, to teach about revelations so that no one would be tricked by them.[110]

Luis de León identified the contemporary need for solid spiritual direction, particularly in the form of dependable mystical treatises, to prevent deception by the devil. For Luis, the positive strategy of the publication of reliable spiritual works was ultimately more effective than the censorship of all books dealing with prayer and contemplation. Further, if the reading of pious books inspired things that could be dangerous to orthodox belief, then

> may the sacred books be obliterated, the ecclesiastical histories burned; let them tear up the *Flos Sanctorum*, the lives of the saints, the *Dialogues* of Saint Gregory, the reports of those who founded and nurtured the Orders. The Church has been mistakened, for until now it has written and wanted people to read what opens the door to the devil.[111]

---

109. Ibid., p. 918: "Mas dirán por ventura que, aunque sean buenas y verdaderas, no se deben publicar y escribir. Si esto dicen, dicen una cosa nueva y nunca oída en la Iglesia; porque, como es notorio, siempre desde el principio de ella se escribieron las revelaciones que hizo Dios a los hombres. En los libros sagrados hay muchas; en las historias eclesiásticas muchas más; en las vidas de los santos, sin número. . . . De las revelaciones de Santa Brígida hay un libro grandísimo; de las de Santa Gertrudis hay otro. La vida de Santa Catalina de Sena está llena de revelaciones y milagros no vistos. Ayer imprimieron en Valencia la *Vida* de Fr. Luis Beltrán, llena de revelaciones y de dichos proféticos. Por qué se ha de encubrir lo que es bueno, lo que hace maravilla de Dios, lo que enciende en su reverencia y amor, lo que pone espuelas para toda santidad y virtud?"

110. Ibid.: "Y más: dicen que el deseo de cosas semejantes abre puertas en las mujeres, que son crédulas, para que el demonio las engañe con ilusiones. El deseo de revelaciones desordenado podrá ser, pero no la lección de revelaciones buenas y verdaderas. Y estos *Libros* ninguna cosa procuran más que quitar deseos semejantes, como por ellos parece."

111. Ibid.: "Bórrense los libros sagrados; quémense las historias eclesiásticas; rómpanse los *Flos Sanctorum*, las vidas de santos, los *Diálogos* de San Gregorio, las relaciones de los que fundaron y multiplicaron las Ordenes. Engañada ha estado la Iglesia, que hasta agora ha escrito y querido que se lea lo que abre puerta al demonio."

"In these things," Luis reminded the censors, "one should look not at the misuse of some but at the common good" produced by mystical books.[112]

> Finally, they say they don't believe them. So what if they don't believe them? For that they have to be prohibited to others? It's intolerable presumption to make themselves lords of judgment for everyone. They don't believe them. Because they don't experience it themselves, they don't want it to be possible for others?[113]

It was her critics, not Teresa herself, who in fact were misguided: "I claim it's beyond doubt that the devil has tricked those who speak of these books without the reverence due them; and beyond doubt that he moves their tongues to obstruct the good they do, if he could do so through them."[114]

Although Teresa's defenders made a strong case for the orthodoxy of her works, many of them still had reservations about making them freely available. We saw such concern in the approbations of Domingo Báñez and Juan de Avila. The anonymous author of the "Defense" also worried about the possible effects of Teresa's works on the unlettered:

> One can only conjecture that it may not be fitting that this book, where it discusses visions, revelations, raptures, and other very sensitive and spiritual things, should find its way in the vernacular into the hands of educated and uneducated alike, religious and laypeople, men and women. Because it seems it can pose a risk, especially for women, of being misled by a wish to imitate things explained in it, or to fake them in order to mislead others.[115]

It is a sign of the times that even those who believed Teresa's doctrine to be orthodox were aware of its potential for misuse.

Some Conclusions

The criticisms of Teresa's mystical doctrine which were submitted to the Consejo indicate several areas of common concern. Several of these issues have to do with the question of authority. The critics question Teresa's au-

---

112. Ibid., p. 919: "En las cosas no se ha de mirar el mal uso de algunos, sino el provecho en común."

113. Ibid.: "Finalmente, dicen que no las creen. Pues porque ellos no las creen, ¿qué? ¿Por eso se han de vedar a los otros? Presunción intolerable es hacerse señores de los juicios de todos. No las creen. Porque no lo experimentan en sí, no quieren que sea posible en otros?"

114. Ibid., p. 920: "Y ansí concluyo diciendo que tengo por sin duda que trae el demonio engañados a los que de estos *Libros* no hablan con la reverencia que deben; y que sin duda les menea la lengua, para, si pudiese por su medio, estorbar el provecho que hacen."

115. Llamas, p. 433: "Solamente se podría con alguna apariencia dudar si cumple que este libro, donde se tratan visiones, revelaciones, raptos y otras cosas muy delicadas y espirituales, ande en romance en manos de doctos y indoctos, religiosos y seglares, hombres y mugeres. Porque parece puede ser ocasión especialmente a mugeres, para ser engañadas, queriendo imitar cosas que en él se dicen, o fingillas por engañar a otros."

thority to teach, and they question the authority granted her by her visions and mystical experiences. Alonso de la Fuente was so certain of women's natural inferiority to men that he doubted that Teresa could even have written the books that bore her name, for such a thing would be "beyond nature."

Juan de Lorenzana thought along the same lines: women could not be theological teachers, and Teresa had overstepped the natural boundary between men and women when she began to write; certainly she had no authority to teach priests or male religious. Like Alonso, Lorenzana focused on Teresa's writings on rapture and union, but he went further than Alonso to accuse Teresa of teaching that the soul was united with God in a union of substances, which implied a state of sinlessness in this life, and that, since the soul was passive in attaining union with God, it must also be passive in the justification process.

When we compare Alonso's criticisms with Teresa's works, we can observe his inquisitorial technique in action. Rather than try to understand Teresa's ideas in their own context—that is, by comparing one text with another to determine the nuances and texture of Teresa's message—Alonso was trying to demonstrate that her behavior fitted an *alumbrado* pattern that he had already detected in other areas. Alonso interpreted any passage in a way that expressly contradicted some other passage. Instead of looking for harmony and coherence, Alonso was seeking any phrase that might resonate with his understanding of the *alumbrado* "doctrine," which he then imposed on Teresa's texts. It is difficult to speak of a well-defined *alumbrado* doctrine, and even more difficult to convict Teresa of such an ideology, but her defense of mental prayer and her visionary theology left her vulnerable to such accusations.

The challenges to the authority of Teresa's mystical experiences are directly related to the doctrine her experience generates. There were several "tests" that could be applied to visions to determine their validity. The inquisitional readers' doubts about Teresa's visions were based on their belief that her teachings included some theological errors. The fact that Teresa led an exemplary life and encouraged others to meet rigorous moral and spiritual standards in their own lives through the reform of the Carmelite order did not always influence these readers. Interestingly, many of them gave her the benefit of the doubt, concluding that she did not intend to mislead others. No one did—or could—call her a heresiarch.

The fact that these readers grappled with issues of personality and intentionality while they tried to decide what the Inquisition should do about Teresa's books indicates that they were not satisfied with the standards for evaluating visions which had developed over the centuries of the Christian mystical tradition. The proliferation of visionary experiences among the laity increased the need for guidelines. The general problem of authority which had emerged so forcefully in the Reformation era required theologians to give more thought to the role of personal revelation in the life of the institutional church, and particularly to the evaluation of visionary phenomena.

If the content of mystical doctrine were the standard by which the authority of mystical experience was to be evaluated, what specifically was there about Teresa's doctrine that aroused such controvery among theologians? The disputed theological points included the manner of Teresa's visions, the experience of union and rapture, the role of the soul in its progress toward mystical union, and the specific ways in which the soul is transformed on this journey. Theologians were wary of any doctrine regarding the passivity of the soul, visionary theology, and the moral behavior of the soul that has experienced rapture. These points have been the most disputed in the history of Christian mysticism, and they were even more suspect in an age when the *alumbrados* were active.

In addition to the general suspicions of Teresa's doctrine was the challenge to institutional authority offered by visionary discourse. As we have seen, Teresa's integration of visionary experience into the mystical journey differentiates her doctrine from other descriptions of mystical union, underscoring a visionary epistemology that makes God more accessible to the unlettered. Teresa's empowering message was in direct conflict with the Inquisition's goal of monitoring and controlling religious practice.

Finally, acceptance of Teresa's doctrine implied acceptance of a woman's role as theologian and teacher, a role prohibited by Paul. Juana de la Cruz had preached while in ecstasy in the 1520s, but by the 1580s holy women were no longer allowed to assume such public teaching roles. The issue, as it was played out in Teresa's life and works, is whether or not the fact that a woman taught was *by and of itself heterodox*. On this issue Luti claims, "From early in the century, one of the clearest signs of the presence of error among the varied movements of spirituality in Spain was the prominence of the *maestra*."[116] Though several women are known to have gained teaching authority in the sixteenth century, the trend toward limiting women's influence certainly grew as the century advanced. Thus, as Teresa's life suggests, a doctrine of gender orthopraxy emerged in sixteenth-century Spain, an orthodoxy that formulated women's religious roles in explicit ways that denied them access to apostolic roles.

The posthumous criticisms of Teresa's works confirm that Teresa was well aware of the theological challenges that might be posed to the mystical doctrine she wanted to teach. Nearly all of the theological issues she qualified

116. Luti, "Teresa of Avila," p. 349.

with *a mi parecer* appeared in one or another of the condemnatory *memoriales*. Although she forsaw the criticism and made a considerable effort to explain her doctrine clearly, Teresa incorporated neither scholastic reasoning nor lengthy citations of Scripture or church authorities in her arguments. Her failure to use the language and modes of discourse that male theologians did permitted them to turn her recourse to divine inspiration against her.

What effect did the posthumous criticism of Teresa's works have in her canonization process? The records of the informative early part of that process reveal that the majority of Teresa's readers found her works entirely orthodox and even miraculous in their ability to teach and convert. The questions posed during the canonization process included a special section asking witnesses to testify to the problems Teresa encountered with the Inquisition. All of those witnesses who do mention any problems speak of the troubles in Seville; none mentions the posthumous criticisms.[117]

Testimonies calling for Teresa's canonization began to be gathered in 1591, and this groundswell of support may well have influenced the Inquisition. Though no document exists to explain why the inquisitors decided not to ban Teresa's works, several historical factors provide insight. First, as Juan de Orellana observes, the prohibition of Teresa's works would necessitate a major effort to discredit Teresa among her followers. Inquisitors must have been hesitant to cause scandal among the faithful. Perhaps, too, the defense of the mystical tradition offered by Luis de León and Antonio de Quevedo persuaded them that the publication of an orthodox treatment of mystical doctrine would be their strongest weapon against the *alumbrados*.[118]

Teresa's doctrine certainly had its problematic areas, but I do not believe that that doctrine was what provoked the most controversy. It seems to me that Teresa was controversial for two major reasons. First, censorship successfully repressed the production of new mystical treatises after the Valdés Index appeared. Teresa's mystical works were the first new texts of this genre to be published. Thus they were a novelty at a time when novelty implied dissent from orthodoxy. The church was struggling to define itself over and against the variety of Christian religious traditions that were emerging in the sixteenth century. Part of that definition involved the de-

---

117. Of the criticisms discussed above, Alonso de la Fuente's *memoriales* must have circulated, because they rapidly generated a response sent to the Consejo. The other criticisms, since they were commissioned by the Consejo, were secret and therefore would not have been accessible.

118. The favorable predisposition of Gaspar de Quiroga, inquisitor general from 1572 until his death in 1593, may also have been a factor in the resolution of complaints against Teresa's works. Although Quiroga's reactions to the posthumous debate are not documented, his support of her during her lifetime suggests that he may have instructed the tribunal to rule in her favor.

velopment and repetition of a standard body of orthodox doctrine that had little to do with mystical experience. Until mystical treatises could be shown to be consistent with orthodox Catholicism, they were considered suspect and potentially dangerous.

Second, Teresa was an "unlettered" woman teaching other women to pray autonomously. At a time when nuns were enjoined to keep to the cloisters, Teresa was out founding convents and monasteries. While the offices of teachers and missionaries were slowly but steadily being taken over by the new Society of Jesus, an order made up of ordained men with a theological education, Teresa was writing page after page of mystical doctrine. The currents of change within the Roman Catholic Church were diminishing the sphere of religious women, defining their function as that of cloistered prayer. Teresa fought against this attempt to marginalize women by teaching that contemplative prayer was a source of great spiritual power. She did not agree with the effort to confine women to a particular religious role, but she worked within that role to define carefully and explicitly what the experience of cloistered prayer should be for the Discalced Carmelites. At a time when written expressions of mystical experience were forbidden, Teresa insisted that women's mystical experience had a place in the life and doctrine of the church.

The challenges to Teresa's authority must be viewed from this perspective. As the head of an influential reform movement and revered by many Catholics, Teresa had become a figurehead of authority in Spanish religious life. By writing about her spiritual experiences, she extended her authority into the teaching realm at a time when women were actively discouraged from taking any role in the doctrinal life of the church. Thus theologians had to wrestle with many issues, not least their prejudice against women as theological teachers and their fear of the influence of mystical doctrine on unlettered female readers. If they approved Teresa's epistemology, they would then be forced to accept the authority of other women who followed in Teresa's footsteps. The challenges to Teresa's authority continued for forty years after her death.

6

Teresa la Santa:
Alone of All Her Sex?

In the aftermath of the Reformation, canonization became an important tool for Roman Catholic propaganda. Living symbols of such key Roman Catholic doctrines as the importance of good works, saints gave bodily affirmation of Catholic theology. Official determinations of sanctity had dropped off significantly, however, in light of the many questions reformers had raised about the intercessory role of saints. Noting that no saint was canonized between 1523 and 1588, Peter Burke claims that this period was "a 'crisis of canonization' at a time when the very idea of a saint was under fire."[1] The sixty-five-year hiatus in the creation of saints suggests a shift in the function of the canonization process at large.

When the first Counter-Reformation saints were canonized in 1588, a series of reforms was also instituted whereby the canonization process, or "the right to define the sacred," was increasingly controlled by the papacy.[2] Saint-making procedures were made increasingly strict and formal by Pope Urban VIII in 1625 and 1634.[3] We may therefore view the earlier Counter-Reformation saints as representative of the religious ideals the papacy sought to promulgate. In other words, while the saints canonized from 1588 to 1622 had some base of popular support, we must not overlook their value to the institutional church, for that was a major reason for their canonization.

As it struggled to redefine itself against the backdrop of Protestantism, the institutional church needed strong Tridentine models for the laity, role models who respected the church hierarchy, adhered to the sacramental sys-

---

1. Peter Burke, "How to Be a Counter-Reformation Saint," in *Religion and Society in Early Modern Europe, 1500–1800*, ed. Kaspar von Greyerz (London, 1984), p. 46. Pierre Delooz dates the final canonization of the early period, that of St. Antonin Pierozzi, at 1525, not 1523: *Sociologie et canonisations* (Liège, 1969), p. 445.

2. Although papal control over the canonization process was not formally decreed until the seventeenth century, it was affirmed by the sixteenth-century writers Petrus Andreas Gambarus, Alfonso de Castro, Domingo Báñez, Robert Bellarmine, and others. See Eric Waldram Kemp, *Canonization and Authority in the Western Church* (Oxford, 1948), pp. 141–50.

3. Burke, "How to Be a Counter-Reformation Saint," p. 46.

tem, and, in short, epitomized what it meant to be a "good Roman Catholic." In retrospect, male role models, such as Ignatius Loyola, founder of the Jesuits, seem to be obvious candidates as the early Jesuits came to embody the Counter-Reformation.[4] There was much disagreement, however, about the orthoprax norms that might lead to sanctity. The clearest disagreement was that between the *letrados* and *espirituales*, which resulted in the controversy over the role of mental prayer and mystical union in the pursuit of holiness. Another area of controversy was the role that a holy person—especially a holy woman—could take in society. Charismatic leaders were often venerated, but their actions in the public arena were subject to intense scrutiny.[5] Displaying the virtues of poverty, chastity, and humility in ways consistent with the Inquisition's norms became critical in maintaining a holy reputation.[6]

What seems clear, both from the imbalance in the number of male and female saints—male saints outnumbered female saints by 4 to 1 in the Counter-Reformation and Baroque periods[7]—and from the widespread devaluation of "little women" is that it was harder to imagine a female saint than a male saint. In view of the climate of suspicion about women's religious experience which we have witnessed, it is clear that the canonization of a sixteenth-century woman would involve quite a bit of reconstruction.

Spirited Teresa de Jesús was a difficult candidate for such a transformation. Yet Teresa's own writings, so carefully crafted to be acceptable to her religious superiors, provided institutional figures with the rhetorical tools to rewrite her life. In the decades after her death Teresa's rhetoric of humility and obedience ceased to be a survival strategy and became a profound weapon in the political struggle for her recognition as a saint.

As we have seen, Teresa's canonization was not at all inevitable. It should be seen as a result of three factors: a rather dogged campaign on her behalf by the Spanish crown and several nobles; the successful construction of a fe-

4. See, e.g., H. Outram Evennett, *The Spirit of the Counter-Reformation*, ed. John Bossy (Notre Dame, 1968), p. 73: "The challenge of the new epoch . . . was met . . . by the new congregations of clerks—priests—regular or secular, of which the Society of Jesus was from the first intrinsically the most significant and very soon became the most influential example. . . . They soon established themselves as an accepted, indeed as an almost essential, constituent element within the church, proliferating in due course." On the orientation of the early Jesuits, see John O'Malley, *The First Jesuits* (Cambridge, Mass., 1993).

5. The many people subjected to scrutiny are not limited to women. Inquisitional proceedings against Ignatius Loyola raised questions about his sexual conduct with women, especially penitents.

6. For a discussion of the complications in expressing these virtues, see Gillian T. W. Ahlgren, "Negotiating Sanctity: Holy Women in Sixteenth-Century Spain," *Church History* 64 (September 1995): 373–88.

7. See Burke, "How to Be a Counter-Reformation Saint," p. 49.

male role model who was able to represent most of the virtues associated with femininity while overcoming the negative attributes associated with womanhood; and, perhaps most important, the Roman Catholic Church's endorsement of the mystical way as an important part of the Counter-Reformation identity. Thus we must distinguish between Teresa as she embodied the Christian life and the growing construction of Teresa as a Christian type to be emulated. Evaluating this process will help us understand why Teresa was the only Spanish woman of the Catholic Reformation to be canonized.

Before we do so, we need to clarify the distinction between sanctity and canonization. Canonization, of course, is the official recognition of a person's sanctity. It automatically moves the discussion of a person's holiness into the realm of the institutional church. While canonization depends on the recollection of a saint's contemporaries (male and female), it places the assessment of sanctity in the hands of men who in most cases have had no experience of the candidate and have to base their judgments on their interpretations of secondhand narratives. Though sixteenth-century Spain certainly had its share of saintly men and women, the climate of suspicion that surrounded religious experience made it difficult for the church to recognize their sanctity officially.

The sociologist of religion Pierre Delooz seems to conflate sanctity and canonization when he suggests that sanctity is the product of a recollected past. "Only the dead can be saints," he writes. "And so sainthood is automatically situated in recollection."[8] Yet a community's recollection of a saint is formed over time, on the basis of a lived experience of the person in question. The social relationships that the candidate establishes, the quality of interaction with his or her contemporaries, and the personality of the saint in some ways predetermine how that saint will be remembered.

More helpful, perhaps, is Delooz's distinction between "real" and "constructed" saints. Beyond the real saint there is a construction of the saint, a process that Delooz suggests occurs through recollection after the saint's death: "All saints are more or less *constructed* in that, being necessarily saints *for other people*, they are remodelled in the collective representation which is made of them. It often happens, even, that they are so remodelled that nothing of the real original is left."[9] I prefer to discuss this construction process in terms of an evolving persona, the persona being the projection of a particular view (or interpretation) of the self to which the saint himself or

8. Pierre Delooz, "Towards a Sociological Study of Canonized Sainthood in the Catholic Church," in *Saints and Their Cults: Studies in Religious Sociology, Folklore and History*, ed. Stephen Wilson (Cambridge, 1983), p. 194.

9. Ibid., p. 195.

herself contributes. The persona can and does take on an independent life as the reputation of the saint, both during and after the saint's lifetime.

The Canonization Procedure

The transformation of Teresa de Jesús into Saint Teresa of Avila can be seen most readily through an examination of her persona as it developed over the course of three decades, from the 1590s testimony of eyewitnesses who had known Teresa through the vita constructed by the promoter for the Congregation of Rites. This analysis makes clear the ways in which Teresa's life was rewritten after her death so that it became a role model for Catholic women acceptable to Counter-Reformation church officials.

The collection of information for Teresa's beatification and canonization began relatively early, on October 16, 1591. As Jodi Bilinkoff has shown, Teresa's canonization offered many potential economic and political advantages. An official determination of Teresa's sanctity might lead to increased pilgrimage and inject new life into the waning local economy.[10] These factors do not, of course, appear in official documents petitioning some recognition of Teresa's sanctity.

As the Roman documents describe it, the key event in the initiation of the "informative process" was the discovery that Teresa's body remained incorrupt nine years after her death.[11] Before that time, several discalced Carmelites had written about Teresa, trying to dispel the shadow cast over her character by the Inquisition's inquiries, but no formal collection of testimonials about her had been undertaken. The original interrogatory for the informative process suggests that, as far as an official inquiry into Teresa's canonization was concerned, the evidence of supernatural intervention after her death—and, most likely, the devotion it inspired in the laity—was at least as noteworthy as the virtues Teresa had practiced during her life.[12]

Testimonials on Teresa's behalf were acquired over nearly twenty years, but most intensely between 1591 and 1597. They constitute over 1,600 pages of typescript and contain a wealth of information about Teresa that

10. See Bilinkoff, *Avila of Saint Teresa*, chap. 6.

11. As the body was kept in the town of Alba, diocesis of Salamanca, the bishop of Salamanca, Jerónimo Manrique, began the procedure. For a summary of the canonization procedure see Kenneth Woodward, *Making Saints* (New York, 1990), pp. 50–86.

12. The three reasons given for opening the process (probably listed in order of importance) were the incorruptibility of her body, the "marvels" (since they were not yet verified miracles) that God was said to have performed through her intercession, and her virtuous life. The text reads: "While she lived in this life the said Mother Teresa led a saintly and exemplary life, and is reputed and held within and outside her religious order to be a holy person . . ." (*BMC* 18:1: "Mientras vivió en esta vida la dicha madre Teresa hizo santa y ejemplar vida, es reputado y tenido dentro y fuera de su Religión por cuerpo santo . . .").

many Teresian scholars have largely ignored.[13] Despite early enthusiasm, the collection of testimonies on Teresa's behalf seems to have suffered from lack of official attention until divine—and monarchical—intervention renewed interest in her cause. In 1595 Diego de Yepes, confessor of Philip II, was on his way to Salamanca from Madrid when he stopped in Alba. There he viewed Teresa's body, and was astonished to see fresh blood flow from the corpse. He soaked it up with some handkerchiefs. Philip had been a supporter of Teresa during her lifetime, and, upon the advice of Diego de Yepes, he urged the papal nuncio Camilo Gaetano to pursue the collection of testimonials from all over Spain.

The pause in the proceedings may well have been due to continuing questions about Teresa's orthodoxy. As we have seen, these debates were most intense between 1591 and 1593. Teresa's canonization could not proceed without a guarantee of her orthodoxy. The doubts raised by Alonso de la Fuente, Juan de Orellana, and Juan de Lorenzana were clearly cause for concern. Further, Teresa was an enigmatic figure. What made her seem a saint to some was considered unattractive and even controversial by others. The problems Teresa presented—particularly her lack of conformity to women's religious roles and her continuing function as a teacher of mystical doctrine—had to be resolved before her canonization could be approved. Additionally, the institutional church had to define for itself the moral and ecclesiastical lessons her canonization could impart.

Probably in response to the continued controversy over the Inquisition's inquiries about Teresa, the Discalced Carmelite Jerónimo Gracián, one of Teresa's confessors and a close friend, wrote a treatise titled *The Defense of the Doctrine of Mother Teresa de Jesús*, which he finished on June 1, 1597.[14] For the next seven years, various individuals and institutions importuned the papacy for Teresa's beatification. The most prestigious Iberian universities—Salamanca, Alcalá, and Coimbra—all wrote formal petitions, as did Juan de Ribera and Diego de Yepes, both authors of vitae.[15] In 1604 the Congregation of Rites opened an investigation into Teresa's miracles, called the *proceso remisorial "in genere."* This collection was translated into Italian, and the final verification process, the *proceso remisorial "in specie,"* began in

---

13. The entire manuscript collection of canonization testimony survives today in the Discalced convent in Salamanca. It was painstakingly transcribed by P. Silverio de Santa Teresa in the 1930s and is available in *BMC* 18–20.

14. See *BMC* 17:324: "Ya se acabó de escribir la obra que dije me costaba gran trabajo, que es *Defensa de la doctrina de la madre Teresa de Jesús*, contra los que la quieren hacer herética."

15. These and other documents are available in *BMC*, vol. 2. All the early testimonials on Teresa's behalf were collected and taken to Rome in 1597 by Bernabé del Mármol with accompanying letters to Clement VIII from Philip II and his sister the empress María asking the pope to move forward in Teresa's canonization process.

1609. In a papal brief dated April 24, 1614, Paul V beatified Teresa, and Gregory XV canonized her on March 12, 1622, along with Ignatius Loyola, Francis Xavier, Felipe de Neri, and Isidore the Worker.

The Testimony of Eyewitnesses

During the first two stages of the canonization process, from 1591–92 to 1595–96, 144 witnesses were deposed. These testimonials represent the informative process instigated by the bishop of Salamanca as well as the witnesses solicited by the papal nuncio. Witnesses were asked a series of questions to focus their testimony in several categories: the quality of Teresa's prayer life; her motives for reforming the Carmelite order; how she embodied the Christian virtues of faith, hope, charity, humility, obedience, poverty, and penitence; her ability to overcome difficulties through perseverance; the circumstances of her death (especially the incorrupt state of her body); and any miracles performed during her lifetime or after her death.

A mixed picture emerges from this testimony, tempered by such variables as how well the witness knew Teresa,[16] whether or not the witness was a Discalced Carmelite, and the religious values of the witness—particularly his or her attitude toward the virtues of humility and obedience. Not surprisingly, the testimony of the many Discalced Carmelites who had known Teresa personally is the richest in intimate details about her life, but it poses several problems of interpretation. First, many of these witnesses had already formed ideas about the meaning of Teresa's life, which influenced their characterizations of her. Second, Teresa's contemporaries, particularly those deeply invested in her reform movement, had obvious reasons to describe Teresa in ways they believed would impress papal representatives. Not content to express their own assumptions about Christian holiness, many of them tried to address the concerns they thought Roman officials might have.

A systematic review of their portraits of Teresa must include the key aspects of saintliness as they emerged in the Christian tradition and were evaluated in the sixteenth century: a heroic pursuit of virtue (control of the body and will through asceticism, humility, obedience, and charity) and extraordinary manifestations of power (visions, mystical phenomena, miracles).[17] Witnesses responded to questions organized around these qualities.

16. In general, those who did not know Teresa directly limited their testimony to a posthumous miracle they had experienced or knew of.

17. Cf. Richard Kieckhefer, "Imitators of Christ: Sainthood in the Christian Tradition," in *Sainthood: Its Manifestations in World Religions*, ed. Richard Kieckhefer and George D. Bond (Berkeley, 1988), p. 12. The following categories were critical in demonstrating sanctity: (1) evidence of special access to God (whether through the performance of miracles, through ec-

Many witnesses testified to Teresa's "many hours" of prayer and her levitation during ecstatic prayer.[18] Others described a glow in Teresa's face when she prayed. A few recounted an episode in which Teresa was taken into a rapture while cooking in the kitchen. Although absorbed in intense prayer, the ever-practical Teresa did not let go of the frying pan and lost not a drop of the convent's only remaining oil.

Those who knew Teresa best bore witness to the intense physicality of her prayer life. María de San José, for instance, declared that "one of the greatest tasks she had in this life was to resist inner feelings in order to attend to external things."[19] The physical components of Teresa's prayer life could be disruptive to the entire religious community.[20] For the Carmelites, the intensity of Teresa's prayer life was rewarded by numerous spiritual gifts, including that of prophecy. Many of them mentioned instances of Teresa's foreknowledge of events or her gift of knowing someone's interior state.

The testimony of many of Teresa's confessors is also very strong on the quality of Teresa's prayer life, although their main concern was its orthodoxy. Their statements often reflect the fact that Teresa won them over from skepticism to confidence about the veracity of her prayer, often because, as one of them says, "she knew things it was impossible to know without revelation."[21]

Many people, both lay and religious, described the edification they experienced from reading Teresa's books, and for some her books were media for miracles of moral and spiritual conversion. María de San Angelo testified that two nuns had entered the Discalced convent in Salamanca as a result of reading Teresa's books.[22] Damiana de Jesús, another Discalced Carmelite in Salamanca, made similar claims about sisters at the convent of

---

stasy and supernatural experiences in prayer, or through prophecy); (2) devotion to asceticism (rigorous fasting, sleep deprivation, withdrawal from society, patience through serious illness, the use of ascetic devices [hair shirts, *cilicios*, whips]; (3) humility (expressed particularly through obedience or self-mortification); and (4) acts of charity. See Donald Weinstein and Rudolph M. Bell, *Saints and Society: The Two Worlds of Western Christendom, 1100–1700* (Chicago, 1982), pp. 141–64.

18. See, e.g., the testimonies of Ana de San Bartolomé (*BMC* 18:168–75), Inés de la Cruz (ibid., pp. 534–37), the Carmelite provincial Angel de Salazar (ibid., 19:1–4), and María de San José Salazar (ibid., 18:487–508).

19. Ibid., 18:491: "Uno de los mayores trabajos que tenía en esta vida era resistir a los sentimientos interiores para así acudir a las cosas exteriores."

20. Recall Juana del Espíritu Santo's description of Teresa in ecstasy in chapter 2.

21. See the testimony of Hernando de Medina, a Calced Carmelite who confessed Teresa on several occasions, in *BMC* 19:274–75.

22. Ibid., 18:55. Her interpretation of the miraculous conversions of these nuns is confirmed by Juana de Jesús in ibid., p. 63.

Santa Ana in Madrid.[23] Dorotea de la Cruz, who entered the Discalced reform in the Valladolid convent, described the spiritual improvement of a secular priest after his reading of Teresa's books.[24] Her books were associated with another miracle as well: they carried the same sweet odor that emanated from her body.[25]

The nexus of similar testimonies about the power of Teresa's books confirmed Teresa's role as a moral and spiritual teacher, a function so adamantly disputed by her Dominican detractors. Though the testimonies do not use the word *maestra* to describe Teresa, they do ascribe teaching credentials to her, stating, for example, that her books are of great benefit,

> especially for women, and particularly for women religious, because they contain great and good counsel and doctrine for any state, particularly that of [vowed] religion, for they treat with great clarity the virtues and habits necessary for it, particularly obedience, humility, mortification, and prayer, with the methods necessary for them and how to achieve them with divine favor.[26]

The descriptions of Teresa's religious virtues focused on humility, obedience, charity, penitence, and poverty. Teresa displayed all of these virtues, but humility, obedience, and penitence were especially significant for female saints.[27]

As we have seen, Teresa's emphasis on humility and obedience was a rhetorical strategy designed to present herself as no threat to a patriarchal and institutional church. Thus her self-deprecating humor is most properly understood not as internalized self-doubt but as an important part of the persona she adopted as a survival strategy. The canonization testimonies suggest that this aspect of Teresa's persona was so developed during her lifetime that it fooled many of her contemporaries. Nearly all witnesses em-

---

23. Ibid., p. 72.

24. Ibid., 19:20. Many other witnesses gave similar testimony.

25. See the testimony of Petronila Bautista, OCD, ibid., 18:180–82.

26. Testimony of Isabel de Santo Domingo, ibid., 19:101: "Preguntada si entiende dichos libros son de mucho fruto, respondió: que de muy grande, y en especial para mujeres, y particularmente para religiosas, porque contienen en sí muy grandes y buenos avisos y doctrina para cualquiera [sic] estado, y particularmente para él de Religión, por tratar ella en ellos con mucha claridad de las virtudes y buenas costumbres necesarias para ella, y en particular de la obediencia, humildad, mortificación y oración con los medios necesarios para ellas y poderlas conseguir con el favor divino."

27. Charity is also an important virtue for women, but there is less to say about its expression vis-à-vis the institutional church or its representatives. Tridentine Catholicism did allow religious women to leave the cloister for charitable work (especially nursing), but the Carmelite vocation did not have that orientation. Certainly Teresa was seen to exercise charity, particularly in nursing and in praying and doing penance on behalf of others. Her Carmelite sisters frequently mention her charity toward ill sisters.

phasized her humility and obedience. The patriarchal context of these virtues is unavoidable, and her contemporaries cited many instances of Teresa's obedience to hierarchical officials and humble acceptance of their suspicions about her religious experience.

Domingo Báñez, for instance, described Teresa's willingness to burn her *Vida* if he had ordered her to do so, and Diego de Yanguas, the confessor who ordered Teresa to burn her commentary on the Song of Songs, declared: "When her confessors ordered her to do something, she did not want them to give their reason for the order."[28] Her Carmelite sisters recalled Teresa's saying that obedience was the most trustworthy virtue, and several quoted her: "In revelation I could be deceived, but not in obedience."[29]

Teresa's more intimate associates, however, were not taken in by such talk. María de San José, testifying from Lisbon, where she had been made prioress after her years as prioress in Seville, said nothing about Teresa's obedience and commented on her humility only as it was expressed in her relationships within the female world of the convent.[30] After the difficulties the Discalced convent in Seville had experienced with the Inquisition, María de San José was in a unique position to understand both Teresa's need to adopt a persona and the importance of humility and obedience to that persona.

María de San José's only comments about humility focused on Teresa's desire to accept the humblest office within her religious community. When she described Teresa's interactions with men, she always vindicated Teresa's position, which her superiors often opposed. Indeed, María de San José used Teresa's canonization process as a platform to make several comments on the narrow circumscription of female sanctity in sixteenth-century Spain. The prioress was arguing, in effect, that the suspicions voiced by Teresa's contemporaries were such a cross that her daily acceptance of these trying circumstances was more than adequate proof of her humility.

Most of Teresa's contemporaries did not share—or at least express— María de San José's nuanced conception of female humility and obedience in a patriarchal world. But Teresa's religious persona was certainly ambiguous enough to permit the religious officials who would be most threatened

28. *BMC* 18:242: "Cuando los confesores le mandaban algo, no quería que le diesen razón por qué se lo mandaban."

29. See, e.g., the testimony of Isabel de la Cruz and Damiana de Jesús, ibid., pp. 29 and 69–73.

30. This approach is consistent with the work of feminist theologians who suggest that women's obedience within a patriarchal society only contributes to collective sin. Thus a woman's fidelity to her experience is a far more important religious virtue than obedience.

by the real Teresa to reconfigure her religious virtues in much more traditional ways.

Those who knew Teresa well also knew about her rigorous—and perhaps, given the state of her health, ill-advised—penitential activity. In a fairly representative statement, Ana de la Trinidad testified, "Nothing gave her more pleasure than to martyr her body for Our Lord."[31] Teresa's attitude toward penance is ambiguous. On the one hand, in her writings she did not advocate harsh penance. Her reformed *Constitutions* say little about penitential practice. Her personal correspondence indicates that she had some concern about individuals who engaged in what she considered excessive penitential practice.[32]

On the other hand, Teresa seemed impressed by the "terrible penances" of Catalina de Cardona, and many of her contemporaries testified that she was well on her way to surpassing such heroic feats with her own severe practices. Several Carmelites described Teresa's *cilicios*, penitential accoutrements worn around the wrists or waist to produce constant discomfort; if they were worn tightly, they would lacerate the skin and draw blood. As Teresa's contemporaries describe them, her *cilicios* were made of tin plates, which caused serious wounds.[33]

Ana de San Bartolomé, Teresa's nurse, testified that Teresa's body was "ulcerated from disciplines and the *cilicios* she wore."[34] Beatriz de Jesús, Teresa's second cousin, concurred: "She was a woman of many disciplines, so much so that her confessors were concerned; and because of her continual *cilicio* she carried wounds on her body, and even with her constant sickness and tremors she always wore it."[35] Alonso de los Angeles, who had known Teresa's confidant Jerónimo Gracián, testified that Teresa's penitential practices got so out of hand that her confessors had to intervene.[36] Such wounds did not stop Teresa from

---

31. *BMC* 18:44: "Ninguna cosa le diera mayor gusto que martirizar su cuerpo por Nuestro Señor."

32. See, e.g., letter 179, to her brother Lorenzo de Cepeda, dated February 10, 1577, in *Obras completas*, pp. 1567–71. See also her comments in *Vida* 13:4 and *CV* 39:3.

33. See in *BMC* 18, e.g., the testimonies of María de San Angelo (pp. 51–56), Ana de los Angeles (pp. 538–43), and Ana de San Bartolomé (pp. 168–75).

34. Ibid., p. 170. Ana de San Bartolomé was Teresa's nurse from 1577 until her death in 1582. Her remarks indicate that, despite lifelong health problems, Teresa continued to engage in penitential practice even as an older woman.

35. Ibid., p. 177: "Era mujer de muchas disciplinas, tanto que sus confesores se estorbaban; y que de la frecuencia y continuación del cilicio traía llagas en el cuerpo, y que con enfermedad continua y perlesía se le traía siempre."

36. Ibid., 19:72: "Preguntado si la dicha madre Teresa hacía penitencia, respondió que sí, y en tanta manera, que era menester irle a la mano sus confesores y prelados. . . ."

wearing her *cilicios* constantly, however, and often her wounds became infected.[37]

One is tempted to view such excesses as the results of internalizing the negative social and theological attitudes toward women, and more particularly toward the female body as the locus of potential evil. However repellent to modern sensibilities Teresa's treatment of her body may be, it is important to view it as an extension of Teresa's role as mediator between Christ and humanity. Penitential exercises were done not for their own sake, or even for the merits they might bring to the penitent, but as extensions of the redemptive power of Christ which Christians could offer up on behalf of others.[38]

Teresa's penitential practice can also be viewed within the framework of "heroic" or "manly" activity. Through such deprecation of the body one could become less embodied; for women a corollary was the possibility of androgyny and escape from theologians' assumptions about their gender. Teresa's transcendence of "womanhood" was duly noted by several of her contemporaries. Domingo Báñez, for example, recalled asking Juan de Salinas, provincial of the Dominican order, "What do you think of Teresa de Jesús?" Salinas answered jocularly, "Oh, you were kidding me when you said she was a woman; by the faith, she's not only a masculine man but one of the manliest [most bearded]."[39] The fact that Teresa was "manly" took the sting out of collaborating with her and taking her orders. Teresa herself urged her nuns to be "strong" and "manly," to pursue the discipline of the monastic rule with vigor. She did not want her nuns to appear womanly in any way, she wrote; she wanted them to be "strong men, for if they do

---

37. See ibid., 18:548, where Ana de la Madre de Dios recounts quite graphically: "Because of the constant *cilicios* she wore, sores formed on her body, and pockets of pus" ("De los cilicios tan continuos que traía, se le vinieron a hacer llagas y bolsas de materia en el cuerpo"); and ibid., p. 194, where Teresa's niece, also called Teresa de Jesús, testifies that her wounds "were so great that they became infected, and on top of them she went on applying nettles" ("Eran hartas que se venían a criar materia en las llagas, y sobre ellas les volvía a tomar con ortigas"). Such details supplied by witnesses who had been physically closest to Teresa lead me to believe that they were not simply constructing Teresa the saint, but were providing accurate reports of her life.

38. For a review of this tradition, see Bynum, *Holy Feast and Holy Fast*. See also Ellen Ross, " 'She Wept and Cried Right Loud for Sorrow and for Pain': Suffering, the Spiritual Journey, and Women's Experience in Late Medieval Mysticism," in Wiethaus, *Maps of Flesh and Light*, pp. 45–59.

39. *BMC* 18:9: "Encontrándole este testigo en otra ocasión, le dijo: ¿Qué le parece a Vuestra Paternidad de Teresa de Jesús? Respondió a este testigo con gran donaire, diciendo: Oh? habíadesme engañado, que deciades que era mujer; a la fe no es sino hombre varón y de los mas barbados; dando a entender en esto su gran constancia y discreción en el gobierno de su persona y de sus monjas."

what's in them, the Lord will make them so manly that men will be shocked."[40]

Teresa's contemporaries clearly understood her to be an exceptional woman in an era when exceptional women seemed threatening. Teresa challenged men's assumptions about her as a woman and therefore about women in general. It was easier to accept Teresa as an anomaly or an honorary man than to acknowledge that perhaps their assumptions were wrong. The stories people shared about Teresa gave abundant examples of her singularity, her "heroic pursuit of virtue," and the abundant grace she had enjoyed. In varying degrees the witnesses understood that Teresa contradicted many of the sixteenth-century assumptions about gender, yet they found her "masculine" achievements acceptable because Teresa as a person remained feminine.

The Hagiographical Reconstruction of Teresa

The hagiographical tradition continued a form of apologia for Teresa's exceptional character rather than a defense of women's virtue more generally. Teresa's biographers used many strategies, but all stressed both the legitimacy of visions as a way of knowing God and Spain's special need for some person to serve as a living model of orthodox visionary experience.

The most extensive biography of Teresa was that of Francisco de Ribera (1537–91), completed in 1590. The book had a wide circulation, as the testimony from Teresa's canonization process makes clear. Indeed, Alonso de la Fuente had read it and incorporated some of it in his denunciations of Teresa. Ribera, a Jesuit who taught in Salamanca, was preparing an edition of Teresa's complete works when he died. His *Vida* gives a complete account of Teresa's life, taken mainly from her own works, and summarizes the early miracle tradition.

To situate the life of the saint, however, Ribera begins with a defense of the visionary tradition; the first chapter is headed "In which is considered which revelations ought to be heeded, and in particular why those of Mother Teresa de Jesús ought to be, so that all may judge what they read in this book."[41] He offers several arguments for the credibility of visions, including historical and biblical precedents, and cites authorities who have

---

40. *CV* 7:8: "No querría yo, hijas mías, lo fueseis en nada ni lo parecieseis, sino varones fuertes; que si ellas hacen lo que es en sí, el Señor las hará tan varoniles que espanten a los hombres."

41. Ribera, *Vida de Santa Teresa de Jesús*, bk. 1, chap. 1: "En que se trata de qué revelaciones se debe hacer caso, y en particular del que se debe hacer de las de la Madre Teresa de Jesús, para que todos estimen lo que en este libro leyeren."

written about visions.[42] To reinforce his point that revelations are an important part of the Christian tradition, Ribera concludes:

> No one should be surprised, as though it were a new language, by all this about revelations and visions and raptures or prophecies, for in the time of the apostles there was so much of that, and since then to this day it has never ceased in those who have dedicated themselves to the service of God and holiness. Nor should anyone be amazed that in these times there have been and are [such revelations], for God has the same goodness and generosity he has always had, and now too he can and will do the same favors for anyone who with his grace prepares himself or herself for them.[43]

Ribera recognizes that not all visions are equal, and he reviews the literature on the discernment of visions. He elaborates five criteria for judging the validity of a vision: (1) whether the revelations themselves are true, in accordance with Scriptures and Roman Catholic doctrine; (2) whether the content of the revelations is substantial and beneficial; (3) whether the effects of the revelations are good or bad; (4) whether the person who had the revelations is of good judgment and discreet, mature, humble, and of conduct that conforms to what one would expect; and (5) whether the revelations have been examined and approved by people who are qualified for the task.[44] After applying these criteria to Teresa's visions, Ribera himself approves them and notes that many experts, including Luis de León and Juan de Orozco, have done so as well.

Finally, Ribera addresses the question of Teresa's gender: "Someone will say that after all she was a woman, and one ought to take little account of a woman's revelations."[45] Not so, says Ribera, for

42. Ibid. Ribera's authorities include Richard of St. Victor, Bonaventure, Gregory the Great, Tertullian, Cassian, Catherine of Siena, Angela of Foligno, Bridget of Sweden, and Ignatius Loyola.

43. Ibid., p. 82: "Nadie debe extrañarse, ni tener por nuevo lenguaje, esto de revelaciones y visiones y raptos o arrobamientos o profecías, pues en tiempo de los Apóstoles hubo tanto de eso, y después acá nunca hasta el día de hoy ha faltado en los que más se han señalado en el servicio de Dios y en la santidad. Ni se espanten tampoco que en estos tiempos lo haya habido y haya, pues tiene Dios la misma bondad y largueza que siempre ha tenido, y ahora también puede hacer y hará los mismos favores a quien con su gracia para ellos se dispusiere. El Santo Concilio de Trento anatematiza a cualquiera que dijere que certísimamente y sin poder faltar, ha de tener el don de la perseverancia, si no es que lo haya sabido por particular revelación que Dios le haya hecho; y nuestro muy santo Padre Sixto V condena a los que dijeren las cosas que han de venir, que dependen de nuestro libre albedrío, de cualquiera manera que ello sea, si no fuere revelándoselo Dios. Por cierto, si en estos tiempos no pudiera o no hubiera de haber revelaciones, demasiada cosa y fuera de propósito era decir, si no fuere revelándoselo Dios, o habiéndolo sabido por particular revelación."

44. See ibid., p. 86.

45. Ibid., p. 88: "Dirá alguno, que en fin era mujer, y que se ha de hacer poco caso de revelaciones de mujer."

those women who with fortitude overcome their passions and submit to God must be called men, and men who let themselves be overcome by them [their passions] are women. This depends not on the difference of the body but on the strength of the soul. Look to see if the Church thinks that way, for when it commands us to pray the office of martyrs to very brave virgins, such as Saint Agnes and Saint Agatha, it is telling us that we must count them as men. So let us pay no attention to women's revelations—that is, those of weak persons who have surrendered to their passions; but much attention must be paid to those of a woman more manly than many big men, so courageous and brave, and of women like her.[46]

Ribera suggests that Teresa's life provides an important example of true visionary experience that will help Catholics recognize false visionaries more easily.

Another of Teresa's biographers, Diego de Yepes (1530/31–1614), took great pains to situate Teresa within the context of suspicion of visions, ecstasy, and mental prayer. As he portrayed Teresa, she was sent by God to give the church a proper model of piety, devotion, and prayer.

> Great are the lies and machinations that the devil and hypocrisy have invented, which not only harm the authors of these deceits but also discredit virtue, because such is the condition of common and ignorant people that with no judgment at all they make rules of individual cases in order to see virtue as evil . . . they would rather take a fall as an opportunity to tarnish it, if they could.[47]

Within this context of deceit, Yepes rejoices in the appearance of Teresa, who, although a woman, was sent by God to provide an example of true Christianity.

> And it is of no less importance that God has revealed in this age such a great display of sanctity, in which such marvelous and rare things are demonstrated—not only admirable virtues and marvelous works, but extraordinary revelations, visions, raptures, conversations with God—so that when the world, having little faith, or confused by the many deceits to which some artful and false people sub-

46. Ibid.: ". . . las que con fortaleza vencen sus pasiones y las sujetan a Dios, hombres se han de llamar, y los hombres que se dejan vencer de ellas, mujeres son. No consiste esto en la diversidad del cuerpo, sino en la fortaleza del alma. Vean si lo siente así la Iglesia, pues a vírgenes muy valerosas, como Santa Inés, Santa Agueda, manda rezar el oficio de los mártires para declararnos que las habemos de contar por varones. Así que no hagamos caso de revelaciones de mujeres, que quiere decir de personas flacas y rendidas a sus pasiones; pero de las de una mujer más varonil que muchos grandes varones, tan animosa y tan valerosa, y de las que a ella se parecieren, mucho caso se debe hacer."

47. Diego de Yepes, *Vida de Santa Teresa de Jesús* (1599; Buenos Aires, 1946), p. 18: ". . . grandes los embustes y tramas que el demonio y la hipocresía han inventado, dañando no sólo a los autores de estos engaños, sino también desacreditando a la virtud, porque es tal la condición del vulgo y gente ignorante, que sin discreción alguna hace reglas de casos particulares para sentir mal de la virtud . . . antes toma ocasión de una caída para escurecerla, si pudiese."

ject it every day, looked from afar at these revelations, visions, raptures, and other gifts and virtues of the saints, thinking that all this had ceased, it could see with its own eyes that the hand of the Lord is no less powerful now than it was then, and that if hypocrisy has cloaked itself in the cape of virtue, trying to pass for it, that is no reason to give less credence to what is [true] virtue and the work of God, even though it appears under the weakness of a woman.[48]

Teresa's biographers realized the inherent conflict between her life and achievements and the gender ideology to which they, too, subscribed. Rather than challenge those assumptions in any meaningful way, they chose to argue for Teresa's circumvention of the natural order. The fact that biographies of Teresa begin rather polemically with a defense of her exceptional nature as a woman underscores the continuing climate of suspicion surrounding religious women, a climate that was so pervasive that most men did not challenge it. Over time, it was the climate that emerged victorious as Teresa's life was increasingly interpreted not as a sign that other women could achieve virtue but as a singular expression of God's grace, all the more remarkable because it was made manifest in a woman.

Teresa's Life and Its Institutional Meaning

By the time the canonization process was far advanced, much of Teresa's message about women's spirituality had been muted. The complex portrait sketched by Teresa's contemporaries did not emerge so clearly in the official *vita* written in 1609–10. This vita can be understood as the institutional church's version of Teresa's life and its meaning. The list of 117 points relied more on Teresa's *Vida* and other accounts of her life than on witnesses' testimonies.[49] Her books, which by 1610 appeared so clearly to contain orthodox mystical doctrine, were declared to have been written while she was in a state of ecstasy[50] and thus completely reliable. Indeed, the author could

48. Ibid.: "Y no es de menos consideración el haber Dios descubierto en esta edad un tan gran espectáculo de santidad, en el cual se muestran cosas tan prodigiosas y raras, y no sólo de admirables virtudes y obras maravillosas, sino extraordinarias revelaciones, visiones, arrobamientos, hablas y trato con Dios, para que cuando el mundo por su poca fe, o por los muchos engaños que cada día experimentaba de alguna gente engañosa y fingida, miraba desde lejos las revelaciones, visiones, arrobamientos y otros dones y virtudes de los santos, pareciéndole que todo aquello había cesado, vea delante de sus ojos que no es menos poderosa ahora que entonces la mano del Señor, y que si la hipocresía se ha cubierto con la capa de la virtud, procurando fingirse cual ella, no por eso se ha de dar menos crédito a lo que es virtud y obra de Dios, aunque venga debajo de la flaqueza de una mujer."

49. For example, the official *vita* includes the childhood incident of running away, her entry into the Encarnación, her illness and recuperation at her uncle's house, her conversion upon reading Augustine's *Confessions*, her early experience of prayer and visions, and the transverberation. Little of this is mentioned in the testimonies.

50. See *BMC* 20:xxxvii.

now claim, "the doctrine of the books not only is holy and Catholic, but also very fruitful for the Church; great improvement has followed from the reading of these books, and marvelous conversions and changes in habits have been witnessed [as a result]."[51]

To demonstrate divine favor, the vita accentuated the incidence of visions in Teresa's mystical experiences, counterbalancing them with her prudent consultation of more than thirty-five theological experts. Because "the servant of God feared being misled by the devil, she was obliged to consult with all the gentlemen [trained] in theology and sanctity who flourished in Spain."[52]

Teresa's consultation with theologians, however, probably had more to do with her need to prove the validity of her experience than with any doubt of her own. This commentary reflects the institutional church's desire to control the discernment of spirits and monitor internal religious experience as much as possible. The vita was careful to make clear that Teresa's experience of prayer was judged to be genuine because it left a "continual glow about her face."[53] Teresa was seen to have been given several gifts of the Holy Spirit that enabled her to take on important pastoral duties. The vita described her gift of prophecy as well as the gift of discerning spirits.

When the vita described Teresa's virtues, it stressed her obedience, giving the example of the famous incident with Diego de Yanguas:

> She burned a book she had written about the Song of Songs, which contained excellent counsel and doctrine, at the order of Father Diego de Yanguas, her confessor, who at that time thought it indecent for a woman to publish commentaries on Sacred Scripture. And when Father Domingo Báñez ordered her to burn the book of her *Life*, which she had written under the orders of very important confessors, she replied that she would obey him immediately if he really commanded her to do it; and the servant of God would have burned it at once if he had not restrained her from doing so.[54]

---

51. Ibid., p. xxxviii: "La doctrina de estos libros, como se echa de ver por su eminencia, y así pública y comúnmente, es tenido y reputado que no fué adquirida o enseñada por industria humana, sino infundida por Dios por medio de la oración; y por esta causa haber sido pintada y pintarse la Virgen con una paloma encima de su cabeza, la cual ella vió sobre de sí en cierto día del Espíritu Santo. Iten, que la doctrina de los libros no solamente es santa y católica, mas muy provechosa a la Iglesia, y que se ha seguido grande aprovechamiento a las almas con la lección de estos libros, y se han visto maravillosas conversiones y mudanzas de costumbres."

52. Ibid., p. xviii: "Como se le multiplicasen los favores y beneficios de Dios, mucho más la sierva de Dios temía de ser engañada del demonio; por lo cual fue forzada a consultar todos los varones que florecían en la universa de España en doctrina y santidad."

53. Ibid., p. liii: ". . . después de la oración tenía el rostro resplaneciente, como se lee de Moisés, hermoseado con una celestial hermosura. . . ."

54. Ibid., p. xxxix: "Quemó un libro que había compuesto sobre los Cantares, que contenía admirables avisos y doctrina por mandado del padre Diego de Yanguas, su confesor, que en-

The vita clearly put Teresa's obedience within the context of the *alumbrados* and the suspicion of women's religious experience. "She used to say that if she did not obey what she was ordered to do by her prelates and confessors, even though they were very arduous and difficult things, she would understand that she was deluded and deceived [by the devil], and from then on she would not dare to ask God for anything or to engage in prayer."[55] Teresa's desire to prove her orthodoxy by being completely obedient to all her confessors was held up as a virtue even when it went beyond reason: "Not only did she reject the discourses of reason in obedience, but she did not even believe divine revelations without the proof of obedience, and she did not write anything in her works that was divinely revealed to her if it were not approved by her confessors and prelates."[56]

Penitential practice received little attention in the iconographic tradition, but the vita noted that Teresa

> beat herself often with disciplines, and many times with keys or with nettles until the blood ran, and the only salve she applied to the wounds was more disciplines. She subjected her body to iron chains, from which protruded iron points; other times she rolled around in thorns. She engaged in these and many other penitential practices until she had completely destroyed her health.[57]

Teresa's poor health was also, according to the vita, related to the fact that she had extraordinary prayer experiences, which literally ate away at her body:

> From this continuous and familiar colloquy [with God] her face would often be luminous after prayer, as one reads about Moses, made beautiful by a celestial beauty, sometimes it shone like crystal, and at other times it seemed to emit rays.

---

tonces pensaba ser indecente que una mujer sacase a luz comentarios sobre la Sagrada Escritura. Como le mandase el padre Domingo Báñez que echase en el fuego el libro de su *Vida*, el cual había escrito por mandado de gravísimos confesores, respondió que al punto le obedecería si él se lo mandaba de veras; el cual la sierva de Dios luego al punto hubiera quemado si no se lo hubiera él prohibido."

55. Ibid.: "Solía decir que si no obedeciese lo que le fuese mandado por sus prelados y confesores, aunque fuesen cosas muy arduas y dificultosas, entendería era ilusa y engañada, y que no se atrevería de allí adelante a pedir a Dios alguna cosa ni ejercitarse en la oración."

56. Ibid., pp. xxxix–xl: "No solamente en la obediencia desechaba los discursos de la razón, mas ni creía las divinas revelaciones sin la prueba de la obediencia, y ninguna cosa ponía por obra que divinamente le fuese revelada si no fuese aprobada por sus confesores y prelados."

57. Ibid., p. xlii: "Azotábase muy a menudo con disciplinas, y muchas veces con llaves o con hortigas hasta derrimar sangre, y no ponía otro remedio a las llagas que se hacía, si no es añadiendo nuevas disciplinas. Sujetaba el cuerpo con cadenas de hierro, de las cuales sobresalían algunas puntas de hierro; otras veces también se revolcaba entre las espinas, en las cuales y en otras muchas obras de penitencia se ejercitó hasta la total destrucción de su salud."

She was constantly transformed in God in such a way that it consumed her body and her life; for this reason she often could not eat.[58]

Teresa was seen as the Counter-Reformation's ideal woman. The vita noted with approval, "She was pleased to be considered a daughter of the church."[59] This clear allegiance with the institutional church was made manifest in many ways. Teresa was understood to have devoted her life to the defense of the Catholic faith, in the same way that the new Jesuit missionaries were doing overseas. Through her devotion to the institutional church, then, Teresa, too, could be considered a "martyr for the faith," as the vita explains: "She ardently wished to suffer martyrdom for the confession of the faith, and she said that . . . for just one ceremony of the Church she would willingly suffer death a thousand times."[60] She continually prayed for the "exaltation of the Holy Church, and for those who engaged in the propagation of the faith and the preaching of the Gospel."[61]

Teresa was also said to have "held the prelates of the church in high esteem and exhorted her nuns to revere the Church and the Pope, and ordered them to keep all the rites of the Church faithfully."[62] Though she wanted her nuns to understand Christian doctrine, she did not encourage them to be learned or curious. In fact, she was so "displeased when her nuns tried to pry into the hidden mysteries of the faith or other curiosities that had nothing to do with women" that she refused to admit one young woman into the order because she wanted to bring her Bible with her into the convent:

> While in Toledo, a young noblewoman asked to receive the habit, and having determined that she could be admitted, she told [Teresa] that she had a Bible in her house that she had to fetch to the convent. Immediately she was excluded by the servant of God: "Don't bring the Bible here or even come back, because we're women who don't know anything but knitting." And not having admitted that young woman to the convent for her excessive curiosity was nothing short of di-

---

58. Ibid., p. liii: "De este continuo y familiar coloquio muchas veces después de la oración tenía el rostro resplandeciente, como se lee de Moisés, hermoseado con una celestial hermosura, algunas veces que lucía a manera de cristal, y también otras veces parece que echaba de sí rayos. En tanta manera estaba continuamente transformada en Dios, que consumía la salud juntamente con la vida; por esta causa no podía comer muchas veces."

59. Ibid., p. lv: "Teníase en mucho cuando se consideraba hija de la Iglesia."

60. Ibid., p. liv: "Deseó ardientemente padecer martirio por la confesión de la fe, y decía que no solamente por la verdad y fe de la Escritura, sino por sola una ceremonia de la Iglesia sufriría de buena gana mil veces la muerte."

61. Ibid., pp. liv–lv: "Continuamente rogaba por exaltación de la Santa Iglesia, y por aquellos que se ocupaban en la propagación de la fe y predicación del Evangelio."

62. Ibid., p. lv: "Estimaba mucho a los prelados de la Iglesia, y exhortaba a sus monjas a la reverencia de la Iglesia y del Sumo Pontífice, y les mandaba que exactamente guardasen los ritos de la Iglesia, que ella en gran manera guardaba."

vine instinct, because, as it later turned out, she was punished by the Inquisition for errors against the faith.[63]

The vita spent comparatively little time on the condition of Teresa's incorrupt body and the continual flow of blood and oil from it, which had so impressed Teresa's contemporaries and had, in effect, kept her canonization process alive. It summarized some twelve miracles attributed to Teresa after her death, and noted that many more had been reported. The vita's clear emphasis on Teresa's virtues, which in many cases it presented as gender specific, suggests that the *vita* and Teresa's canonization in general were part of a strategy to develop the Counter-Reformation ideal of "woman." What Teresa achieved was much less important than the virtues that she embodied and that other women could imitate.

The Holy Woman Teresa

The papal bull of Teresa's canonization, signed by Gregory XV in 1622, reiterated the virtues described in the vita, which had become the cornerstones of Tridentine Catholicism. First, Gregory held up as exemplary Teresa's devotion to the sacraments and to Roman Catholic doctrine: "She believed and confessed the Holy Sacraments of the Church and the other dogmas of the Catholic Religion with such firmness and truth that, as she often said, she could not have been surer of anything else."[64] Her religious experience, he declared, affirmed the truth of Roman Catholicism. Thus she was gifted with visions of the body of Christ present in the Eucharist. In addition, she so mourned the gross ignorance of the unfaithful and the heretics that she turned to prayer and penance to effect their conversion: "Not only did she make many prayers [on their behalf], but she also offered up fasts and disciplines and with other exquisite torments she afflicted and mortified her body."[65] Finally, the bull presented her as absolutely obedient to her religious superiors:

63. Ibid.: "Llevaba mal que sus monjas anduviesen escudriñando los misterios escondidos de la fe u otras curiosidades que no pertenecían a mujeres. Habitando en Toledo, le pidió el hábito de religión una doncella, a la cual habiendo determinado de admitir en la Religión, la dijo la doncella que tenía en su casa la Biblia, la cual había de traer al monasterio. Al punto fué excluida por la sierva de Dios: no traigáis acá la Biblia ni volváis, porque somos mujeres que no sabemos otra cosa más que hilar; y no haber admitido la sierva de Dios a esta doncella por la demasiada curiosidad, no fué sino instinto divino, porque como después sucedió, fué castigada por el Santo Oficio de la Inquisición por causa de algunos errores que tuvo contra la fe."

64. See *Bula de canonización de Santa Teresa de Jesús*, in *BMC* 2:421: "Con tanta firmeza y verdad creía y confesaba los Santos Sacramentos de la Iglesia y los demás dogmas de la Católica Religión, que no podía, como muchas veces ella aseguraba, tener mayor certeza de otra ninguna cosa."

65. Ibid., p. 422: "Lloraba con perpetuas y continuas lágrimas las tinieblas y el poco conocimiento de nuestra fe de los infieles y herejes, y por su reconocimiento y conversión, no tan solamente hacía muchas oraciones, sino también ofrecía ayunos y disciplinas, y con otros exquisitos tormentos afligía y maceraba su cuerpo."

The vows and promises concerning the observance and profession of her religion which she had offered to God she kept with great precision, care, and diligence, and not only did she perfect and accomplish all her outward acts with great humility in accordance with the will and opinion of her superiors, but she firmly proposed in her heart to subject and offer all her thoughts and works to them. . . .[66]

As examples of Teresa's complete lack of self-will, Gregory recalled that at the command of her confessors she at first scorned her visions, and that she burned her commentary on the Song of Songs.

Teresa was the first woman to be canonized in the seventeenth century. It seemed quite natural for the pope to make an official statement about Teresa as a model of holiness for women. Indeed, Gregory's bull hailed Teresa as a "new Deborah," a woman who,

having conquered and triumphed over her flesh with perpetual virginity, and over the world with admirable humility, and over all the machinations and temptations of the devil with great and abundant virtues . . . exceeded and surpassed feminine nature with admirable courage and strength of will.[67]

Clearly the pope was caught in the same dilemma as Teresa herself had been. Women had to struggle "manfully" for virtue, yet they had to conform to social and institutional expectations of femininity so as not to "subvert" the established hierarchial order of the sexes.[68] Ironically, the pope adopted the same stance toward "womanhood" that Teresa had. As the bull explains, by

66. Ibid.: "Los votos y promesas que en lo tocante a la observancia y profesión de su Religión había ofrecido a Dios, los cumplió con grande puntualidad, cuidado y diligencia, y no tan solamente perfeccionaba y acababa todos los actos exteriores con grande humildad al arbitrio y parecer de sus superiores, sino que propuso firmemente en su corazón de sujetar y rendirles todos sus pensamientos y obras, de cuya intención y proposición nos dejó grandes ejemplos."

67. Ibid., pp. 419–20: ". . . después de haber vencido y triunfado de su carne con perpetua virginidad, y del mundo con admirable humildad, y de todas las artes y lazos del demonio con grandes y exuberantes virtudes, abatiendo y desechando de sí las cosas grandes y habiendo excedido y sobrepujado con admirable valor y fortaleza de ánimo la naturaleza femenil. . . ."

68. According to the psychologist Ellyn Kaschak, the challenge to conform to gender identities has characterized Western society for centuries, and continues to be a problem today. "Simply put, while males may be ridiculed and humiliated for behaving or sounding or looking like females, so may females. Women are subject to censure not only for behaving too much like men but for behaving too much like women. . . . While a man in our society can attain approval and avoid humiliation by behaving in socially prescribed masculine ways, a woman does not have this same uncomplicated alternative. She may be admired for responding in an appropriate (feminine) way, but she is also subject to social sanction for this behavior, just as she would be for responding in an inappropriate (masculine) way": *Engendered Lives: A New Psychology of Women's Experience* (New York, 1992), pp. 40–41.

becoming exaggeratedly feminine (particularly through her embrace of humility), Teresa approached manliness, thus avoiding all the problems associated with the "feminine nature." Dissociated from her body, and thereby freed from demonic influence, Teresa had overcome "womanhood" and was no longer truly a woman.

The pope's verdict was echoed by many members of Teresa's own order. When Teresa was declared the patron saint of Spain, Francisco de Jesús, a Carmelite friar, proclaimed: "This woman ceased to be a woman, restoring herself to the state of a man to her greater glory than if she had been [a man] from the beginning, for she corrected nature with her virtue, returning to the bone from which she sprang."[69] Later observers, such as Silverio de Santa Teresa, have used Teresa's detachment, purity, and strict observance of her order's rules to establish models of femininity in the twentieth century:

> Woman, according to the Holy Spirit, must be the grace of the house, and if a certain disdain and harshness of character are tolerable in a man, in a woman only gentle and mild virtues are appropriate. . . . In religion, culture, and feminine virtues, Saint Teresa is the greatest synthesis and personification [of virtue]. She is, as well, the model of practical and sacrificial works.[70]

The Parameters of Female Sanctity

Teresa's canonization demonstrates how narrow the parameters for women's sanctity were. Institutional definitions of virtue were conditioned by the post-Tridentine agenda to control public space and to confine women to increasingly smaller spheres of influence. In such a context, women's spiritual expression, which traditionally had offered them many options otherwise denied them, proved to be a minefield.

Teresa, who vacillated from stereotypical forms of feminine humility and obedience to public activities judged to be male prerogatives, was able to negotiate these difficult times. Indeed, in Teresa of Avila the institutional church found a powerful spokesperson for the Counter-Reformation church. Having proclaimed her allegiance both to hierarchical officials and

---

69. *Relación sencilla y fiel de las fiestas . . .* (1627), quoted in Francis Cerdán, "Santa Teresa en *Los sermones del patronato* (1627)," in *Santa Teresa y la literatura mística hispánica*, ed. Manuel Criado de Val (Madrid, 1984), p. 606: "Esta . . . ya dejó de ser mujer, restituyéndose en el ser de varón con mayor gloria suya que si lo hubiera sido desde principio, pues enmendó a la naturaleza con su virtud, volviéndose con ésta al hueso de adonde salió." On this point, see also Weber, *Teresa of Avila*, pp. 17–18.

70. Silverio de Santa Teresa, *Santa Teresa: Modelo de feminismo cristiano* (Burgos, 1931), p. 93: "La mujer, según el Espíritu Santo, debe ser la gracia de la casa, y si cierta esquivez y aspereza de condición es tolerable en el hombre, a la mujer encuadran exclusivamente las virtudes apacibles y blandas. . . . En religión, cultura y virtudes femeninas, Santa Teresa es la síntesis y la personificación más levantada. Es, además, modelo de acción práctica y sacrificada."

to the sacramental life of the church, Teresa was an exemplary model of Roman Catholic piety. The interpretive "problems" of Teresa's embodied experience of prayer—the inquisitors' major concern—could be overcome when they were understood as supernatural favors properly monitored by trained theologians. Finally, Teresa's independence, originality, and spiritual power were acceptable as long as the woman who embodied them was seen as exceptional, not in these respects to be emulated. Teresa's singularity at once separated her from other women and confirmed the abundance of grace that had allowed her to overcome her womanhood. Thus the Teresa who came to be canonized was increasingly a solitary figure, so circumscribed by her virtues that she would encourage women to exist within the margins of the institutional church.

"Saint Teresa" reduced an astute and ingenious woman to a set of patriarchal values essential to the Counter-Reformation agenda, an image that perpetuated stereotypes of holy women and effectively blocked other women's bid for autonomy and authority within the Roman Catholic Church. The clash between reality and gender ideology prevented many women from achieving official recognition of their sanctity. In a twist of irony, Teresa of Avila, who had fought so hard for women's spiritual autonomy, became the instrument by which the Roman hierarchy propagated its own gender ideology.

Conclusion

The complex political and religious situation of sixteenth-century Europe encouraged new formulations of Roman Catholic socioreligious control. The institutional church seemed initially to be caught off guard by Protestant developments, but by the 1550s it had reemerged in a considerably more authoritarian form. At this point, mental prayer had become a symbol of spiritual and religious autonomy, for which Tridentine Catholicism had little use. In Spain the Inquisition went to work on the *alumbrados* and others who taught prayer techniques in efforts to maintain control over the various forms of esoteric authority that were embedded in the experience of mental prayer.

Repression of mystical experience and rigid authoritarianism could not sustain religious identity, however. As Catholicism moved into the seventeenth century, the papacy began to reaffirm much of the medieval traditions that had come under fire. Caught up in the debate over the role of human participation in justification, Catholics had to affirm the role of human participation in salvation; thus mystical experience had a "natural" place on the Catholic agenda. But Spain had already become embroiled in trials of *alumbrados*, and those trials gave rise to new concerns about how much authority should be granted to mystical experience and whether or not such experience complemented the Catholic sacramental life. Further, descriptions of mystical union that assigned a passive role to the soul raised objections because of their implications in the question of justification. When Teresa's published works appeared in 1588, they generated controversy but also offered creative possibilities. Teresa's early critics did not see her agenda—the development of mystical treatises in the vernacular—as an important source of Roman Catholic identity. The growing recognition of the need for an orthodox, authoritative mystical text was a major factor in the resolution of the procedures against Teresa's works. Her books could not be used, however, until Teresa's stature as a woman in the church was resolved.

The Roman Catholic orientation toward a highly ordered church had special implications for women. Understood as the descendants of Eve, who had introduced chaos into the universe, women were viewed as more susceptible than men to the devil's deceptions. In Spain the esoteric authority of women became, abstractly and concretely, an impossible reality.[1] The climate of suspicion and the process of censorship imposed on mystical writers—particularly women—forced them to search for new sources of authority within their own experience, because they received more challenges to their internal authority. Mystics were called upon to demonstrate that the internal authority they received from visions or other kinds of spiritual experience neither clashed with the institutional authority of the hierarchy nor encouraged others to challenge it. In this struggle women had an especially difficult time. The Tridentine decrees on the claustration of nuns emphasized contemplation as the central role of religious women, but the fruits of women's contemplation were then subjected to close scrutiny and not always accepted by the religious hierarchy. Limited primarily to the vernacular and to an elementary level of theological discourse, these women struggled to express the spirituality confirmed as their vocation by Tridentine reforms.

In chapter 1 we encountered several women who aspired to holiness but were not institutionally recognized because they were not seen to conform to the virtues of humility and obedience, to practice penance, or to have achieved special access to God in ways appropriate to their gender. One of the clearest differences in religious expectations of men and women is seen in the matter of humility. Proud and independent women could not expect recognition. The test of obedience applied to women to see if they were truly humble was a conflict of authority and epistemology unlike tests that spiritual men faced. The devotion of women to their inner spiritual experiences was set against their allegiance to the verdict (often negative) of representatives of the institutional church. For women the problem was how to affirm the authority of their religious experiences while accepting the authority of institutional figures in the framework of patriarchal forms of humility. Women's survival strategies and their acceptance of external authority produced heavily encoded public and written expressions of self which historians are just beginning to decipher and interpret.

We have seen how Teresa de Jesús responded to the challenges to women's spirituality, that her tremendous struggle to gain credibility among her peers was the norm for women in sixteenth-century Spain. Teresa drew her strong

---

1. One indication of the Spanish inquisitors' success in silencing women's voices is in the number of spiritual works that never reached the printing presses. A wealth of these texts remain in manuscript form in convents and libraries; others fall out of the Inquisition's records, where they were kept after the theological review process.

sense of vocation as an author of mystical texts from the void in spiritual literature created by the Valdés Index. She adapted her style and ideas to the standards of the times, expressing her doctrine within the context of obedience to institutional authorities. Further, she deliberately located her mystical experience and the esoteric authority it gave her within the sacramental life of the Roman Catholic tradition. Concerned about the survival of other spiritual women whose religious experience was primarily visionary, she shared her strategies with other women, helping them to express their visions in ways that would not attract negative attention. She worried about the survival of her doctrine and wrote the *Moradas* because she believed that the *Vida* might not emerge unscathed from the Inquisition's tribunal. Teresa did not allow censorship and repression to keep her from writing. She cooperated with the system to the extent that she had to. She incorporated the censor's comments in the second version of her *Camino de perfección*, yet she did not destroy the earlier Escorial edition. She did not allow her commentary on the Song of Songs to disappear, even though one of her confessors instructed her to burn it. Teresa was frustrated by the strictures placed upon her, yet she had great confidence that in another era her works would be read and would gain influence.

Teresa's life was a struggle to define and legitimate both her mystical experience and the ecclesiastical roles that that experience encouraged her to claim. Over time Teresa became increasingly adept at encoding her experience and at breaking into the male-dominated realm of spiritual direction and mystical treatises. To do so she took on a persona that mimicked the feminine character idealized by her male contemporaries. She achieved significant reforms because her willingness to shape her behavior to accord with men's expectations and to hide behind "feminine" subterfuges when necessary allowed her to survive harsh criticisms of "womanhood" and women.

She knew, too, that her church lacked a mystical text with its own intrinsic authority, a body of ideas deemed orthodox yet authoritative, expressed in a nonauthoritative way and therefore nonthreatening. Teresa's works answered the needs of her times perfectly. Inspired by the dearth of vernacular mystical treatises produced by the Valdés Index, Teresa employed considerable rhetorical skill in developing a body of works that addressed the spiritual needs of her contemporaries without openly challenging the authority of church officials, the sacramental system, or any other aspect of orthodox Catholic doctrine or practice. The ultimate verdict on Teresa was that not only was she orthodox, but she represented orthodoxy. Over time she became a model of sanctity and a doctor of the Roman Catholic Church. Teresa's canonization finally resolved her quest for authority as a woman in the church and ensured the survival of her works.

The decision to canonize Teresa in 1622 indicates the recognition of a distinct, Catholic mystical spirituality codified by both Teresa and her contemporary John of the Cross, one of the major achievements of the so-called Counter-Reformation.[2] The Inquisition's censors repressed spiritual literature that they feared might incite its readers to challenge the institutional authority of the Roman Catholic Church. Ironically, however, the indexes of prohibited books inspired Teresa, John of the Cross, and others to produce new authoritative texts that eventually formed one of the pillars of Roman Catholic identity.

Yet Teresa's canonization contributed to a different Roman Catholic agenda as well: the production and maintenance of gender ideology. To some degree, all of Teresa's contemporaries grappled with the fact that Teresa shattered sixteenth-century assumptions about gender. Many of her contemporaries found her unconventionality acceptable because they understood it to be consistent with her religious vocation. Her critics, however, were profoundly disturbed by her subversion of gender roles, and viewed it as evidence of a tendency toward heresy. By the end of the sixteenth century, as Teresa's canonization looked promising, the institutional church had to come to grips with the fact that Teresa straddled its conceptions of masculinity and femininity.

In its endorsement of Teresa's sanctity, the Roman Catholic hierarchy promoted her hyperfeminine traits in order to establish a model for women that was consistent with the Counter-Reformation's orientation toward masculinity. Though women did indeed need to overcome "womanhood" in order to advance spiritually, they had to do so in "womanly" ways. Women's religious lives were secure only with the explicit recognition of their social and theological inferiority; humility and obedience were the yardsticks of women's conformity to this law. Women were considered suitable for subordinate roles in the church; they could provide the support network of prayer and penitential activity, the nursing and domestic activities that permitted men to engage in religious activity in the secular world. Teresa's call for women to play a more active role in the mission of the church fitted into this process, especially since her critiques of the contemporary church could be muted in the contemplative's cell.

What is so paradoxical about Teresa is that her identity as a woman came to have very different meanings for the women who came after her. The hagiographical treatises and the official canonization documents make it clear

2. Michel de Certeau recognizes the creation of mysticism as a category during the second half of the sixteenth century, and considers that the appearance of Teresa's works marks "the moment of its greatest formalization": *La fable mystique* (Paris, 1982), p. 29.

that many men viewed her as upholding their prescriptions for female behavior; yet she gave birth to a new generation of spiritual women, encouraging their literary expression of themselves and their world. These women's texts, suggest Electa Arenal and Stacey Schlau, "contain almost the only record we have of the consciousness of early modern women in Hispanic lands."[3]

Teresa's message and contributions to women were very complex. My own assessment is that she taught women more about the process of survival in the church than anything else. In other words, although I agree that the literature produced by Teresa's successors has important social-historical value—or, as Arenal and Schlau put it, "we regard the written material produced by the nuns who claimed her as spiritual mother to be essential to an understanding of the history, psychology, literature, spirituality, and sexual politics of the period"—it is overly optimistic to call it a "reclaiming of the 'mother tongue.'"[4] A "mother tongue" would imply freedom from the patriarchal language and assumptions that clearly impeded Teresa. There is ample material in Teresa's works to enable women to intuit how the mystical way might involve "an alternative mode to patriarchy,"[5] but the rhetorical survival strategies and the limitations on women which they represent are at least as striking to the reader. As we continue to recover and interpret the texts of spiritual women in Spain, we must be sensitive to the climate that produced Saint Teresa's persona while recognizing her keen insights into the politics of sanctity in her day.

3. Arenal and Schlau, *Untold Sisters*, p. 2.
4. Ibid., p. 2.
5. See Lerner, *Creation of Feminist Consciousness*, p. 152.

Appendix:
Primary and secondary sources
of inquisitional inquiries
regarding Teresa de Jesús and her works

Date of inquiry	Tribunal	Primary sources	Secondary sources
1570	Pastrana	Relación de Isabel de Santo Domingo[1]	BN MS. 13.483: Andrés de la Encarnación, "Memorias historiales," fol. 179r
January–June 1575	Valladolid	AHN, Inq., lib. 578, fol. 266v AHN, Inq., leg. 3192, exps. 98, 109	Llamas, pp. 44–52
March 1575	Córdoba	AHN, Inq., lib. 578, fol. 282r AHN, Inq., leg. 2395	Llamas, pp. 32–42
January–April/May 1576	Seville	AHN, Inq., lib. 578, fol. 365v AHN, Inq., leg. 2946	Llamas, pp. 53–127. Efrén de la Madre de Dios and Otger Steggink, *Santa Teresa y su tiempo*, vol. 2, pt. 1 (Salamanca, 1984)
1578–79	Seville	AHN, Clero, legs. 3820, 3821	Llamas, pp. 127–94
1579–80	Valladolid	Ana de San Bartolomé, *Autobiografía* (Madrid, 1969), pp. 57–58	—

continued

Date of inquiry	Tribunal	Primary sources	Secondary sources
1589–93	Consejo	AHN, Inq., leg. 4442, no. 43 AHN, Inq., leg. 2706 AHN, Inq., leg. 3198 AHN, Inq., leg. 3081, no. 21	Llamas, pp. 227–392

1. Andrés de la Encarnación reviewed this document in his "Memorias historiales," but its whereabouts are not known at this time.

2. Llamas's transcription of this document lists the sources as AHN, leg. 1063; elsewhere it has frequently been cited as AHN, Inq., leg. 1063. Neither citation is correct. María Dolores Alonso, head of the Inquisitional section of the Archivo Histórico Nacional, informs me that the material is in the Papeles de Clero there, under the numbers cited here.

Selected
Bibliography

Primary Sources

Unpublished Works

Archivo Histórico Nacional, Madrid (AHN). Inquisición, legajos 104–13, 1856,
2072, 2075, 2395, 2706, 2946, 3081, 3192, 3198, 4442; libros 578, 579.
Biblioteca Nacional de Madrid (BN)
    MSS. 13.482–84. Andrés de la Encarnación. "Memorias historiales."
    MS. 19.389. Ana de San Bartolomé. "Vida de la madre Ana de San Bartolomé."
    MS. 12936(37). María de San José (Gracián). "Notas marginales a la Vida de la
    M. Teresa de Jesús, escrita de su misma mano."
    MS. 2176. María de San José (Salazar). "Historia de la fundacion de los descalzos
    y descalzas carmelitas que fundo Santa Theresa de Jesus nuestra madre."
    MS. 3508. María de San José (Salazar). "Libro de las Recreaciones."
    MS. 3537. María de San José (Salazar). "Ramillete de mirra."

Published Works

Ana de San Bartolomé. *Autobiografía*. Madrid: Editorial de Espiritualidad, 1969.
Avila, Julián de. *La Vida de la Santa Madre Teresa de Jesús*. Ed. Vicente de La Fuente.
    Madrid: Antonio Pérez Dubrull, 1881.
Bujanda, Jesús Martínez de, ed. *Index de l'Inquisition espagnole, 1551, 1554, 1559*.
    Sherbrooke, Québec: Centre d'Etudes de la Renaissance, 1984.
—, ed. *Index des livres interdits*. Sherbrooke, Québec: Centre d'Etudes de la Re-
    naissance, 1985–93.
Castañega, Martín de. *Tratado de las supersticiones y hechicerías*. Madrid: Bibliófilos
    Españoles, 1946.
Córdoba, Martín de. *Tratado que se intitula Jardín de las nobles doncellas*. Ed. Fer-
    nando Rubio. Biblioteca de Autores Españoles 171. Madrid: Atlas, 1946.
Francisco de Santa María. *Reforma de los descalzos de Nuestra Señora del Carmen de la
    primitiva observancia, hecha por Santa Teresa de Jesús*. 2 vols. Madrid, 1644–55.
Gracián, Jerónimo de la Madre de Dios. *Anotaciones al p. Ribera*. In Antonio de San
    Joaquín, *Año Teresiano, diario histórico, panegyrico moral, en que se descubren las
    virtudes, sucesos y maravillas de la seráphica y mýstica Doctora de la Iglesia Santa
    Teresa de Jesús*. 12 vols. Madrid, 1733–69.

——. *Declaración en que se trata de la perfecta vida y virtudes heróicas de la Santa Madre Teresa de Jesús y de las fundaciones de sus monasterios.* (Brussels, 1611.) In *Biblioteca Mística Carmelitana,* ed. Silverio de Santa Teresa, 16:485–510. Burgos: El Monte Carmelo, 1933.

——. *Dilucidario del verdadero espíritu; en que se manifiesta la verdadera oración, pureza, luz, charidad y trato del alma con Dios.* (Brussels, 1608.) In *Biblioteca Mística Carmelitana,* ed. Silverio de Santa Teresa, 15:1–242. Burgos: El Monte Carmelo, 1932.

——. *Escolias y adiciones al libro de la Vida de la M. Teresa de Jesús que compuso el P. Doctor Ribera, hechas por fray Jerónimo Gracián de la Madre de Dios, carmelita descalzo.* Ed. Juan Luis Astigarraga. *Ephemérides Carmeliticae* 32 (1981): 358–430.

——. *Peregrinación de Anastasio.* In *Biblioteca Mística Carmelitana,* ed. Silverio de Santa Teresa, vol. 17. Burgos: El Monte Carmelo, 1933.

Granada, Luis de. *Historia de Sor María de la Visitación y Sermón de las caídas públicas.* Ed. Bernardo Velado Graña. Barcelona: Juan Flors, 1962.

Herrero Bayona, Francisco, ed. *Reproducción Foto-litográfica y fieles traslados impresos del "Camino de Perfección" y el "Modo de Visitar los Conventos," escritos por Santa Teresa de Jesús, que se veneran en El Escorial.* Madrid: Luis N. de Gavina, 1883.

Horozco y Covarrubias, Juan de. *Tratado de la verdadera y falsa prophecia.* Segovia: Juan de la Cuesta, 1588.

Juan de la Cruz. *Obras completas.* Ed. Jucinio Ruano de la Iglesia. Madrid: Biblioteca de Autores Cristianos, 1982.

León, Luis de. *De la vida, muerte y virtudes y milagros de la Santa Madre Teresa de Jesús.* In *Biblioteca mística carmelitana,* ed. Silverio de Santa Teresa, 2:474–89. Burgos: El Monte Carmelo, 1934.

——. *Obras completas.* 2 vols. Madrid: Biblioteca de Autores Cristianos, 1957.

Llorca, Bernardino, ed. *Bulario Pontificio de la Inquisición Española en su período constitucional (1478–1525) según los Fondos del Archivo Histórico Nacional de Madrid.* Rome: Pontificia Universita Gregoriana, 1949.

María de San José. *Libro de las recreaciones. Ramillete de Mirra. Avisos, máximas y poesías.* Ed. Silverio de Santa Teresa. Burgos: El Monte Carmelo, 1913.

María de Santa Domingo. *The Book of Prayer of Sor María de Santo Domingo.* Ed. Mary E. Giles. Albany: SUNY Press, 1988.

Ribadeneyra, Pedro de. "Tratado de la tribulación." In *Obras escogidas del padro Pedro de Rivadeneira de la Compañía de Jesús,* ed. Vicente de La Fuente. Biblioteca de Autores Españoles 60. Madrid: Atlas, 1952.

Ribera, Francisco de. *La Vida de la madre Teresa de Jesús, fundadora de las Descalzas y Descalzos, compuesta por el Doctor Francisco de Ribera, de la Compañía de Jesús, y repartida en cinco libros.* (Salamanca, 1590.) Ed. Jaime Pons. Barcelona: Gustavo Gili, 1908.

Silverio de Santa Teresa, ed. *Biblioteca mística carmelitana.* 35 vols. Burgos: El Monte Carmelo, 1934–49.

Teresa de Jesús. *El camino de perfección.* Ed. Tomás Alvarez. Facs. ed. 2 vols. Rome: Vatican, 1965.

——. *Escritos de Santa Teresa,* 2 vols. Ed. Vicente de la Fuente. Biblioteca de Autores Españoles 53 and 55. Madrid: Real Academia Española, 1952.

——. *El libro de la vida*. Ed. Guido Mancini. Madrid: Taurus, 1982.

——. *Obras completas*. Ed. Enrique Llamas Martínez, Teófanes Egido, Daniel de Pablo Maroto, José Vicente Rodríguez, Fortunato Antolín, and Luis Rodriguez Martínez, under the direction of Alberto Barrientos. Madrid: Editorial de Espiritualidad, 1984.

——. *Obras completas*. Ed. Efrén de la Madre de Dios and Otger Steggink. Madrid: Biblioteca de Autores Cristianos, 1974.

Vitoria, Francisco de. *Obras de Francisco de Vitoria: Relecciones teológicas*. Madrid: Biblioteca de Autores Cristianos, 1960.

Yepes, Diego de. *La Vida de Santa Teresa de Jesús*. (1599.) Buenos Aires: Emecé Editores, 1946.

Bibliographies

Alcocer y Martínez, Mariano. *Catálogo razonado de obras impresas en Valladolid, 1481–1800*. Valladolid: Casa Social Católica, 1926.

García López, Juan Catalina. *Ensayo de una tipografía complutense*. Madrid: Manuel Tello, 1889.

Jiménez Salas, María. *Santa Teresa de Jesús: Bibliografía fundamental*. Madrid: Cuadernos Bibliográficos, 1962.

Matías del Niño Jesús. "Indice de manuscritos carmelitanos existentes en la Biblioteca Nacional de Madrid." *Ephemerides Carmeliticae* 8 (1957): 187–255.

Paz y Meliá, A. "Expedientes de Inquisición conservados en la Biblioteca Nacional." *Revista de Archivos, Bibliotecas y Museos* 10 (July-December 1907): 276–86.

——. *Papeles de Inquisición: Catálogo y extractos*. Madrid: Patronato del Archivo Histórico Nacional, 1947.

Pérez Pastor, Cristóbal. *La imprenta en Toledo: Descripción bibliográfica de las obras impresas en la imperial ciudad desde 1483 hasta nuestros días*. Madrid: Manuel Tello, 1887.

Serrano y Sanz, Manuel. *Apuntes para una Biblioteca de Escritoras Españolas*, 4 vols. (1898, 1903.) Biblioteca de Autores Españoles 268–71. Madrid: Atlas, 1975.

Secondary Sources

Alberto de la Virgen del Carmen. *Historia de la reforma teresiana*. Madrid: Editorial de Espiritualidad, 1968.

Alcalá, Angel, et al. *Inquisición española y mentalidad inquisitorial*. Barcelona: Ariel, 1984.

Alonso Cortes, Narciso. "Pleitos de los Cepedas." *Boletín de la Real Academia Española* 25 (1946): 85–110.

Alvarez, Tomás. "Esta monja: Carisma y obediencia en una relación de la Santa." *El Monte Carmelo* 78 (1970): 143–62.

——. "El ideal religioso de Santa Teresa de Jesús y el drama de su segundo biógrafo." *El Monte Carmelo* 86 (1978): 203–38.

Alvarez Suárez, Aniano. *Itinerario del alma a Dios: según la doctrina del Carmelo Teresiano primitivo*. Madrid: Editorial de Espiritualidad, 1986.

Andrés Martín, Melquíades. *El misterio de los alumbrados de Toledo, desvelado por sus contemporáneos, 1523–1560.* Burgos: El Monte Carmelo, 1976.

——. *Los recogidos: Nueva visión de la mística española (1500–1700).* Madrid: Fundación Universitaria Española, 1975.

——. *Reforma española y reforma luterana: Afinidades y diferencias a la luz de los místicos españoles (1517–1536).* Madrid: Fundación Universitaria Española, 1975.

——. *La teología española en el siglo XVI.* 2 vols. Madrid: Biblioteca de Autores Cristianos, 1976.

Andueza, María. *Agua y luz en Santa Teresa.* Mexico City: Universidad Nacional Autónoma de México, 1985.

Arenal, Electa, and Stacey Schlau. *Untold Sisters: Hispanic Nuns in Their Own Works.* Albuquerque: University of New Mexico Press, 1989.

Astrain, Antonio. *Historia de la Compañía de Jesús en la asistencia de España.* 2 vols. Madrid: Sucesores de Rivadeneyra, 1905.

Auclair, Marcelle. *Teresa of Avila.* New York: Doubleday, 1959.

Avellá Cháfer, Francisco. "Beatas y beaterios en la ciudad y arzobispado de Sevilla." *Archivo Hispalense* 65 (1982): 99–132.

Azcona, Tarsicio de. *Isabel la Católica.* 2 vols. Madrid: Sarpe, 1980.

Barrientos, Alberto, ed. *Introducción a la lectura de Santa Teresa.* Madrid: Editorial de Espiritualidad, 1978.

Baruzi, Jean. "Un moment de la lutte contre le protestantisme et l'illuminisme en Espagne au XVIᵉ siècle." *Revue d'Histoire et de Philosophie Religieuses* 7 (1927): 541–53.

——. *Saint Jean de la Croix et le problème de l'expérience mystique.* Paris: Felix Alcan, 1924.

Bataillon, Marcel. *Erasmo y España.* Trans. Antonio Alatorre. Mexico City: Fondo de Cultura Económica, 1986.

Beinart, Haim. *Conversos on Trial: The Inquisition in Ciudad Real.* Jerusalem: Magnes, 1981.

Beltrán de Heredia, Vicente. "Los alumbrados de la diócesis de Jaén: Un capítulo inédito de la historia de nuestra espiritualidad." *Revista Española de Teología* 9 (1949): 161–222, 445–88.

——. "Un grupo de visionarios y pseudoprofetas que actúa durante los últimos años de Felipe II: Repercusión de ello sobre la memoria de Santa Teresa." *Revista Española de Teología* 7 (1947): 373–97; 9 (1949): 483–534.

Bertini, Giovanni Maria. *Ensayos de literatura espiritual comparada hispano-italiano (siglos XV–XVII).* Turin: Facultad de Magisterio, Universidad de Turin, 1980.

Bilinkoff, Jodi. *The Avila of Saint Teresa: Religious Reform in a Sixteenth-Century City.* Ithaca: Cornell University Press, 1989.

——. "Confessors, Penitents, and the Construction of Identities in Early Modern Avila." In *Culture and Identity in Early Modern Europe (1500–1800): Essays in Honor of Natalie Zemon Davis*, ed. Barbara B. Dierendorf and Carla Hesse. Ann Arbor: University of Michigan Press, 1993.

Brink, Jean R., Alison P. Coudert, and Maryanne C. Horowitz, eds. *The Politics of Gender in Early Modern Europe.* Kirksville: Northeastern Missouri State University Press, 1989.

Burke, Peter. "How to Be a Counter-Reformation Saint." In *Religion and Society in Early Modern Europe, 1500–1800*, ed. Kaspar von Greyerz, pp. 45–55. Boston: George Allen & Unwin, 1984.

Bynum, Caroline Walker. *Holy Feast and Holy Fast: The Religious Significance of Food to Medieval Women.* Berkeley: University of California Press, 1987.

Caimari Frau, Francisca. *La lengua en el epistolario de Santa Teresa.* Mallorca: Muro, 1984.

Caminero, Juventino. "Dialéctica de la experiencia y la erudición en Santa Teresa." *Letras de Duesto* 12 (July–December 1982): 99–146.

Castro, América. *Teresa la santa y otros ensayos.* Madrid: Alianza, 1982.

Certeau, Michel de. *La fable mystique.* Vol. 1, *XVIe–XVIIe siècle.* St-Amand: Gallimard, 1982.

Chevalier, Maxime. *Lectura y lectores en la España de los siglos XVI y XVII.* Madrid: Turner, 1976.

Cilveti, Angel L. *Introducción a la mística española.* Madrid: Cátedra, 1974.

Corrientes espirituales en la España del siglo XVI: Trabajos del II Congreso de Espiritualidad. Barcelona: Juan Flors, 1963.

Criado de Val, Manuel, ed. *Santa Teresa y la literatura mística hispánica.* Madrid: EDI-6, 1984.

Cruz, Anne J., and Mary Elizabeth Perry, eds. *Culture and Control in Counter-Reformation Spain.* Minneapolis: University of Minnesota Press, 1992.

Cuevas García, Cristóbal. "El significante alegórico en el castillo teresiano." *Letras de Duesto* 12 (July–December 1982): 77–97.

Dalmases, Cándido de. "Santa Teresa y los jesuitas, precisando fechas y datos." *Archivum Historicum Societatis Jesus* 35 (1966): 347–78.

Delooz, Pierre. *Sociologie et canonisations.* Liège: Faculté de Droit, 1969.

Domínguez Ortiz, Antonio. *El antiguo régimen: Los Reyes Católicos y los Austrias.* Vol. 3 of *Historia de España Alfaguara*, ed. Miguel Artola. Madrid: Alianza, 1980.

——. *Los judeoconversos en España y América.* Madrid: Istmo, 1971.

Douglas, Mary. *Purity and Danger: An Analysis of Concepts of Pollution and Taboo.* London: Routledge & Keegan Paul, 1966.

Efrén de la Madre de Dios. *Santa Teresa por dentro.* Madrid: Editorial de Espiritualidad, 1982.

——. *Teresa de Jesús.* Madrid: Biblioteca de Autores Cristianos, 1981.

Efrén de la Madre de Dios and Otger Steggink. *Santa Teresa y su tiempo.* 3 vols. Salamanca: Universidad Pontificia de Salamanca, 1982–84.

Egido, Teófanes. "La familia judía de Santa Teresa." *Studia Zamorensia* 3 (1982): 449–79.

——, ed. *Perfil histórico de Santa Teresa.* Madrid: Editorial de Espiritualidad, 1981.

Egido Martínez, Teófanes, Víctor García de la Concha, and Olegario González de Cardenal, eds. *Congreso Internacional Teresiano (4–7 octubre, 1982).* Salamanca: Universidad de Salamaca, 1983.

Eire, Carlos M. N. *From Madrid to Purgatory.* New York: Cambridge University Press, 1995.

Elizalde, Ignacio. "Teresa de Jesús y los Jesuitas." In *Teresa de Jesús: Estudios histórico-literarios*, pp. 151–75. Rome: Teresianum, 1982.

Elliott, J. H. *Imperial Spain*. Harmondsworth: Penguin, 1963.

Fernández Alvarez, Manuel. "El entorno histórico de Santa Teresa." *Studia Zamorensia* 3 (1982): 357–447.

García Cárcel, Ricardo. *Herejía y sociedad en el siglo XVI*. Barcelona: Península, 1980.

García de la Concha, Víctor. *El arte literario de Santa Teresa*. Barcelona: Ariel, 1978.

——. " 'Sermo humilis,' coloquialismo y rusticidad en el lenguaje literario teresiano." *El Monte Carmelo* 92 (1984): 251–86.

García-Villoslada, Ricardo, ed. *La Iglesia en la España de los siglos XV y XVI*. Vol. 3, pt. 2, of *Historia de la Iglesia en España*. Madrid: Biblioteca de Autores Cristianos, 1980.

——. "Santa Teresa y la contrarreforma católica." *Carmelus* 10 (1963): 231–62.

Garrido, Pablo M. "Magisterio espiritual de Santa Teresa de Jesús entre los carmelitas españoles." *Carmelus* 18 (1971): 64–121.

Giovanni della Croce. "Peculiaridades de la mística teresiana." *Revista de Espiritualidad* 29 (1970):462–78.

Gracia Boix, Rafael. "Los autos de fe de la Inquisición." *Boletín de la Real Academia de Córdoba de Ciencias, Bellas Letras y Nobles Artes* 54 (July–December 1983): 61–82.

Green, Dierdre. *Gold in the Crucible: Teresa of Avila and the Western Mystical Tradition*. Longmead: Element Books, 1989.

Groult, Pierre. "Les courants spirituels dans las Peninsule Ibérique aux XVe, XVIe, et XVIIe siècles." *Lettres Romances* 9 (1955): 218–21.

——. "Las fuentes germánicas de la mística española." *ARBOR* 1 (1961): 22–39.

——. *Les mystiques des Pays-Bas et la littérature espagnole du seizième siècle*. Louvain: Librairie Universitaire, 1927.

Haliczer, Stephen, ed. *Inquisition and Society in Early Modern Europe*. London: Croom Helm, 1986.

Hamilton, Alastair. *Heresy and Mysticism in Sixteenth-Century Spain*. Toronto: University of Toronto Press, 1992.

Hatzfeld, Helmut. *Estudios literarios sobre mística española*. Madrid: Gredos, 1955.

——. *El hogar espiritual de Santa Teresa: En torno al estado del Carmelo español en tiempo de la santa*. Rome: Insitutum Carmelitanum, 1983.

Henningsen, Gustav, and John Tedeschi, eds. *The Inquisition in Early Modern Europe: Studies in Sources and Methods*. De Kalb: Northern Illinois University Press, 1984.

Herraíz García, Maximiliano. *Introducción a "Las moradas."* Desierto de las Palmas, Castellón: Centro de Espiritualidad Santa Teresa, 1981.

——. *Introducción al "Camino de perfección" de Santa Teresa*. Desierto de las Palmas, Castellón: Centro de Espiritualidad Santa Teresa, 1981.

——. *Introducción al 'Libro de la Vida' de Santa Teresa*. Desierto de las Palmas, Castellón: Centro de Espiritualidad Santa Teresa, 1981.

——. *Solo Dios basta: Claves a la interpretacion de Santa Teresa de Jesús*. Madrid: Editorial de Espiritualidad, 1985.

Hoornaert, Rodolphe. "Le progres de la pensée de Sainte Thérèse entre la 'Vie' et le 'Château.' " *Revue des Sciences Philosophiques et Théologiques*, 1924, pp. 20–43.

Huerga, Alvaro. *Historia de los alumbrados 1570–1620*. 5 vols. Madrid: Fundación Universitaria Española, 1972–94.

——. *Predicadores, alumbrados e inquisición en el siglo XVI*. Madrid: Fundación Universitaria Española, 1973.

Imirizaldu, Jesús. *Monjas y beatas embaucadores*. Madrid: Editora Nacional, 1977.

Jorge Pardo, Enrique. "Rectificaciones necesarias en la cronología teresiana." *Manresa* 22 (1950): 317–35.

——. "Las visitas a Avila de San Francisco de Borja." *Manresa* 23 (1951): 195–210.

Juberias, Francisco. *Guía para la lectura de "Las Moradas" de Santa Teresa de Jesús*. Madrid: Claune, 1985.

Kagan, Richard L. *Lucrecia's Dreams: Politics and Prophecy in Sixteenth-Century Spain*. Berkeley: University of California Press, 1990.

Kamen, Henry. *Inquisition and Society in Spain in the Sixteenth and Seventeenth Centuries*. Bloomington: Indiana University Press, 1985.

——. *The Phoenix and the Flame: Catalonia and the Counter-Reformation*. New Haven: Yale University Press, 1993.

Kemp, Eric Waldram. *Canonization and Authority in the Western Church*. Oxford: Oxford University Press, 1948.

Kieckhefer, Richard. "Imitators of Christ: Sainthood in the Christian Tradition." In *Sainthood: Its Manifestations in World Religions*, ed. Richard Kieckhefer and George D. Bond, pp. 1–42. Berkeley: University of California Press, 1988.

Kleinberg, Aviad M. *Prophets in Their Own Country: Living Saints and the Making of Sainthood in the Later Middle Ages*. Chicago: University of Chicago Press, 1992.

La Pinta Llorente, Miguel de. *La Inquisición española y los problemas de la cultura y de la intolerancia*. Madrid: Editorial Cultura Hispánica, 1953.

Lea, Henry Charles. *Chapters from the Religious History of Spain Connected with the Inquisition*. New York: Burt Franklin, 1967.

——. *A History of the Inquisition of Spain*. 4 vols. New York: Macmillan, 1906–7.

Lerner, Gerda. *The Creation of Feminist Consciousness: From the Middle Ages to 1870*. New York: Oxford University Press, 1993.

——. *The Creation of Patriarchy*. New York: Oxford University Press, 1986.

Llamas Martínez, Enrique. *Santa Teresa de Jesús y la Inquisición española*. Madrid: Editorial de Espiritualidad, 1972.

Llorca, Bernardino. *La Inquisición española*. Madrid: Sarpe, 1986.

Llorente, José A. *La Inquisición y los españoles*. (1812.) Madrid: Gráficas Goya, 1973.

Longhurst, John E. "Alumbrados, erasmistas y luteranos en el proceso de Juan de Vergara." *Cuadernos de Historia de España* 27 (1958): 99–163; 28 (1958): 101–65.

——. "Luther in Spain, 1520–1540." *Proceedings of the American Philosophical Society* 103 (1959): 69–93.

Luis de San José. *Concordancias de las obras y escritos de Santa Teresa de Jesús*. Burgos: El Monte Carmelo, 1982.

Luti, J. Mary. "Teresa of Avila, 'Maestra Espiritual.'" Ph.D. diss., Boston College, 1987.

Maldonado, Luis. *Experiencia religiosa y lenguaje en Santa Teresa*. Madrid: Promoción Popular Cristiana, 1982.

Mancini, Guido Giancarlo. *Espressioni letterarie dell' insegnamento di Santa Teresa de Avila*. Modena: Società Tipografica Modenese, 1955.

Márquez, Antonio. *Los alumbrados: Orígenes y filosofía (1525–1559)*. Madrid: Taurus, 1980.

——. *Literatura e Inquisición en España, 1478–1834*. Madrid: Taurus, 1980.

——. "Orígen y caracterización del iluminismo (según un parecer de Melchor Cano)." *Revista de Occidente* 63 (1968): 320–33.

Márquez Villanueva, Francisco. "Santa Teresa y el linaje." In *Espiritualidad y literatura en el siglo XVI*. Madrid: Alfaguara, 1968.

Martín, Felipe. *Santa Teresa de Jesús y la Orden de Predicadores*. Avila: Sucesores de A. Jiménez, 1909.

Martínez Millán, José. "El catálogo de libros prohibidos de 1559: Aportaciones para una nueva interpretación." *Miscelanea Comillas* 37 (1979): 179–217.

McGinn, Bernard. "Love, Knowledge, and *Unio mystica* in the Western Christian Tradition." In *Mystical Union and Monotheistic Faith: An Ecumenical Dialogue*, ed. Moshe Idel and Bernard McGinn. New York: Macmillan, 1989.

——. *The Growth of Mysticism: From Gregory the Great through the Twelfth Century*. New York: Crossroad, 1994.

Menéndez Pidal, Ramón. *La lengua de Cristóbal Colón: El estilo de Santa Teresa y otros estudios sobre el siglo XVI*. Madrid: Espasa-Calpe, 1958.

Michel-Ange. "La vie franciscaine en Espagne entre les deux couronnements de Charles Quint." *Revista de Archivos, Bibliotecas y Museos* 1 (1912): 157–214, 345–404; 1 (1913): 167–225; 2 (1913): 1–63, 157–216.

Miles, Margaret. *Carnal Knowing: Female Nakedness and Religious Meaning in the Christian West*. New York: Vintage, 1989.

Mir, Miguel. *Santa Teresa de Jesús: Su vida, su espíritu, sus fundaciones*. 2 vols. Madrid: Jaime Ratés, 1912.

Mir, Miguel, and Justo Cuervo, eds. "Los alumbrados de Extremadura en el siglo XVI." *Revista de Archivos, Bibliotecas y Museos* 9 (1903): 203–6; 10 (1904): 64–67; 11 (1904): 179–91; 12 (1905): 459–63; 13 (1905): 57–62.

Moliner, José María de la Cruz. *Historia de la literatura mística en España*. Burgos: El Monte Carmelo, 1961.

Morel-Fatio, A. "Les lectures de Sainte Thérèse." *Bulletin Hispanique* 10 (1908): 17–67.

Nalle, Sara T. *God in La Mancha: Religious Reform and the People of Cuenca, 1500–1650*. Johns Hopkins University Studies in Historical and Political Science, 110th ser., 2. Baltimore: Johns Hopkins University Press, 1992.

——. "Literacy and Culture in Early Modern Castile." *Past and Present* 125 (1989): 65–96.

Peers, E. Allison. *Handbook to the Life and Times of Saint Teresa and Saint John of the Cross*. Westminster, Md.: Newman Press, 1954.

——. "Literary Style of St. Teresa." *Cross and Crown* 5 (1953): 208–22.

——. *Mother of Carmel: A portrait of St. Teresa of Jesus*. London: SCM Press, 1946.

——. *Saint Teresa of Jesus and Other Essays and Addresses*. London: Faber & Faber, 1953.

——. *Studies of the Spanish Mystics*. 3 vols. London: S.P.C.K., 1960.

Pelisson, Nicole, and Robert Ricard. *Etudes sur Sainte Thérèse*. Paris: Centre de Recherches Hispaniques, 1968.

Pépin, Jean. " 'Stilla aquae modica multo infusa vino, ferrum ignitum, luce perfusus aer': L'origine de trois comparaisons familières a la théologie mystique médiévale." In *Miscellanea André Combes*, 1:333–75. Rome: Vatican, 1967.

Pérez, Quintin. "Santa Teresa de Jesús y sus confesores." *Estudios Eclesiásticos* 2:3–23, 152–82.

Pérez Villanueva, Joaquín, ed. *La Inquisición española: Nueva visión, nuevos horizontes.* Madrid: Siglo XXI, 1980.

Perry, Mary Elizabeth. *Gender and Disorder in Early Modern Seville.* Princeton: Princeton University Press, 1990.

Petroff, Elizabeth Alvilda, ed. *Medieval Women's Visionary Literature.* New York: Oxford Univrsity Press, 1986.

Pinto Crespo, Virgilio. "Biblias publicades fuera de España secuestradas por las Inquisición de Sevilla en 1552," *Bulletin Hispanique* 69 (1962): 236–47.

———. "La censura: Sistemas de control e instrumentos de acción." In Angel Alcalá et. al., *Inquisición española y mentalidad inquisitorial.* Barcelona: Ariel, 1984.

———. *Inquisición y control ideológico en la España del siglo XVI.* Madrid: Taurus, 1983.

———. "Nuevas perspectivas sobre el contenido de los indices inquisitoriales hispanos del siglo XVI." *Hispania Sacra* 33 (1981): 593–641.

Poitrey, Jeannine. *Vocabulario de Santa Teresa.* Salamanca: Universidad Pontificia, 1983.

———. "Vocabulario teresiano de 'Vida' y 'Camino de perfección': Filones lexicales del castellano vivo." Thesis, Universite de Lille, 1977.

Poutrin, Isabelle. "Souvenirs d'enfance: L'apprentissage de la sainteté dans l'Espagne moderne." *Mélanges de la Casa de Velázquez* 23 (1987): 331–54.

Redondo, Agustin. "Luther et l'Espagne de 1520 à 1536." *Mélanges de la Casa de Velázquez* 1 (1965): 109–59.

Ricard, Robert. "Quelques remarques sur les 'Moradas' de Sainte Thérèse." *Bulletin Hispanique* 47 (1945): 187–98.

———. "Le symbolisme du 'Château intérieur' chez Sainte Thérèse." *Bulletin Hispanique* 67 (January–June 1965): 25–41.

Rodríguez, Isaias. *Santa Teresa de Jesús y la espiritualidad española.* Madrid: Instituto Francisco Juárez, 1972.

Román de la Inmaculada. "El fenómeno de los alumbrados y su interpretación." *Ephemerides Carmeliticae* 10 (1958): 49–80.

Ros, Fidèle de. *Un inspirateur de Sainte Thérèse, le frère Bernardin de Laredo.* Paris: J. Vrin, 1948.

———. *Un maître de Sainte Thérèse: Le père François d'Osuna, sa vie, son oeuvre, sa docrine spirituelle.* Paris: G. Beauchesne, 1936.

Rossi, Rosa. *Teresa de Avila: Biografía de una escritora.* Trans. Marieta Gargatagli. Barcelona: ICARIA, 1984.

———. "Teresa de Jesús." I, "La mujer y la iglesia," and II, "La mujer y la palabra." *mientras tanto* 14 (1983): 63–79; 15 (1983): 29–45.

Saint-Saens, Alain. *La nostalgie du désert: L'ideal érémitique en Castille au Siècle d'Or.* San Francisco: Edwin Mellen, 1993.

———, ed. *Religion, Body, and Gender in Early Modern Spain.* San Francisco: Mellen Research University Press, 1991.

Sáinz Rodríguez, Pedro. "Influencia de los místicos italianos en España." In *Trabajos del Segundo Congreso de Espiritualidad de Salamanca*, pp. 543–60. Barcelona: Juan Flors, 1963.

——. *La siembra mística del Cardenal Cisneros y las reformas en la Iglesia*. Madrid: Fundación Universitaria Española, 1979.

Sala Balust, Luis. "En torno al grupo de alumbrados de Llerena." In *Corrientes espirituales en la España del siglo XVI: Trabajos del II Congreso de Espiritualidad*, pp. 509–23. Barcelona: Juan Flors, 1963.

——. "Introducción a las obras completas del santo maestro Juan de Avila." In Juan de Avila, *Obras completas*, pp. 1–63, 320–53. Madrid: Biblioteca de Autores Cristianos, 1970.

Sánchez Moguel, Antonio. *El lenguaje de Santa Teresa de Jesús*. Madrid: Imprenta Clásica Española, 1915.

Selke, Angela. *El Santo Oficio de la Inquisición: Proceso de fray Francisco Ortiz (1529–1532)*. Madrid: Guadarrama, 1968.

Selke de Sánchez, Angela. "Algunos datos nuevos sobre los primeros alumbrados: El Edicto de 1525 y su relación con el proceso de Alcaraz." *Bulletin Hispanique* 54 (1952): 125–52.

Seris, Homero. "Nueva genealogía de Santa Teresa." *Nueva Revista de Filología Hispánica* 10 (1965): 363–84.

Silverio de Santa Teresa. *Historia del Carmen descalzo en España, Portugal y América*. Burgos: El Monte Carmelo, 1935–52.

——. *Santa Teresa: Modelo de feminismo cristiano*. Burgos: El Monte Carmelo, 1931.

Slade, Carole. *St. Teresa of Avila: Author of a Heroic Life*. Berkeley: University of California Press, 1995.

Smet, Joaquin. *Los carmelitas: Historia de la Orden del Carmen*. Trans. Antonio Ruiz Molina. 2 vols. Madrid: Biblioteca de Autores Cristianos, 1987–90.

Steggink, Otger. *Arraigo e innovación en Teresa de Jesús*. Madrid: Biblioteca de Autores Cristianos, 1976.

——. *La reforma del Carmelo español: La visita canónica del general Rubeo y su encuentro con Santa Teresa (1566–1567)* Rome: Institutum Carmelitanum, 1965.

Surtz, Ronald E. *The Guitar of God: Gender, Power, and Authority in the Visionary World of Mother Juana de la Cruz (1481–1534)*. Philadelphia: University of Pennsylvania Press, 1990.

Tellechea Idígoras, José Ignacio. "La censura inquisitorial de Biblias de 1554." *Anthologica Annua* 10 (1962): 89–142.

——. *Tiempos recios: Inquisición y heterodoxias*. Salamanca: Sígueme, 1977.

Trueman Dicken, E. W. *The Crucible of Love*. New York: Sheed & Ward, 1963.

Urbano, Luis. *Las analogías predilectas de Santa Teresa de Jesús: Estudio crítico*. Valencia: Real Convento de Predicadores, 1924.

Vázquez de Prada, V. *Historia económica y social de España*. 5 vols. Madrid: Casa de Socorro, 1978.

Villar Degano, Juan F. "Ideas recurrentes en los prólogos y epílogos de las obras de Santa Teresa." *Letras de Duesto* 12 (July–December 1982): 147–71.

Villoslada, R. G. "Santa Teresa de Jesús y la contrarreforma católica." *Carmelus* 10 (1963): 231–62.

Weber, Alison. *Teresa of Avila and the Rhetoric of Femininity*. Princeton: Princeton University Press, 1990.

Weinstein, Donald, and Rudolph Bell. *Saints and Society: The Two Worlds of Western Christendom, 1000–1700.* Chicago: University of Chicago Press, 1982.

Wiesner, Merry E. *Women and Gender in Early Modern Europe.* Cambridge: Cambridge University Press, 1993.

Wiethaus, Ulrike. *Maps of Flesh and Light: The Religious Experience of Medieval Women Mystics.* Syracuse: Syracuse University Press, 1993.

Williams, Rowan. *Teresa of Avila.* Harrisburg, Pa.: Morehouse, 1991.

Wilson, Stephen, ed. *Saints and Their Cults: Studies in Religious Sociology, Folklore and History.* Cambridge: Cambridge University Press, 1983.

Woodward, Kenneth. *Making Saints: How the Catholic Church Determines Who Becomes a Saint, Who Doesn't, and Why.* New York: Simon & Schuster, 1990.

Wright, A. D. *Catholicism and Spanish Society under the Reign of Philip II, 1555–1598, and Philip III, 1598–1621.* Studies in Religion and Society 27. Lewiston, N.Y.: Edwin Mellen, 1991.

Index